Moral Textures

To Jeff Alexander,
For all he knows.

Moral Textures

Feminist Narratives in the Public Sphere

Maria Pia Lara

University of California Press
Berkeley   Los Angeles   London

University of California Press
Berkeley and Los Angeles, California

University of California Press, Ltd.
London, England

Published by arrangement with Polity Press in association with Blackwell
Publishers Ltd.

ISBN 0-520-21776-4 (hardcover)
ISBN 0-520-21777-2 (paperback)

9   8   7   6   5   4   3   2   1

Typeset in 10 on 11 pt Palatino
by Ace Filmsetting Ltd, Frome, Somerset
Printed in Great Britain by TJ International Ltd, Padstow, Cornwall

This book is printed on acid-free paper.

Contents

Author's Note

This book would not have made its way into English without the patient assistance, hard work and personal involvement of my good friend and translator, Laura Gorham. Having translated some early drafts from Spanish into English, she later helped me find ways to formulate my English drafts into more fluent prose. At the start of this project, she was fundamental in helping me find financial support from the Fideicomiso Mexico/USA. I am deeply grateful to her.

Acknowledgements

The preparation and completion of this book, as with any creative work, has incurred profound debts to many persons, from those who heard the arguments in their initial form, through those who helped shape and sharpen the viewpoints offered here, to those who read many different versions of the manuscript and offered valuable suggestions about how it could be improved and revised.

The book received vital support from the Fideicomiso Mexico/USA, funded jointly by the Rockefeller Foundation and the Bancomer Foundation through the Fondo Nacional Para la Cultura y las Artes in Mexico (FONCA). A fund established to strengthen academic and literary ties between Mexico and the United States, this institution facilitated the translation of the early drafts of my book from Spanish into English. I am also indebted to my university, Universidad Autonoma Metropolitana (UAM)-Iztapalapa, not only for its continuing financial support throughout the years but for the fellowship that allowed me to spend a year in Berlin, a trimester in Sweden and two trimesters in Los Angeles. I am especially thankful to Dr Julio Rubio, General Rector of UAM, Dr José Luis Gazquez, Rector of my campus at UAM, Gregorio Vidal, Dean of Social Sciences and Humanities, and José Lema, Chair of my Department of Philosophy. Without their help and support, this book would not have been completed.

I also wish to record my gratitude to the Institut für Hermeneutik at the Freie Universität, Berlin, and especially to its Director, Professor Albrecht Wellmer, for allowing me to spend my 1994–5 sabbatical year in the Institut and to participate in its many fruitful activities throughout the year. Christoph Menke made possible my initial connection with the Institut, and Ina Maria Gumbel, its secretary, helped me in innumerable and generous ways during my year in Berlin. I am also grateful to Professor Axel Honneth for allowing me to participate in his

Colloquium at the Social Science Institute of the Freie Universität. I was very fortunate to be at the Freie Universität at such a stimulating moment.

I wish particularly to acknowledge and thank the friends I made in Berlin, Marion Rudzki and Hermann Steffens, Maeve Cooke and Martin Santer, and Begonya Saez and Daniel Saez, all of whom gave me invaluable support.

Professor Alessandro Ferrara allowed me to present an early draft of one chapter from this book to his Multicultural Seminar at the University of La Sapienza in Rome. Bjorn Wittrock, Director of the Swedish Collegium for Advanced Studies in the Social Sciences (SCASSS) in Uppsala, also gave me an opportunity to present a lecture drawn from this book and to share my research with the exciting group of feminist scholars in residence there in spring 1996.

I am also grateful to those who have participated in the annual meetings of the Philosophy and Social Sciences group in Prague; these were initiated by Jürgen Habermas in Dubrovnik and are now held under the auspices of the Institute of Philosophy of the Czech Academy of Sciences. Especially I wish to thank the recent directors of these meetings, Jean Cohen, Seyla Benhabib, Sandro Ferrara and Axel Honneth, through whom I have been able to establish a permanent dialogue with many scholars who have become my colleagues and friends.

David Held gave my typescript his initial support. His trust throughout the reviewing and revising process was invaluable to me, as were his open and encouraging suggestions for improvements. I was also very lucky in the anonymous reviewer chosen by Polity Press. The clarity and insight of this detailed evaluation not only showed me possible weaknesses in my arguments but ways to strengthen them, and it deepened my understanding of the whole field of critical feminist studies. I only hope that I have sufficiently profited from this reviewer's great help. I would like to thank Ruth Thackeray, whose work as copy editor has been painstaking and Julia Harsant and Sue Leigh at Polity Press for all their help.

I also wish to thank Joan B. Landes for her constant commentaries, advice and support as she read various drafts of the chapters of this book. Her personal and intellectual friendship means a great deal to me, first in Sweden, later in Mexico and Los Angeles.

I am also deeply indebted to Nora Rabotnikof, who gave this manuscript the last and very important critical reading and offered final suggestions for revision. Throughout our many years of friendship, Nora has taught me how emotional and intellectual solidarity can be deeply interrelated.

Jeff Alexander, to whom this book is dedicated, also helped edit my English prose, but, much more importantly, he shared the whole creative process with me, through sharing readings, engaging in innumerable discussions, and much, much more. This book is the expression of the many things I have learned from him, and of his generosity in helping me to crystallize my ideas.

Finally, I wish to thank my parents, Nydia and Hernan Lara, who have supported my work and life in all its various stages of development, in the most profound and important ways.

I would like to thank the following presses and journals for permission to reprint some of the earlier versions of the chapters of this book. Parts of chapter 2, 'Communicative Rationality: Between Spheres of Validity', previously appeared as 'Albrecht Wellmer: Between Validity Spheres', in _Philosophy and Social Criticism_, vol. 21, no. 2 (1995), pp. 1–23, and is reprinted here by permission of Sage Publications Ltd. Parts of chapter 3, 'Feminism as an Illocutionary Model', appeared in the Mexican journal _Debate feminista_, vol. 15 (1997), pp. 315–34. Parts of chapter 5, 'Narrative Cultural Interweavings: Between Facts and Fiction', appeared in Italian in the journal _Parolechiave_, no. 10–11 (1996), pp. 287–96. Parts of chapter 6, 'Justice and Solidarity: Women in the Public Sphere', appeared in _Justice and Democracy: Cross-cultural Perspectives_, edited by Ron Bontekoe and Marietta Stephaniants (Hawaii: The University of Hawaii Press, 1997), pp. 37–50. Part of chapter 7, 'The Moral Foundation of Recognition: A Critical Revision of Three Models', appeared as an article written with Jeffrey C. Alexander in the _New Left Review_, no. 220 (1996), pp. 126–36.

Introduction

This book seeks to contribute to a new understanding of the women's movement by philosophically interpreting its historically unprecedented contributions to late modernity. I frame this research within the tradition of critical theory, which understands philosophical accounts as reconstructive theories that are in need of empirical references, viewing the accounts as falsifiable, postmetaphysical and normative. My goal has been to elaborate a theory of how social movements, through their interventions in the public sphere, create and generate solidarity through narratives which demand recognition and, at the same time, aim to redefine the collective understanding of justice and the good life by proposing new visions of institutional transformation. While I place these contributions in the public sphere, the originality of my position lies in the particular way I approach this newly public participation. I argue that women made (and make) use of the public sphere by interrelating two different validity spheres, the moral and the aesthetic. In making this unusual connection, I argue, feminists have created both new forms of social relationship and new forms of theoretical understanding. The feminist movement provided (and provides) a much more comprehensive understanding than was previously available of how the realms of justice and the good life must be interconnected and how a critical view of them promotes transformations of democratic conceptions and institutions.

In order to demonstrate that the women's movement achieves this new level of clarification, I cannot concentrate only on its public role as a participatory democratic movement. I must also look closely at the discursive level. I seek to demonstrate how the aesthetic and moral interweaving of women's discourses establishes a new viewpoint that profoundly reorders social values and needs. I argue that the women's movement, in its struggle to achieve public recognition of women's rights and needs, has developed an 'illocutionary form'. Before entering into the explanation of how I conceive these social and cultural dynamics, I will clarify the terms that I introduce as the basis of my theory, as well as the theoretical sources from which I draw them. The works of Jürgen Habermas, Hannah Arendt, Albrecht Wellmer and Paul Ricoeur enable me to build up the core of my model.

A Cultural Interpretation of Speech-Acts

The term 'illocutionary' comes from Habermas' effort to combine J. L. Austin's speech-act theory with the normative ambition of the critical theory tradition. By illocutionary force, Habermas refers to a speech-act in which 'alter' and 'ego' understand one another solely on the basis of well-argued reasons. The goal of such illocutionary action is to achieve a consensus based on mutual understanding. While I follow Habermas in this normative approach to illocutionary force, I wish to elaborate it in a new way. To attain such a mutual understanding, I claim, one must first address the other with powerfully imaginative speech, not only to attract the attention of 'alter', but also to open up possibilities for creating different kinds of recognition and solidarity between both parties. The aim of an illocutionary act is simultaneously to transform preceding views of 'alter' and 'ego' such that after the action is performed neither party remains the same. In this way, the initial asymmetry of a dialogue is contemplated as a first step. The possibility of engaging others through a powerful dialogue conceives of language as possessing a disclosive capacity. The term 'disclosure' is taken from its original Heideggerian source, which refers to the aesthetic and ontological roots of language, which according to Arendt's interpretation are inextricably linked. The normative element, however, remains important insofar as language is conceived as a self-reflexive and critical tool. Language and reason are linked insofar as the moral and the aesthetic dimensions are both seen as communicative and differentiated spheres of validity. This viewpoint leads to an understanding of how, with the subjects of the speech-acts focusing on newly problematic social issues, it is possible to transform them by creating new narratives in the public sphere. I call the dynamics of such efforts 'illocutionary force'. I understand the consensual element of this force as an action that includes two analytically differentiated moments empirically bound together and which can create, simultaneously, a pragmatic effect on both parties. The first moment refers to the capacities of a speech-act to disclose new meanings and understandings in relation to 'justice'. The other moment comes after 'alter' and 'ego' have transformed themselves via this act of mutual understanding, and refers to their ability to reorder their values and beliefs in light of it. This reordering implies a public agreement about a new definition of justice and its connections to the good life.

In performative terms, this approach to speech-acts suggests the interrelation of agonistic and consensual moments. The agonistic refers to the initial asymmetry of ego's position and her capacity to produce a powerful narrative that provides an account of the lack of justice created by situations about marginalization, oppression or exclusion. The other moment consists in the consensual act of reaching agreement about the normative content of this claim for recognition, which must relate such accounts to the moral sphere and depends upon the capacity to propose a better understanding of what justice means and how it can be reconceived through institutional transformations. I claim that women's narratives have this emancipatory content whatever their particular viewpoints, and provide the best example of how 'claims for recognition' are conceived as 'illocutionary forces'. By contrast, discourses which aim at exclusion and separation cannot be considered illocutionary; rather than having a moral ambition, 'polluted' discourses assert the superiority of their particularities. By entering into the public sphere and struggling for public recognition, emancipatory narratives mediate between particular group identities and universalistic moral claims, providing new frameworks that allow those who are not members of the group to expand their own-self conceptions and their definitions of civil society.

Women's narratives show how this can be done. They have reordered understandings of what the public sphere is, by casting doubt on previous views of the reasons for cultural, social and political marginalization. These feminist 'illocutionary forces' have fought imaginatively, building a bridge between the moral and the aesthetic validity spheres across the rigidly traditional gendered division between private and public. This bridge-building provides a critical example of how questions related to self-determination and questions related to self-realization have been redefined as specific historical linkages between autonomy and authenticity, as suggested in chapter 4. Indeed, I wish to argue that these specific links between two validity spheres have provided a new approach to the definition of moral subjects.

That I build upon an interpretation of Habermas' early research on the public sphere in order to link critical theory with a more cultural understanding of emancipation is by no means arbitrary. In my view, it is possible to trace in this early work a clear connection between the aesthetic and the moral dimensions of modern identities. However, Habermas makes this cultural-aesthetic connection only at an empirical level. Such empirical references appear again in his late writing, when he thematizes the simultaneous processes of individualization and socialization in relation to George Herbert Mead's theory, as explained in chapter 1. In these discussions, Habermas shows a clear understanding of how groups employ fictional narratives to contest and restructure conceptions of subjectivity, notions of morality and expectations about the good life. The problem is that Habermas does not accompany these empirical insights with a philosophical account of justification; neither does he connect an emancipatory theory of the public sphere with a discussion of how the cultural identities of groups and individuals are related to moral claims for justice on a universalistic basis. In his book *Between Facts and Norms* (1996), Habermas shifts from his earlier empirical focus on cultural struggles in the public sphere to an institutional account of law, which he describes as a 'strong public' that provides the space for emancipatory discourses contesting the empirical contents of norms. Habermas is offering here a philosophical account of the integrative role of the public sphere in its procedural dimension, but he loses sight of his important earlier insights about the interaction between moral and aesthetic spheres, the communicative spheres of reason that are equally important in creating new understandings of the self and of societies' self-representations which could provide for the link between particularistic claims of recognition and universal demands of justice. The task of conceptualizing the interrelation of normative and cultural-aesthetic accounts of justice and the good therefore remains.[1]

This critical perspective on Habermas' resistance to conceptualizing the interconnections of justice and the good informs my discussions of women's narratives and their sucessful effort to reconceptualize the liberal view. In order to overcome the limitations of Habermas' viewpoint, I conceptualize the public sphere as a cultural arena where 'public' meanings of justice and the good permeate democratic institutions, and where the tensions produced between facts and norms are seen as the dynamics that allow for the possibility of interventions by emancipatory movements. By introducing a cultural content into Habermas' speech-act theory, I will be able to develop further the approach to the 'disclosive' capacities of language, viewing speech-acts as communicative tools that provide new meanings and contest earlier ones. Making use of Wellmer's deep insight into the communicative interrelation of aesthetic and moral spheres (see chapter 2), I develop a systematic theory about the connection between public narratives and their 'disclosive' potentialities for emancipatory transformations. According to this new approach, I conceive narratives of emancipation as forms of 'recognition' (see chapters 3 and 8). Contrary to the suggestions of many post-structuralists, it is by no means the case that contestatory discourses, or narratives, are necessarily tied only to strategies of resistance *vis-à-vis* strategic power and ideological domination.[2] I demonstrate that emancipatory narratives can themselves create new forms of power, configuring new ways to fight back against past and present injustices, thus making institutional transformations possible. This is the power I call 'illocutionary force'.[3]

If the public sphere is the mediating space where justice and solidarity meet in concrete ways, I need to clarify precisely how it is that 'narratives' demanding recognition from others actually can aim at the redefinition of justice. To be sure, cultural contestations of identity are not necessarily of a virtuous kind; numerous group efforts aim publicly to exclude others. However, while I would acknowledge that such 'polluted' discourses do flow throughout public channels of information, according to my model they do not achieve illocutionary force. It is in order to make this normative distinction that I wish to follow Habermas in the moral reinterpretation he gave to the speech-act theory of Austin and John R. Searle. Justice reframes the terms in which 'alter' and 'ego' find a normative perspective of a 'we' in the act of mutual understanding. This condition points at the possibility that narratives can only be successful when they are integrative, not exclusionary. Within this normative framing, I add the aesthetic connection: subjects engaging in speech-acts learn to configure 'disclosive' possibilities of new understandings, to relate in different ways things that were once seen otherwise. An action that occurs performatively can produce new and simultaneous understandings between the two sides of the performative relation. This is the 'disclosive' effect.

The conception of disclosure I employ here is clearly connected to a new reading of Hannah Arendt's philosophy of language and action in its relation to the aesthetic sphere.[4] Arendt relates Heidegger's ontological conception of language with that of Walter Benjamin, a point that has not escaped Dana Villa's rigorous examination of the relation of Arendt's political project to Heidegger's.[5] I wish to argue that it is precisely because she grasps the connection between the normative dimension of storytelling – where experience is relearned in the political world – and the aesthetic effects of language that Arendt can overcome Heidegger's aestheticism. Developing further Benjamin's initial concern with 'moral responsibility', Arendt is able to grasp the similarity between Heidegger's and Benjamin's conceptions of language and time. Yet Arendt gets beyond the traditionalism of Heidegger's conception by rescuing Benjamin's submerged hope for a utopian future. She conceives this as the capacity of action to perform new 'beginnings', a capacity that points away from repetition and traditionalism to moral responsibility. The aesthetic effect of 'disclosure' can provide a new way of understanding justice. Once the story is retold, it is possible to grasp the narrowness of previous conceptions of justice; debts to the past that take the form of moral responsibilities in the present are thereby incurred. Narratives that possess such 'illocutionary force' have the 'disclosive' ability to envision normatively – that is, in a critical way – better ways of being in a world of 'equality and distinction'.⁶ Such collective narratives acquire normative legitimacy because they are filtered through the public sphere, where actors create fragile and falsifiable agreements about what needs to be done in the social world. It is certainly a virtue of Arendt's conception of the public sphere that she relates it to power. Whenever people are gathered together – through speech and action – they act in concert to achieve practical ends. But they can do so, argues Arendt, only because 'the force that keeps them together, as distinguished from the spaces of appearances in which they gather and the power which keeps this public space in existence, is the force of mutual promise or contract'.⁷ This connection allows a conception of power, seen as related to collective agreements, to avoid the charge of being overly rationalistic. For Arendt, the political realm allows actors to produce agreements conceived as 'promises' which are neither 'essentialist' truths or arbitrary opinions but the result of concerted speech and action, that is, of illocutionary effects. In my reinterpretation of Arendt's work, this normative warranty produced through stories about new beginnings is a legitimation process that depends on critical acceptance by other groups in the public sphere. My model departs from Habermas' conception, then, not only by systematically connecting it to the aesthetic domain in a general way but by relating it specifically to notions elaborated by Arendt about the public sphere as a source of storytelling.⁸ Her work is of prime importance for reconceptualizing the public sphere in relation to narratives as performances. I am well aware of the doubts that many Arendt specialists have expressed in regard to efforts of Habermasians to reinterpret her work merely as one step in the development of his communicative action theory. Dana Villa, for example, has written a lucid book on Arendt's originality and the theoretical difficulties that arise when one wants to frame her work as only Aristotelian, Habermasian or even postmodern.⁹ Villa makes a great effort to show that the primary source of Arendt is Heidegger, although he is forced to acknowledge that Arendt actually builds her own theory 'against Heidegger'. In my interpretation of Arendt, I argue that the possibility of taking Heidegger against Heidegger depends on sources other than Heidegger himself.

These sources do not come from political theory but, rather, from the aesthetic field, mainly from the works of Walter Benjamin and the literary Jewish tradition, which includes other important Jewish writers such as Herman Broch and Franz Kafka. As Villa himself has argued, 'it is the spirit of Benjamin, not Heidegger, that informs [Arendt's] search for hidden treasures – moments of pure initiatory action – covered in wreckage by the "angel of history"'.[10] Villa's goal – to interpret Arendt's Heideggerianism as 'against Heidegger' – opens up the possibility of seeing that Arendt aimed at conceiving action and speech as primary sources of plurality, and narratives as society's ways of coping with the past, the present, and a possible, utopian future. By connecting Arendt with Habermas, my aim is not to bring Arendt into the Habermasian model, but rather to use both sources as a means towards a more complex and coherent understanding of the normative content of the public sphere and the important cultural role of emancipatory narratives that can crystallize in transformations of our self-understandings about democracy and the good life.

The difference of my approach lies precisely in this emphasis on the moral significance of cultural efforts to reformulate 'values', 'beliefs', 'self-images', 'boundaries' and 'frontiers'. It is in this scenario of contested meanings that the *cultural* contents appear as a frame for struggles of recognition and transformation. My notion of the symbolic order refers to the processes by which societies utilize language as a collective institution to publicly construct self-representations, images and rules, which create and configure symbolic frames that make possible, and permeate, all our actions, beliefs and thoughts. My understanding of 'symbols' emphasizes the public character of meaningful articulation, which points clearly not to their pyschological operation but to how they allow meanings to be incorporated into action.[11]

Women's narratives provide a critical illustration of a positive understanding of the emergence of social movements as emancipatory interventions. With the help of Arendt's conception of 'storytellings', I develop a reconstruction of how the normative and the aesthetic contents of narratives allow the multiple projects of women's identity to express themselves positively in the public sphere. I claim that emancipatory social movements must fight first for a 'new meaning' of justice that provides emancipatory institutional transformations in which the boundaries of what should be considered public and what private need to be redrawn. Feminist interpretations, in 'fact' and in 'fiction', have transformed our previous notions of what these boundaries are, providing a new space for emancipation and integration. What Habermas could not explain, or even envision, is precisely such variegated strategies of deconstructing, retelling and reconfiguring the symbolic order and its historical sources. I would contend, nevertheless, that in cultural boundaries and frontiers, women's success in attaining recognition has been intimately linked with how they have drawn a new meaning of the 'public'. This is the subject of my book.

I take up the challenge Habermas set up in his 'Further Reflections on the Public Sphere' (1996), when he expressed the hope that further elaborations of public sphere theory 'could give cause for a less pessimistic assessment and for an outlook going beyond the formulation of merely defiant postulates'.[12] Contrary to post-structuralist theories that conceive of speech and narratives as strategies of resistance only, my aim is to show how it is possible to conceive resistance and emancipation as something other than two different positions. Women have shifted from being victims – who can offer only resistance – to being owners of their own lives. Historical understanding of past narratives can give place to new meanings, allowing new definitions to be created in a positive and not only in a negative sense. With these new understandings comes the possibility of transformation. Women's efforts have made it possible to retell the story of the public sphere and the paradoxes of democratic theories. They have done so, I claim, not only by resisting but by asserting a utopian viewpoint that describes how gender plurality allows all individuals to flourish and how a more complex and multicultural public sphere is better suited to the embodiment of democratic ideals. This process of utopian enrichment occurs through what might be called the 'communicative power of solidarity'. This power expands the space for public discussion and creates an environment in which the cultural understandings of groups can interact and influence one another. As some critics have pointed out, the rationalism of Habermas links communication to integration. I claim that such a sphere is also a field of conflict, of contested meanings and of exclusion. It is because the public sphere is an arena where symbolic mediating processes shape the public's opinion that one has not only to address the consensual and normative aspects of opinion but also the interpretative struggles to resist domination and agonistic performances to attract the attention of other groups. The agonistic dimension of struggles is revealed in the narrative speech-acts themselves, for 'the self is an exclusively public phenomenon that only action can disclose'.[13] In Arendt's conception, narratives depend on the capacity to construct imaginative ways of holding the attention of others, of 'performing' differences in such a way that they embody the quality of plurality as it permeates the frames of the public sphere.[14] The channels by which new forms of solidarities are fuelled rely on the capacity of narratives to disclose previously unseen marginalization, exclusion and prejudice. There is competition over the public space for relocating those new meanings. My aim is to provide for a new theory of the public sphere as a concrete mediation in which justice connects to solidarity in a narrative fashion.

As in the case of Habermas, I am aware that many feminist criticisms have focused on Arendt's lack of interest in women's issues and on her 'traditionalist' view of politics, which are conceived by her critics as 'Aristotelian' or opaquely 'Heideggerian'. I wish to develop evidence to indicate that both charges are untrue. Arendt understood herself as an 'agonistic' thinker, a 'pariah', refusing to be classified by any particular tag. She resisted being called a philosopher, and used 'disclosive' terms to configure a new conceptualization of democracy and politics. Nor did she wish to give particular weight to her birth as a woman and a Jew. Nonetheless, I believe that she gave weight to both particularities in her own theoretical narratives, and that it was for this reason that her work provides a 'new beginning' – as a special kind of judgement – in the form of a new story for democracy after the moral collapse of the holocaust. Her example could be taken as suggesting a narrative of how the 'uniqueness' of a writer's position makes her account of human action meaningful, a point that such feminists as Bonnie Honig have described with significant clarity.[15] While it is also true that Arendt's vision of the public can appear as a 'traditional' or 'nostalgic' account of the relation between public and private life, through the interconnection between different traditions she makes her theory capable of responding to the major threats and challenges of contemporary societies. She provides for the most emphatic theory of plurality as a source of democratic societies, while, at the same time, her notion of plurality intertwines with a strong conception of the 'individual'. No one regarding 'plurality' as a basic condition of democracy can be called a conservative, especially one who gives such a significant role to human individuality. By understanding the role that narratives perform in the public sphere, Arendt is able to give an account of just how plurality and the uniqueness of individuals are embodied. It is in the political world of the public where 'the action he begins is humanly disclosed by the word, and though his deed can be perceived in its brute physical appearance without verbal accompaniment, it becomes relevant only through the spoken word which he identifies himself as the actor, announcing what he does, has done, and intends to do'.[16] In focusing in various chapters of this book on the elements that make Arendt one of the most relevant thinkers for contemporary democracy, I will show how she herself has become a 'narrative' for a new beginning for women.[17]

In the process of this new incorporation of Arendt, I hope to throw doubt on Dana Villa's assumption that any 'attempt to recast the public sphere in accordance with a universalistic model of practical reason (whether deontological or discursive) is invariably an attempt to eliminate the performative dimension of politics'.[18] Because my model provides for a theory of contested meanings in the symbolic order, as well as the communicative side of language, I can show how the performative and the consensual sides of speech-acts are interrelated. The rules governing political speech in terms of validity can now be seen as a specific interaction between two validity spheres, the moral and the aesthetic. The agonistic dimension refers back to the expressive sphere, where the validity is granted by an appeal to the quality of an authentic or sincere expression. The moral dimension, by contrast, introduces normative contents into speech-acts through the capacity to configure critically elements of a description that seeks to provide evidence of injustice or past injury. With the introduction of narratives into the deliberative dimension of the public sphere, the performative dimension of politics is restored, even while the normative stance is preserved through the comprehension of how it is an impossible task to build democratic institutions and practices without collective agreements. 'Justice' is a normative concept that stands as a space where critical and contesting historical 'meanings' and 'understandings' are brought into public deliberation to transform our lives. In this way, the public sphere integrates performance and persuasion, deliberation and initiation, agonism and agreement.

There are other theoretical works on narrative which I have also drawn on here, some of which have striking affinities with Arendt's. This is certainly the case for Ricoeur's major book *Time and Narrative*.[19] In this work, Ricoeur succeeds in systematizing the structural interrelation of the two dimensions of narrative, the philosophical and the literary. Furthermore, he is able to give an account of how stories are capable of 'innovating' life.[20] In elaborating the interrelation between the moral and the aesthetic spheres, he provides important reasons for clarifying the relation of narratives to projects of identity, as I suggest in chapters 3, 5 and 8. Yet only in his later work, *Oneself as Another* (1992), does Ricoeur seem to have become aware of the similarities between his project and Arendt's. However, in contrast to her work, Ricoeur's notions of the political and the public sphere display little of the complexity of his narrative theory. I examine this problem in detail in chapter 7, in which I address Ricoeur's model of recognition as the hermeneutical model.

Like Arendt, Ricoeur has an explicit theory of the ontological level of narratives, as well as a profound understanding of Heidegger's conception of time and language. He, too, develops his theory of narratives by returning to such classical sources as Aristotle and Augustine, philosophers who allow him to develop the interrelation between 'mimesis' and 'action' and 'time' and 'plots'.[21] Differences in Arendt's and Ricoeur's approaches, however, become apparent when one focuses on the different strategies they employ to put some distance between their ideas and the purely Heideggerian attitude to time and language. In her early writings, Arendt admired Augustine because he allowed her to reframe the conceptualization of the political world in terms of experience of becoming 'human'. Later on, she recovered Aristotle's conception of community as well as his understanding of human beings as political animals. Through her deep critical understanding of Aristotle, Arendt refurbished the concepts of 'praxis', 'speech' and 'action'. She also grasped the resemblance between Benjamin's and Heidegger's notions of time and language, and, most importantly, the fact that they both were connected in different ways to the aesthetic realm. What Benjamin provided was a highly moral concern that was lacking in the purely aestheticized Heideggerian view. On this basis, Arendt connected her conception of the public sphere as the human creation of plurality with a conception of narratives as the sources of a reflexive judgement capable of envisioning utopian futures. Unlike Heidegger, it is not the aesthetization of the moral sphere that interests her, but, rather, the interconnection of these realms as communicative spheres.

By contrast, Ricoeur employs Aristotle and Augustine to counteract the 'deadly' effects of Heidegger's notions of being and time. Ricoeur's strategy is to counteract Heidegger with Augustine: 'Augustine's break-through is exploited in the most decisive way, even though this occurs, as we shall see, beginning from Heidegger's meditation on being-towards-death and not, as in Augustine, from the structure of the threefold present'.[22] Ricoeur's theory of recognition is structured by a moral concern; on the basis of a profoundly religious orientation, he views narratives as ways to 'configure and transfigure the practical field' in a manner that can 'encompass not just acting but also suffering, hence characters as agents and victims'.[23] The problem is that Ricoeur has difficulty in drawing out the political implications of this position. The reason is clear. Where Arendt succeeded in providing for a contemporary account of the political in her notion of the public sphere, in the later theory of recognition he elaborated in *Oneself as Another*, Ricoeur had to develop his connection of narratives with emancipatory content via the Aristotelian conception of solidarity as esteem and friendship (as discussed in chapter 7).

Until now, much of the work done by critical theory has been carried out on the basis of 'discourse theory', based on familiar features of Habermas' model of deliberation. As I indicated earlier, criticisms have been raised against this model for over-emphasizing the rationality of deliberation, by employing a restricted conception of rationality which seems to exclude disagreement, contested exclusions and heterogeneity. The highly Kantian view of critical theory has also been a target for criticism from feminist, communitarian and post-structuralist positions. Nonetheless, I chose a critical theory frame because I wish to develop a theory that can relate identities as processes of social relations that are inherently normative. I open up the critical theory perspective by suggesting that there are multiple, not restricted, forms of interactive rationality. In addition to the sources mentioned above, and within this critical theory tradition, in making this argument I draw on the work of Albrecht Wellmer, who has provided deep insights into the dynamic relation of the moral and the aesthetic validity spheres (see chapter 2).

A Bridge Between Critical Theory and Post-structuralist Narratives

I would certainly wish to acknowledge that very significant efforts have already been made to counter criticisms of the restricted scope of Habermasian critical theory. I use some of those efforts as examples of feminist narratives. Seyla Benhabib, for example, has built her feminist critical view on a wider model relating issues of the good life to the realm of moral issues.[24] Portraying Arendt's contradictions as a kind of 'reflexive grist' for her own mill, she has creatively attempted to bring Arendt's most important categories into a deliberative model of discourse ethics.[25] Benhabib's creative interpretations of Arendt's work have strongly influenced my own approach, but she stays much more carefully than I within Habermasian limits. Rather than mixing Habermas and Arendt, she seeks to rescue Arendt from her own contradictions by bringing her to a discourse ethics model. My own approach is to use Arendt as a complementary balance against some of the thinly procedural notions of the Habermasian model. Simply put, I believe one needs Arendt to be able to give some cultural content to the Habermasian notions of language and to the contestatory dimension of 'emancipatory movements' in the public sphere.

Nancy Fraser's critical theoretical writings have also been important for me. By acknowledging the existence of several publics, both strong and weak ones, they have clarified the radical potential of contestatory movements. Fraser has also given a great deal of attention to establishing bridges with feminists from other traditions.[26] With her ability to see the impact of the political in relation to the moral, she has fundamentally clarified the history of feminism and its impact in social life over the last thirty years. My differences with Fraser are related to her analytical separation of 'distribution' and 'recognition' as two different kinds of claim, and with her rather negative view of what she calls the 'cultural turn'. I wish to propose, by contrast, that justice can be incorporated into a cultural frame without any damage to traditional egalitarian concerns about class, race or, of course, gender.

Jodi Dean has recently taken the critical feminist turn in critical theory one step further by trying to integrate the concerns of other traditions into a model of solidarity that provides for an expanded space for 'the other'.[27] Offering an original reading of Mead's concept of the generalized other, she hopes to avoid potentially restrictive implications of conventional and affectional solidarities. Her strategy is to open up our conceptions of the 'we' by making the cognitive and emotional concept into a normative one. With this twist, Dean can approach some of the challenges that feminists confront when they emphasize only the conventional or affectional sides of solidarity. I share her ambitions in this regard; my difference has only to do with the manner in which it should be carried out. What is missing from her account is a cultural understanding of how the normative conception of the 'we' is developed. It is precisely the struggle to expand the 'we', through symbolic interventions in the public sphere, that this book is about.

As will be evident in the chapters that follow, the ideas of many other critical theorists have been helpful to me in the formulation of my arguments, among them such thinkers as Thomas McCarthy, James Bohman, Axel Honneth, and Jean Cohen and Andrew Arato. Like Honneth and Cohen and Arato, and unlike many of the other critical theorists who have influenced this book, the way in which the theory is built is fundamental to my philosophical methodology. I have gone back to the approach to critical theory of Habermas himself, viewing it as an effort at normative reconstruction that is rooted in empirical development. For me, these developments have to do with the emergence and development of feminism, as social movement, literary efflorescence and intellectual critique, a development I take to be more or less continuous with modernity. While I take various feminists' interventions in the public sphere to be of equal significance in this empirical sense, this does not mean that I do not have critical differences with many of them (see especially chapter 8). Yet, while it is by no means the case that every approach to the public sphere or to women's identity seems equally convincing to me, from my methodological standpoint it will be important to bring to light the illocutionary effects that have been produced by different feminist strategies. It is for this reason that I have investigated and try to understand sympathetically a wide variety of feminist traditions and approaches. For example, I have found Martha Nussbaum's connection with the Aristotelian tradition very fruitful. Her work can now be considered by some postmodern critics as metaphysical and her intentions universalistic. Yet her books provide a clear example of how an influential feminist narrative interweaves the moral and the aesthetic, and, in this sense, it offers incomparable insights for my theory. Nussbaum also provides a clear example of a tradition that has fought to rescue the universal claim for justice in terms of 'human capabilities'.[28]

Another issue I would like to clarify in terms of the relation to the feminist literature is 'the normative'. With this term, I refer to certain kinds of concept that are related to the 'ought' as compared to the real. It is the reference to 'oughtness' that characterizes core arguments in the spheres of law, morality and politics. Some feminists have expressed horror at including such 'metaphysical' allusions in their accounts, claiming that the normative reference of such supposedly universal moral, political and legal theories merely camouflages particularistic masculine conceptions. My opinion, on the other hand, is that it is precisely because of an inherently normative dimension referring to the 'ought' that it is always possible to question what purportedly universal theories aim to define. Universalistic theories are theories related to justice, thus to the possibility of enlarging the scope of integration and emancipation. A normative approach is not metaphysical insofar as it allows for an historical falsifiable criticism. To give a space to reflection about what needs to be done does not refer to essences,[29] to ahistorical claims, or to the conflation of the 'ought' with the 'is'. It is in that sense that my theory is postmetaphysical, connecting with other feminists who have tried to defend the possibility of making critical claims about how things should be while escaping the 'aporias' that are at stake when feminism wants to be framed as a discourse of justice. This seems to me precisely Linda Alcoff's concern. 'If metaphysics is conceived not as any particular ontological commitment but as the attempt to reason through ontological issues that cannot be decided empirically', she argues, 'then metaphysics continues today in Derrida's analysis of language, Foucault's conception of power, and all poststructuralist critiques of humanist theories of the subject'. From this viewpoint, she concludes, 'the assertion that someone is doing metaphysics does not serve as pejorative'.[30]

My use of the notion of narratives may also seem vulnerable to criticism from the point of view of feminist post-identity projects. The worry here is the way in which this notion has often been tied to traditionalist concerns. This is the path that Alasdair MacIntyre takes in the communitarian model he develops in *After Virtue*, where he conceives of narratives as reinforcing ideas about people's identities. In religious traditions like the Jewish one, the reading of stories has, similarly, been a means for maintaining a sense of the traditional community. Here again, critics have seen narratives as exclusionary devices that undermine heterogeneity and difference. Yet, there have been recent post-structuralists and postmodern feminist theories that have tried to develop more critical narrative models *vis-à-vis* more traditionalist and universal ones. Some of these efforts display radical scepticism about any 'privileged' critical standpoint and about the possibility of normative consensus. Narratives are seen, in this view, as ways to historicize 'experience', a process that creates a place for asserting its indeterminacy.[31] The aim of this critical approach to narratives is not that stories can illuminate what it is like to be oppressed or marginalized, but, rather, that stories can expose power relations. Subjectivity here is understood as determined by macro-social forces of power and domination. At the bottom of this position lies the idea that we are all merely social constructions. Our experience is a construct – a 'technology of the self'[32] – mediated only by social discourse. Thus, since the early 1980s, feminists like Teresa de Lauretis have argued that 'a starting point may be to think of gender along the lines of Michel Foucault's theory of sexuality as a "technology of sex" and to propose that gender, too, both as representation and self-representation, is the product of various social technologies, such as cinema, and of institutionalized discourses, epistemologies, and critical practices, as well as practices of everyday life'.[33] With this turn, post-structuralist conceptions of narrative have stressed the 'fictional' part of the construction of the subject. To understand historically some of the self's 'fictitious' content is certainly an achievement. The emphasis on social explanations of individual practices and experiences has forced some theorists to take a 'deconstructive' look at social life and to understand the historical dimensions of social institutions as well as societies' own self-representations. However, I disagree with the absolute claim that the construction of the subject is purely fictional. If this is so, there would be only biological explanations of what humans have shared across history and societies or, alternatively, no explanation of ourselves at all.[34] Paradoxically, such a negative approach would deny the possibility of thinking that emancipatory efforts could make things realistically better. I have developed my book to show exactly the contrary. Indeed, I demonstrate that such narrative efforts at deconstruction – as well as efforts that can be characterized as cultural and critical – have developed their multiple strategies of re-reading history, social institutions and conceptions of the self, in order to sustain the normative and non-relative claim that such cultural and social devices have deprived half of humanity of the necessary conditions of life. I will try to demonstrate this strong claim in the 'aesthetic laboratory' provided by women's biographical and autobiographical accounts. These accounts, I will argue, are increasingly tied up with feminist efforts to recover their lives by retelling their stories in the public sphere.

Post-structuralism is right to emphasize that action does not develop entirely through the subjects' intentions, but that does not mean necessarily that intentions have no importance at all in relation to the challenge of transforming social structures and social discourses. The striking thing about such an argument is that it erases the possibility of giving any weight to individual agencies, falling into the same kind of determinism as did Marxists when they conceived the force of history to be the only real and material force. In the history of Western democracies, however, there is enough empirical evidence to suggest the very opposite, namely, that social movements have challenged previous ways of understanding how justice should be implemented. It is because of human intentions, and not because of some extra-individual force, that justice itself, as a term, has acquired a new meaning in this century. Of women's struggles Alcoff asks the right question: 'Why is a right wing woman's consciousness constructed via social discourse but feminist consciousness not?'[35] How can critical feminist theories explain this without giving a place for contingencies and intentions in the emancipatory and altruistic movements led by women themselves?

In her widely read book *Alice Doesn't*, De Lauretis offered a careful semiotic analysis of what narratives have meant in the symbolic development of male identity. Through a revision and from other treatments she tried to demonstrate the continual recurrence of the 'Oedipal tale' as a childhood experience that created male dominance and female submission. She concluded by suggesting 'it may well be, however, that the story has to be told differently'.[36] Indeed, the fact that women have written critical and influential works of art (and philosophy, and social science) over the last century has shown that we do not need to enter an 'Oedipal tale' to make a woman's life story meaningful. This provides compelling empirical evidence about the limitations of the post-structuralist argument about our so-called 'incapacity' to define who we are. Take, for example, Virginia Woolf's *Orlando*, where her character, at times a man, at times a woman, has no story in which the 'symbolic' configuration of an 'Oedipal' plot is enacted. There is no 'male' violence in Orlando's plasticity. One morning, after many adventures as a man, Orlando simply becomes a woman. She feels and lives these body changes despite repressive social structures and her experience is far more enriching once she grasps her own female consciousness. It has been this kind of new reading of Woolf's novels that created the possibility for developing new versions of the story, as Sally Potter did in her film of *Orlando*. In fact, one need go no further than Virginia Woolf's classic novel *To the Lighthouse* to discover a sense of self that is rather different from traditional or even modern plots. Here the female author's voice is decodified in six different characters.[37] Such aesthetic experiments always offer new forms of subjectivities. Stories have been, for more than a century, inventing a variety of new profiles for women. Self-identification is not a simple lineal task but a great and complex process that relates two different fields. The freedom of imagination allows one to grasp the levels of experience in the institutional frame of language, and these fragments are then projected into a moral sphere, where new and more effective processes of learning and judging emerge. In this framework, reflexivity becomes a principal feature of the contemporary subject. One process of reflexivity starts when an author is creating an exploratory moral quest for identity through the written word. The second level is related to that of the readers in the 'act of reading', which is itself a highly reflexive moral search. Ricoeur argues that 'the call for verisimilitude could not long hide the fact that verisimilitude is not just resemblance to truth but also a semblance of truth'.[38] I argue that it is indeed a different kind of truth, one that refers to the aesthetic sphere of validity. To the extent that the narratives of art have an effect, they bring something new into the world. In my opinion, it is here, in narratives as action, that every myth can be challenged.

As Arendt argues, no story belongs to one person in particular; every one of them is rewoven into new stories that bring to life a variety of different meanings and experiences and thereby provide new possibilities for action.[39] My argument is that there has been more than 'empirical evidence' from women's narratives to demonstrate how the appropriation of stories has been an empowering technique aimed at the recovery of 'women' and their intentional capacities.

Another post-structuralist view with which my book takes issue is 'nominalism'.[40] Post-structural conceptions of narratives owe much to Jean-François Lyotard's idea that the postmodern condition is best expressed as fragmentation and discontinuity. Only local knowledges are possible, and it is only such knowledges that can provoke contestation and produce new ideas. Here too, the category of 'women' is only a fiction, and it must be appropriately dismantled.[41] The problem here lies in the logical impossibility of asserting a 'better' or 'worse' interpretation about the content of any identity text, for if they are all equally fictions then they are all equally unjudgeable. Yet here too, there are feminists who are seeking to find a way out of the paradox that is inherent in such positions, for at the bottom of these critical post-structuralist discourses there is, inevitably, a critical reflexivity linked to consciousness and intention. Some feminist theorists find themselves once again suggesting the reality of some normative points of departure. This is the case with De Lauretis' notion of subjectivity, which relates itself critically to the pragmatist view experience offered by Charles S. Peirce.[42] It is only after De Lauretis is able to give a notion of agency 'through political interpretation' that she can overcome the dilemma I earlier described in relation to _Alice Doesn't_, for it is through agency that political interpretations are possible. Instead of conceiving the 'symbolic order' as 'unchangeable' or stressing a pure 'fragmented self', she now envisions 'particular discursive configurations' as strategies of women's narratives.[43]

It is precisely this viewpoint that allows me to explore the consequences of an emancipatory social movement that has struggled, through interventions in the public sphere, to redefine justice and the good. I claim that it is the many different efforts of women's narratives that have made it possible to answer political questions about the viability of democratic ideals. Examining these narratives gives me the possibility of moving between past, present and future, connecting different stories which are in the continuous process of being retold. Methodologically speaking, the reader will have to travel through the same discourses as they are performed by different authors at different times. In this way, I can provide for readers themselves the experience of the 'concrete ways by which textual configuration mediates between the prefiguration of the practical field and its refiguration through the reception of the work'.[44] Only through this device is it possible to illustrate how pre-signified human action can be over- or re-signified in relation to earlier stages, and more traditional modes of symbolic articulation. Through this continuous signifying process one can see the different levels of illocutionary force that have allowed women to display and enact new understandings of themselves as moral subjects.

Thus, the readers will be able to follow the philosophical structure of this book. Part I, entitled 'From the Aesthetic to the Moral Sphere', opens with a chapter called 'Autobiographies and Biographies: The Construction of Women's Identity', which develops its conceptual structure by taking Habermas and Arendt as its main sources. It shows how women's autobiographies are reconstructed narratives, not objective accounts, and describes how these imaginative reconstructions have functioned as illocutionary forms. It describes Habermas' first approach to the cultural sphere through his empirical research on *The Structural Transformation of the Public Sphere*. It goes on to rescue Arendt's conception of storytelling and then provides examples of how projects of self-realization and self-determination come together as moral demands for recognition.

Chapter 2, 'Communicative Rationality: Between Spheres of Validity', interprets Albrecht Wellmer's work as developing a decentred conception of rationality and its dynamic feedbacks. I connect this general philosophical discussion to the women's movement, showing how its discourses have been related to aesthetic boundaries in a way that allows women's identities to be imagined and constructed in novel ways.

This is followed by 'Feminism as an Illocutionary Model', a chapter that develops a philosophical definition of what recognition means, viewing it as the successful result of an interaction between social groups and the public. I examine how a wide range of different kinds of feminist effort can be understood as constructions of new public narratives which retell the stories of women, interrelating the aesthetic and the moral spheres and redefining the relationship between justice and the good.

Chapter 4, 'Autonomy and Authenticity as Textures of the Moral Subject', deals with the way in which feminism has opened up a new paradigm for thinking about autonomy and authenticity. It involves first describing the demands for self-determination and self-realization as two inseparable strands in the project by which the moral subject constructs her identity as a life worth living. It reveals also the ways in which two validity spheres, the aesthetic and the moral, are closely linked.

Part I concludes with a chapter called 'Narrative Cultural Interweavings: Between Facts and Fiction', which investigates the new meaning of human capabilities that can be drawn out of the feminist model. Drawing on a further elaboration of narratives and the dynamics established between the public sphere and the new emergent publics, I explain how such moral narratives constitute the symbolic order in three stages of 'mimetic representation'. The model articulates the feedbacks between specific historical moments when 'lay narratives' are invented in response to a particular challenge and the subsequent creative process of the initial construction of the literary narrative which is followed by a return to the experiential dimension of the readers, where narratives gain influence and transform previous ways of seeing things, a process that can occur both contemporaneously, and also decades or centuries later.

Part II takes this philosophical investigation further, under the heading 'From the Moral to the Political Sphere'. Its opening chapter, 'Justice and Solidarity: Women in the Public Sphere', relates my model of narratives to a discussion of the relation of a group's claim for recognition and the emergence of new public self-understandings. I consider feminist strategies, focusing on recent discussions about deliberative democracy and the transformation of institutions through the 'disclosive' process of criticism stemming from this new female public. I then proceed to argue that, because of these developments, earlier and more abstract models of solidarity are currently being revised. Because feminist criticisms have gained acceptance in public opinion, conceptualizations about solidarity in relation to justice can be reframed.

Chapter 7, 'The Moral Foundation of Recognition: A Critical Revision of Three Models', investigates different models of recognition by contemporary philosophers. Only recently have political philosophy and morality become concerned with this issue, for only with contemporary discussions of how to revalue heterogeneity and plurality have the moral contents of the term 'recognition' become so clearly important for understanding post-traditional societies. Hegel's legacy has now been reinterpreted through the traditions of hermeneutics, philosophy of language and critical theory, and most importantly, through the works of Charles Taylor, Axel Honneth and Paul Ricoeur. This chapter critically examines these three models of recognition.

The final chapter, 'Feminist Models of Recognition: Problems of Multiculturalism', approaches feminism as a basic model for rethinking problems of multiculturalism and continues the themes of chapter 7. In the conclusion I show how the model of illocutionary force can be applied to other emancipatory social movements and refer to the works of scholars that have affinities with the model developed in this book.

Part I

From the Aesthetic to the
Moral Sphere

1 Autobiographies and Biographies: The Construction of Women's Identity

I propose a model of recognition based on narratives performing simultaneously identity claims and institutional transformations. Today, almost all of the literature devoted to moral issues is linked, one way or another, to questions of moral identity. Since the 1980s the configuration of moral identities has been clearly related to narratives,[1] primarily because theories of language connect issues of the self to the 'narrative constructions of stories'.[2] However, until the late 1990s the tradition of critical theory had shown little interest in this interrelation, which, nonetheless, can be traced through important aspects of theories of various authors. I intend to develop a connection between the thematization of narratives and the moral dimension through a new approach to Jürgen Habermas' discussions of identity and narratives and to Hannah Arendt's conception of storytelling from the point of view of critical theory. I focus first on Habermas' notion of the public sphere and its relation to autobiographies as tools for presenting a self-fashioned moral model, which originated with Rousseau's autobiography. I then broaden this approach via Arendt's conception of storytelling as one of the most important elements for building a culture that deals with the past and envisions a utopian future. Both viewpoints have a common link: the use of the public sphere. In this chapter I aim to show how by recovering some insights in Habermas' original formulation of autobiographies and in Arendt's concept of storytelling, the idea of narratives as self-presentations can be developed, as can a theory of culture that sees moral identities as products of performative narratives between social groups and civil society that simultaneously create and reconfigure the symbolic order.

In order to do this, I must first return to the problematic of the relationship between the moral and the aesthetic domains. While they are implicitly related in the theories of Habermas and Arendt, this

connection must be made explicit if the claim that narratives are vehicles of emerging moral and political identities is to be substantiated.
After making this argument, I then return to my model of feminism to
illustrate these interconnections, showing how women's autobiographies and biographies have already performed illocutionary transformations of conceptions of moral identities.

A New Formulation of the Interconnection between
Justice and the Good Life

The differentiation between the fields of ethics (*Sittlichkeit*) and morality (*Moralität*), which Habermas examined in depth on several occasions,[3] has led to an analysis of the pertinence of this separation or, as
the case may be, of the difficulties which this conceptualization promoted in the division between moral life and matters of public order,
inasmuch as both clearly affect the integral nature of daily life. In
passing, I should like to note that Habermas' critics have pointed out
ideas which are relevant to this debate. For example, Thomas McCarthy
indicated the difficulty with the conception of practical discourse that
supposedly separates the 'ethical' from the 'moral'. If discussion arises
on the issue of the interpretations of needs, McCarthy argued, we will
find ourselves involved in the consideration of the values in 'terms of
which [those] needs are interpreted'.[4] And if we go further, he suggests,
we will enter into a discussion of 'strong evaluations' that can easily
'lead to a consideration of who we are and who we want to be'. Thus,
Habermas' insistence on leaving behind the 'evaluative frames' does
not allow value standards to be criticized and revised, for they are
embodied in particularistic conceptions. Therefore, argues McCarthy,
Habermas needs to consider that 'these modes of communication' are
closely tied to the contexts of actions and experiences of the participants. By not allowing 'practical discourses' to be related to value
standards, and by conceiving such discussions as scrutinizing only
'arguments', Habermas not only misses the close link between values,
experiences and selves, but also closes the door on the possibility of
seeing 'practical discourses' as 'reflective discussions' with the
transformative power to get to know the 'experiences of significant
others, life crises, alien cultures, countercultures'.[5] Habermas' position,
then, would fail to clarify the problems of recognition that plural societies entail. Discourse is not a substitute for experience; rather, it guides
us by expressing experiences.
    A very similar point was raised by Albrecht Wellmer, when he
argued that moral arguments are almost 'exclusively concerned with
the interpretation of situations attendant upon actions and needs, as

well as with the way that those who act or suffer the consequences of actions see themselves'.[6] Discourse ethics, argues Wellmer, must begin any critique or clarification in the field of validity, where identities are thematized.[7] For her part, Seyla Benhabib suggests that the idea of a moral point of view, as conceived by Habermas, leaves us in a dilemma similar to the 'Archimedean point of view' in the field of cognition. It portrays the moral point of view as something empty and oversimplified. Benhabib argues that even though Habermas defends his position as a dialogical model of reasoning, the standpoint of 'practical discourse' seems to be articulated only in 'theoretical terms', where a 'central procedure is presented to moral agents as the "privileged description" corresponding to _the_ moral point of view'.[8] Thus, according to Benhabib, 'discursive argumentation' should be the new procedure by which universalization itself is interpreted 'discursively'. These arguments, in turn, bring us to feminist criticism pointing to the need to reconsider the interrelationship between questions of justice and those of the good life, a criticism generated simultaneously by the communitarians.[9]

If one considers these issues in terms of Habermas' theory itself, it is possible to see which of his ideas have changed and why. In the process, Habermas' initial position can be shown to lead to a totally new interpretation of the interconnections between moral and ethical discourses, viewed in terms of narratives and the public sphere. Although Habermas has made only empirical references to this possibility in various parts of his work, in my view, he has never fully addressed its implications on a normative basis. Thus, while carefully reconstructing some of his arguments, I develop my own viewpoint on how critical theory can provide a model of narratives in the public sphere.

In the first place, we must consider that Habermas thinks that the separation between morality and ethics is part of a historical process of intersubjective configuration, in which social subjects evolve until they achieve reflexive and normative thought.[10] This postconventional stage is capable of dealing with moral rules and norms, the verification and internalization of moral values, and a socialization which recognizes human rights and duties. This is no trivial matter, since it postulates that the acceptance of human beings as such has been a struggle producing an internalization and an intersubjective acceptance of all human beings as worthy of consideration. It attributes to them the reflexive capacity for rational thought so that they may reason about questions of moral and political life. This means that the processes of abstraction and universalization also imply a moral evolution, allowing individuals to adopt these reflexive attitudes as well as to assume hypothetical ones and to question the concrete foundations on which their norms are validated. Such individuals are also able to stand back from their own worlds in order to reach a more abstract plane on which they may or may not validate a norm or action.

This formulation, however, leaves unexamined the role of experience in morality or in the construction of a moral identity. Carol Gilligan provided a variety of examples about the different ways in which practical experience leads women to a postconventional level.[11] Furthermore, the experience of women in their struggle for recognition in the public sphere has illuminated the close interrelationship between questions of the good life and issues of justice. Precisely because such voices were heard, public arguments were able to make explicit the lack of recognition and the injustice that was preserved by an aprioristic separation between these two spheres. This connection, as shown in Gilligan's examples of women as narrators of their moral concerns and their own specific point of view, has been established through a recovery of the 'narratives' of the lives of women as they have been recaptured in the public sphere.

Yet, despite these systematic gaps in his approach, which feminist critics have illuminated, I maintain that there is a conception of the connection between justice and the good life that is present from the very beginning of Habermas' theoretical career. Paradoxical as it might seem, it is in his sociological writings on the origins of the public sphere that this interconnection first appeared, on the empirical level; this insight later crystallized theoretically in Habermas' conception of self-determination and self-realization as interrelated processes of a simultaneous development of individuation and socialization. In his later works, the interconnection is between private and public autonomy relating questions of deliberative politics to a normative conception of the public sphere.

Society's Processes of Self-Fashioning

In *The Structural Transformation of the Public Sphere*,[12] Habermas documents how the 'self-fashioning' features of letters and autobiographies performed and displayed new forms of subjectivity that broadened and transformed the public of readers. Habermas conceived the bourgeois public sphere as emerging from the creation of new literary genres, new social practices of reading political journals and pamphlets, and new habits on the part of readers. The impact in salons, coffee houses and public spaces was immediate. A significant part of this historical reconstruction lay in its focus on the tensions generated between a catalogue of 'human rights', constitutive of the idea of the liberal public sphere, and the particularity required to view those subjects who were the bearers of such 'rights'. These tensions produced a dynamic in which the 'body politic' was the mediating force that allowed groups and people to integrate into a larger society.

However, the importance of Habermas' conception of the public sphere that I wish to stress is related to the connection that he establishes between the aesthetic and the moral realms. That is, he focuses not only on the dimension of the public sphere in its political expression, but on the 'cultural' interaction between the emergence of new literary genres and the interest of society in areas that, until then, were perceived as intimate or private.[13] The cultural dynamic connected this emergence of literary genres with a new approach to the worth and authenticity of life achievements in the moral sense.[14] That is precisely why Habermas returns again and again, long after the publication of his first book, to the example of *The Confessions* of Jean-Jacques Rousseau, which provides the best example of an autobiographical self-presentation that is, at the same time, an intended moral claim on how to lead life.[15]

By focusing on this dimension, Habermas is able to grasp the importance of the cultural and symbolic meanings interwoven in the public sphere, and, particularly, the exploration and presentation of new identities configured inside it. Moreover, Habermas clearly links the two validity spheres in this process of striving for an identity, and, at the same time, of conceiving oneself as a moral example of a new kind of human being. Interestingly, Habermas sees this dynamic as a 'performative discourse': 'The dialogue form too, employed by many of the articles, attested to their proximity to the spoken word. One and the same discussion transposed into a different medium was continued in order to reenter, via reading, the original conversation medium'.[16] The public was concerned with itself and 'sought agreement and enlightenment through the rational-critical public debate of private persons with one another which flowed from the wellspring of a specific subjectivity'.[17]

At the same time, one of the basic definitions of the public sphere in *The Structural Transformation of the Public Sphere* is the relation between public and private. Habermas defines the bourgeois public sphere as 'the sphere of private people [that] come together as a public'.[18] Habermas offers an original idea when he focuses on the interrelationship between the codes of intimacy, characteristic of fiction, and the new and expanding subjectivities.[19]

The importance of this early historical reconstruction is Habermas' accent on the specific interrelation between emerging identities and the creation of new literary genres. In this sense, his reconstruction opens a dimension in which to conceptualize the symbolic order and culture as key elements of the public sphere. Habermas' account of the emergence of the public sphere distinguishes between the literary and the political spheres that together constitute a historical fusion in the understanding of bourgeois society. However, in this work he focuses on practices of social actors, their public access to education, their new habits in creating and attending public gatherings for theatrical representations and musical concerts. The aesthetic dimension is explored through his understanding of how the relations between author, work and the public changed: 'They became intimate mutual relationships between privatized individuals who were psychologically interested in what was "human", in self-knowledge, and in empathy'.[20] The result of this process was the creation of the genre of 'fiction',[21] which, at the same time, allowed people to enter into 'the literary action as a substitute for his own, to use the *relationships between the figures, between author, the characters, and the reader as substitute relationships for reality.'*[22]

Habermas argued that the family was the intimate sphere differentiated from the private realm, the latter being related to the logic of the market. It was in the former space that individuals were able to experiment with their growing subjectivities, and they could do so, not only through the dynamics of their intimate relations of love and friendship, but also because of the transformative social dynamics embedded in those subjectivities, which mediated between readers and the influence of the novels and books creating new ideas of society's self-understanding in the symbolic order. It was then, according to Habermas, that the living-room and the salon were relocated under the same roof. Publicity and privacy needed each other for 'converting the public sphere in the world of letters already equipped with institutions of the public and with forums for discussion'. With their help, Habermas wrote, 'the experiential complex of audience-oriented privacy made its way also into the political realm's public sphere'.[23] The public made out of private persons transformed itself into a critical public sphere, one which gave rise to publicity and new platforms for discussion. In the same way, the experimental side of privateness then appeared as being mediated by political publicity. The political task of bourgeois publicity was the regulation of civil society; it achieved self-understanding through the legal norm, and the legal norm also was mediated by self-conscious institutionalized practices of literary publicity.

In spite of the fact that this early work has been criticized by many feminists, one of its main focuses was precisely the *performative* features that developed a specific critical dynamic between the 'private versus public',[24] which, in time, gave place to the creation of new ways of conceiving moral lives, their struggles, and their need for recognition. In this sense, I regard Habermas' insight into the dynamics of 'illocutionary forces' – performances – as very important to my own thesis and the exemplification of women's narratives.

On the basis of this conceptualization, the interrelationship between

the aesthetic and the moral domains and the performative configuration of identities can now be explored further, with Habermas' early
idea reinterpreted in the light of the way in which he used Mead's
formulation of the simultaneous process of socialization and individuation to develop his later theory. In Mead, Habermas finds 'the
connection between differentiation within the structure of roles, on the
one hand, and the formation of conscience and gain in autonomy by
individuals who are socialized in increasingly differentiated conditions, on the other hand'.[25] Habermas develops the concept of
intersubjective identity from Mead as well as from Durkheim and his
own later theory of language. Self-realization and self-determination
are the conditions under which subjects develop their identities, and
both require a reflexive attitude. It is precisely in the quest for identity
that the interrelationship between self-determination and self-realization becomes apparent. Social subjects can be autonomous to the degree
to which they are able to choose a form of self-realization in which
responsibility is assumed as a reflexive tool that often expresses itself as
a narrative. The moral values one assumes as conditions for the choice
of a life identity show that the project of autonomy cannot be based on
an a priori separation of moral issues and the good life. But this also
indicates the importance of moral support, which provides a normative
basis for justifying who we are and who we want to be within a
narrative.

In the first step, Habermas reconstructs the idea of individuation as
an identity process within socialization. He goes back to Johann Gottlieb
Fichte (1762–1814), who brought the issues of individuality and biographical identity to the fore.[26] Karl Wilhelm von Humboldt accounts
for them in the linguistic acknowledgement that comprehension of an
ego and an alter are necessary for a common understanding to be
reached.[27] But it was Søren Kierkegaard who saw public confession as
the assumption of a project of identity through self-affirmation.[28] However, as mentioned above, Habermas considers that the great change in
the affirmation of a projection of choice comes about in autobiographical texts, whose essence is a public dialogue. These can no longer be
seen simply as historical documents, but fall within the sphere of expressive validity, which now needs closer examination.

Habermas, in referring to Rousseau's _Confessions_, notes that its private nature has an unquestionable public goal, as it really appeals to
future generations in his project of authenticity. Thus, to employ a
concept of individuality that goes beyond purely descriptive intentions
requires a receiver of the confession in order to complete the performative act. In this dialogue, the focus is on the individuality which takes on
a special relevance in two simultaneous dimensions. On the one hand,
individuality requires a moral character in struggles to become a

worthy human being; on the other, it is implicated in an aesthetic relevance, in which the self-description becomes unique. These two dimensions, however, appear relevant only when addressed to the public, for only then does the performance entail the appearance of the specific 'human being' as a 'model' of a moral agent. There is a change in the validity claim that autobiographies like Rousseau's pursue: they want recognition of their specific struggle to become a worthy human being. Experiences and moral goals are now interwoven.[29] We are no longer dealing merely with descriptions, or reports, but with self-presentations which are only justified by their aim: 'The claim of recognition of the unexchangeable identity of a self which is manifest in a consciously assumed life style'.[30] As narratives of identity, argued Habermas, autobiographies always remain fragmentary. 'Rousseau's confessions can be most properly understood as an encompassing ethical self-understanding with justificatory intent, put before the public in order for the public to take a position on it'.[31]

Habermas claims that the performative knowledge expressed by the speaker has to be aided by an 'illocutionary act', which means that the explicit knowledge contained in the propositional content provides for the enactment of such a knowledge only when it is performed. This conceptualization avoids the essentialism of considering that an identity is fixed or can ever be completed.[32] Different moments allow us to reframe our narrative, and different publics grant us a historical perspective. In both cases, it is clear that no definitive meaning is assumed when a project of identity is exposed to the public, as Habermas argues when he described Rousseau's many different attempts at autobiographical works.

In the second step of his argument, Habermas turns to Mead's theory of socialization and individuation as simultaneous processes, where the 'me' performs as a 'generalized other', and the 'I' relates to this agency as 'spontaneity' that eludes consciousness. 'Through the fact that I perceive myself as the social object of an other, a new reflexive agency is formed through which ego makes the behavioral expectations of others into his own. To the normative character of these expectations, however, there corresponds a transmuted structure of this second "me" as well as a different function of the self-relation. . . . Self-reflection here takes on the specific tasks of mobilizing motives for action and of internally controlling one's own modes of behaviour'.[33] Whereas the 'me', as bearer of moral consciousness, adheres itself to conventions and practices of specific groups, the 'I' appears as the pressure of 'presocial', 'natural' drives that, through the impulse of imagination, strives for the innovative transformation of a 'way of seeing'.[34] Habermas argues that this distinction drawn from Mead allows us to account for the experience 'we have of the *difference* between the way in which institutionalized forms of social intercourse are placed in question by the revolt of split-off motives and repressed interests, and the way in which they are placed in question by the intrusion of a revolutionary renewed language that _allows us to see the world with new eyes_'.[35] Through Mead's psychological distinction between the 'me' and the 'I', Habermas reflects on the cultural and institutional dimensions of his conception of autonomy. This cultural paradigm allows him to argue that self-determination and self-realization become differentiated depending on the degree to which the accent is placed on 'the subject's own achievements'.[36] Subjects, in their individual projects, aim at the direction of a 'larger society': 'We are already familiar with the appeal to posterity from Rousseau, who regards the process in which he reaches self-understanding as being subjected to similar conditions of communication, conditions for a universal discourse that is counterfactually directed into the future'.[37] In Habermas' view, Mead gives the concept of self-realization a 'communication-theoretical formulation', similar to the one already achieved by the concept of self-determination in moral theory. 'Progressive individuation is measured,' according to Habermas, 'just as much against the _differentiation of unique identities_ as it is against the _growth of personal autonomy_'.[38]

Faced with this proof of the importance of the documents which made Rousseau and Kierkegaard the craftsmen of this new form of sensitivity, Habermas, through his discussion of Mead's model, posits that any project of autonomy as self-determining and self-realizing identity leads to a conscious effort to submit to public dialogue in order to gain recognition, and he envisions this as the utopian projection of a larger society. In my view, the most important features of this discussion are not how they inform Habermas' later model of moral evolution, but rather, their insight into how these new narratives become fundamental parts of the struggle for group recognition. This point has been fully argued by Axel Honneth in his _Struggles for Recognition_ (see chapter 7 below). The processes of self-determination and self-realization, which Habermas believed to be the means to achieving stage six of morality – the postconventional one – have been more the fruit of a permanent tension on the part of various collective and personal efforts than merely a developmental moral evolution. Moreover, Habermas seems to focus on the way contextualized reasoning and judgement are transformed when projects of identity are displayed in the public sphere and individuals grasp the interconnections of values and experiences and develop the new horizons that illuminate the moral scenario which envisions a 'larger society'. To explore these dynamics is to explore the possibility of retelling the story of justice as it has been conceived in such struggles. However, this perspective is more appropriately framed when we focus on Hannah Arendt's conception of 'narratives' as a key element of the collective reordering of society's self-interpretation into a new beginning.

In *Between Facts and Norms: Contributions to a Discourse Theory of Law and Democracy*,[39] Habermas explores the sociological and philosophical aspects of law as a tension between facticity and validity. He still insists here on the separation of discourses, yet he is revealing about the problem of identities in his claim that moral and ethical dimensions can be related in political discourses. Questions of self-determination and self-realization must interact.[40] Self-reflexiveness adds a tension between 'consciousness of contingency, self-reflection, and liability for one's own existence'.[41] Though the intrusion of reflexiveness has fostered individualism in personal life projects and pluralism in collective life, Habermas insists that moral discourses and ethical deliberations remain analytically differentiated. The mediating link between these two types of discourses is law, conceived by Habermas thus: 'At the post-traditional level of justification, individuals develop a principled moral consciousness and orient their action by the idea of self-determination. What self-legislation or moral autonomy signifies in the sphere of personal life corresponds to the rational natural-law *interpretations of political freedom, that is, interpretations of democratic self-legislation in the constitution of a just society*'.[42] The ideas of self-determination and self-realization generate a tension which liberals and republicans had to face and try to solve. Habermas then alludes to his pragmatic search for an internal connection between 'popular sovereignty' and 'human rights', through the normative content of the 'mode of exercising political autonomy'.[43]

From the sociological point of view, law must have the authority to achieve social integration, since traditional religious views have lost their normative authority. From the philosophical point of view, law must have its basis in notions of justice that allow democratic societies to legitimate them. This is why Habermas develops his legal discourse theory, which tries to find a normative basis, on the one hand, and, on the other, to account for the institutional dimensions in which this discursive theory is embedded. The tensions between facticity and validity are shown in the claims of social groups that demand recognition of their rights, more democratic structures, and channels to build their identities publicly, along with claims that focus on the lack of freedom and justice that these groups have experienced in the past. Yet law is also coercive, and it has been articulated to impose regulations on social relations. Recovering the notion of 'civil society', Habermas conceptualizes this social function in terms of social integration. He argues that the integration of all of its members into a free and equal association is a task that depends on moral grounds that relate to the validity of the modern system of law. The need for social integration arises from the new ways in which the modern processes of differentiation take place.

As a result of the juridification of all social relations, democratic citizenship has become universalized. The core of this citizenship is the right to participate politically. The new flourishings of public political participation arise from civil society, a web of voluntary associations protected by basic rights that enforces new ways of communicating in the public sphere. In this sense, law appears as a regent of 'society' that has transformed itself into 'civil society', and is able to take the claims of solidarity within an abstract configuration that grants it legitimacy. Modern law must admit the claims of solidarity through the universalization and specificity of citizenship. From this point of view, the law is a system of knowledge and a system of action.[44]

Nevertheless, laws can only be considered legitimate if they are derived from 'democratic legislative procedures' that allow participants to sustain normative expectations of their claims achieving a collective good. This interpretation connects human rights with collective sovereignty. This is what makes Habermas' interpretation of the legal system so original. Private autonomy and collective autonomy are co-originated; they presuppose each other. Demands of equal respect and fair application are parts of the discursive process of reaching an intersubjective understanding of autonomy in both senses. Therefore, the internal connections between popular sovereignty and human rights are the normative content of the ways in which political autonomy is exercised. These are not simply granted by the grammatical body of the law, but rather arise from the communicative channels of discursive processes in the formation of public opinion.[45]

Thus, Habermas argues that the 'discourse theory of democracy corresponds to the image of a decentred society, albeit a society in which the political public sphere has been differentiated as an arena for the perception, identification, and treatment of problems affecting the whole of society'.[46] In this sense, power springs from the interactions between institutionalized means of opinion formation and culturally mobilized plural publics. Deliberative politics acquires its legitimating force from the discursive structure of public opinion formation, and it assumes an integrative force because the citizens can see transformations on the level of the reinterpretation of the system of law. The discursive level of public debates is the most important variable.

What is so important to understand about this discussion is that Habermas now agrees that discourses of application and justification 'have to be open to a *pragmatic* and an *ethico-political use of practical reason*', for as soon as we are faced with concrete legal problems 'it must cross the boundaries of justice discourses and include problems of value (that depend on the clarification of collective identity) and the balancing of interests'.[47] With this subtle yet fundamental revision of his approach to the public sphere, he has also acknowledged a wide variety of publics and counterpublics. Opinions interact informally with each other and can reach into the strong public – the parliament – that Habermas conceives as a context of justification. The 'weak publics' are the 'vehicles of public opinion'. 'The issues that are raised in deliberative political discussions can also be about the interpretations of needs and desires'.[48]

Yet, even this new outlook can be criticized on the grounds that Habermas has still not fully developed the underlying content of language, apart from its purely communicative pragmatic dimensions. At the root of this problem is the fact that the ways in which different levels of discourse interact with each other remains unclarified. One way to do so would be to think of the category of 'speech-acts' in a wider framework, which can then be traced back to Habermas' initial understanding of the interaction between genres of literature and societies' self-conceptions. In my opinion, this reformulation allows us to understand when an argument can become a potential claim for solidarity and recognition. Illocutionary power depends on the way in which the problem can be *presented*, regardless of the pragmatic, ethical or moral grounds. The ability to seek a connection with the interest of others is the ability to connect all the issues of life into a framework of justice. The symbolic content, as well as the cultural reframing of needs and values, and their interrelation to justice, can be recovered on the grounds of what Habermas has potentially developed with his concept of 'illocutionary speech-acts'.

Thus clarified, Habermas' conception of the interrelation of the legal system and the public sphere offers new grounds for 'narratives' to be considered an important tool in achieving power by transforming previous views of justice and freedom. I believe that deliberative politics adopts two structures of demand, one for social integration, the other for the recognition of institutional transformations. On the one hand, there is the institutionalization of opinion formation. On the other, there are the informal fluid interactions with other levels of the public sphere. Therefore, public opinion is displayed here as feeding into the institutional level – what I propose to call the 'constitutional narrative' – and also into the informal arenas where cultural transformations shape new definitions of justice and the good. Although Habermas has not fully explored the concept of language in its cultural dimension, it is possible to glimpse a link with the new spaces opened by communication that are necessarily shared by practices. Thus, communication has both a linguistic and an action dimension. Communication and praxis intersect within a common space: the public sphere. Communication is the manner in which praxis is expressed. At the same time, praxis qualifies communication as a performing action and as the accomplishment of identities striving for a redefinition of justice and the good life.

Following what Calvin O. Schrag calls the third term mediating between communication and praxis, there is the concept of 'textures'.[49] Schrag says: 'We want to set forth the _texture_ of communicative praxis. In the end this may be the most important term because it indicates the bonding of communication and praxis as an intertexture within their common space'.[50] In my opinion, it is this shift that allows us to conceive of communicative praxis as narrative. With this conceptualization, we are able to see that the world is experienced as a 'script' of thought and action. As Schrag maintains, 'communicative praxis includes also the texture of human projects, of motivations and decisions, of embodiment, and of wider processes of social formation'.[51] Focusing on a theory of language that considers the textures of communicative praxis, we can capture the array of meanings within the text of everyday speech and the text of various narratives. At the same time, we are able to grant a specific space to the play and display of 'meanings' within the field of perception and of human action. I have tried to develop Habermas' conception of illocutionary performances as a dynamic of specific communicative praxis that attempts to interweave discourse and action, language and non-discursive practices, speech and perception, where the core is the interaction between the expressive and the moral validity spheres.

Storytelling: Autobiographical Narratives as Identity Projects

With our revised view of language as more than a tool for communicating, as also an important part of reality construction, part of its very texture, we are now able to return to narration, this time as a highly significant genre of language usage. Disciplines such as history, sociology, psychology, philosophy, literary theory and semiotics have become increasingly concerned with how narratives provide a way to embody our understandings of the world, our experience and ourselves. Narratives, as mentioned above in connection with Habermas' treatment of Rousseau's autobiographical texts, tend to offer some kind of unifying action that, through a historical connection between past and future, gives meaning to our lives. Narratives are a privileged medium for understanding human experience, but also, as demonstrated in the rest of this chapter, for giving meaning to our lives. Narratives, seen as conceptualizations of what Foucault has called 'the technologies of the self', are products of historical embeddedness and highlight the emergence of specific understandings of such practices.

Because Hannah Arendt conceived of storytelling as one of the most important tools for creating a space for a new beginning, the debt to her is substantial in at least two regards. She had a cultural interpretation of storytelling that played an important role in her conceptualization of the public sphere: for her, the political domain has a cultural frame that encompasses language and action. Arendt's focus on the importance of narratives in displaying human experience and the different textures of meaning is a basic reference point in the rest of this chapter. In her view of the public sphere, narratives become the vehicle for the construction of collective and individual identities, and it is this dimension that is explored here. In my view the connections between Arendt's books *Rahel Varnhagen: The Life of a Jewish Woman, The Human Condition* and *Men in Dark Times* reveal the most interesting features of her narrative theory. Connecting the two validity spheres – the moral and the aesthetic – she sees narratives not only as 'historical reorderings' or discourses, but also as stories that contain a normative argument. Through memory and recollection, narratives reorder past injustices and envision the possibility of a new start through the powers of judgement. Arendt's conception of storytelling provides a cultural arena where action and speech intertwine. She also believes that social narratives have a specific task in democratic societies, for through them we personally expand our understanding of society's debt to the past.

Despite the fact that Arendt's best-known book, *The Human Condition*,[52] has been widely criticized as a nostalgic appeal to the past, attitudes to her work have shifted and it is increasingly seen as illuminating not only premodern but very modern phenomena, as pointing to a view of democracy that allows for the plurality and diversity of human life projects. Two examples provided by these recent readings of her work enable me to develop my own thesis.

In her article 'Politics as Culture: Hannah Arendt and the Public Realm',[53] Margaret Canovan, one of the most influential interpreters of Arendt's works,[54] focuses on the link between politics and culture. According to Canovan, in *The Human Condition* Arendt defines the 'public' as two related phenomena. On the one hand, the 'public realm' appears as a space of common attention and interests. But she also speaks of the 'public' that connects action with the public scenario, where the dimensions that appear to be illuminated by collective concerns are seen as the 'world'. This category of 'world', argues Canovan, is a social creation – 'it gives permanence and significance to human existence because it outlasts individual life'.[55] Thus, world and action are the two essential aspects that complement each other, and the public realm is where the 'affairs of the world in a blaze of publicity' display their meanings and attract the attention of society. Canovan points out the importance of the artificiality of the category of 'world', through which 'we provide humanity with a visible, lasting memorial, and by acting in a space of appearance we keep that world alive and make our mark in it as individuals'.[56] It is the space of the world, which includes cultural achievements, where civilization and politics coincide. Thus, politics is perceived as a highly cultural achievement, as being immersed in cultural preoccupations. Furthermore, Canovan argues that Arendt's assimilation of politics to _performance_ is not accidental. The artificiality of political life, together with her consideration of the spatial quality of the public realm and the separation between private and public, are at the bottom of Arendt's major insight into democracy: 'Politics to her was not a direct outcome of man's natural life: instead, like the rest of civilization, it was an achievement imposed upon nature, _an artificial world making possible highly skilled performances by actors'_.[57] Politics becomes a cultural achievement which, according to Canovan, helped Arendt to articulate the fragility of civilized politics as a human achievement.

My second example is Seyla Benhabib's essay 'Hannah Arendt and the Redemptive Power of Narrative',[58] which provides another interpretation of Arendt that seeks to recover her as 'decidedly modernist and politically universalist'. Benhabib argues that Arendt developed a conception of political theory as 'storytelling', suggesting that it was her specific links to the Jewish culture that made her a modernist.[59] Despite the many criticisms offered by feminists, I agree with Benhabib and others that Arendt also situated herself as a woman.[60]

I have adopted a twofold strategy in dealing with the recent readings of Hannah Arendt's conception of storytelling. On the one hand, I trace the various approaches she developed, mainly in _The Human Condition_. In doing so, I show that some feminists have analysed these aspects of Arendt's work in a creative fashion, adopting her conceptualizations as original tools to develop their own points of view about women, democracy and the importance of the categories of identity and difference in modern societies. However, I would also like to show how Arendt became her own narrator and, despite her lack of concern for women's issues, developed an original frame which reveals her unmistakable position as a woman. She was a pariah in two senses, as a Jewess and as a woman. My argument, therefore, pursues the connection between autobiographies and biographies as narrative tools that offer a specific historical self-presentation – a performative action – in the quest for identity.

Benhabib's essay delves into the complexities and contradictions in Arendt's works, and through this hermeneutic approach finds some clarification of Arendt's methodology. In both this study and that on Arendt's biography of Rahel Varnhagen, Benhabib clearly attempts to unfold the layers of meaning in Arendt's conceptualizations. In her essay on Varnhagen, Benhabib applies Arendt's ideas of the 'pariah' and 'parvenu' to the issues of identity and gender. She situates herself within Arendt's narrative, arguing that 'Rahel's Jewish identity and Arendt's own changing understanding of what this means in the 1930s in Germany are the central hermeneutic motifs in the Varnhagen story. In telling Rahel's story, Arendt was bearing testimony to a political and spiritual transformation that she herself was undergoing. There is thus a mirror effect in the narrative. The *one narrated about becomes the mirror in which the narrator also portrays herself*.[61] Benhabib grasps the importance of narratives to moral identity projects, how it is possible to build up one's identity through the recovery of the identity of someone else in the past. By retelling Rahel's story, Arendt assumes her own conscious position as a pariah, and Benhabib reflexively places herself as the person that will retell Arendt's story.

It is not by 'inwardness' that Arendt achieves her purpose of connecting narration to moral processes, according to Benhabib. Rather, it is 'Arendt's literary success in conveying this sense of endless expectation, of an endless yearning without fulfillment, of inaction coupled with the wish to live and experience most intensely'.[62] Benhabib offers an interpretation without romantic conceptualizations of 'inwardness', pointing rather to a specifically reflexive need, a longing to be able to perform something that Rahel cannot do on her own. According to Arendt's recovery, Rahel needed to construct a meaning for her being in action in the 'world'. She could not, however, obtain that meaning in a 'world' that marginalized Jews and women from the public sphere. 'The category of the "world"', argues Benhabib, 'is the missing link between the "worldless" reality of Rahel Levin Varnhagen and her contemporaries and Arendt's own search for a recovery of the "public world" through authentic political action in her political philosophy'.[63] With Benhabib's interpretation, we move to another level. We are now able to grasp the importance of narratives that connect to the public realm, and a specific recovery of the concept of political action. It is possible, now, to see why Benhabib believes that Arendt offers us a new interpretation of narratives as identity projects for her own feminist point of view.

In her own account of Rahel Varnhagen, Arendt reveals with extraordinary clarity that Rahel's mistake was to believe that she could accomplish her goal of making her life a 'work of art' through a solitary act. Arendt attempts to show the level on which she understands that her telling of Rahel's story must begin by breaking away from traditional ways of making biographies: 'Following this principle, she could neither choose nor act, because choice and action in themselves would anticipate life and falsify the purity of life's happenstance. All that remained for her to do was to become a "mouthpiece" for experience, *to verbalize whatever happened. This could be accomplished by introspection, by relating one's own story again and again to oneself and to others; thereby one's story became one's Destiny'*.[64] Thus, Arendt clearly understood that Rahel's story would be recovered through her own contemporary intervention, that the act of telling Rahel's story would inaugurate a new level of understanding and give new meaning to both Rahel's life and her own. Rahel's significance as a human being is her embodiment of uniqueness; she believed herself extraordinary, but was unable to assign any meaning to this quality, for 'her view of the source of that quality differed from that of others'.[65] It therefore became important to Arendt to demonstrate that our uniqueness is something that can be developed only socially, for only in the political dimension, where culture and action generate the concrete meanings of plurality, is it possible to create the 'world'.[66] Arendt recovers the 'uniqueness' of Rahel once she is able to grasp that it connects with her as an 'equal'. Arendt believes that the fact that Rahel 'remained a Jew and a pariah' is why she found 'a place in the history of European humanity'.[67] Benhabib understands this dimension of Arendt's narratives. In telling us the life of Rahel – 'as she herself might have told us' – Arendt needed to connect her concerns regarding Jewishness with a much broader conception of what storytelling meant for the life of humanity and its resonance in the public sphere. By refusing to take Arendt as a one-sided sociological curiosity, Benhabib opened the space for a feminist interpretation that relies more on contemporary philosophical construction than on scholarly historical reconstruction. Benhabib is using a narrative perspective, the one that I claim feminists have best developed to make their claims on the public sphere.

Rahel's origins and her problems acquire new meaning because Arendt's biographical account is clearly linked to the political dimension. Through Rahel's story, Arendt is able to grasp the importance of 'German-speaking Jews and their history [which] are an altogether unique phenomenon; nothing comparable to it is to be found even in the other areas of Jewish assimilation. To investigate this phenomenon, which among other things found expression in a literally astonishing wealth and talent and of scientific and intellectual productivity, constitutes a historical task of the first rank, and one which, of course, can be attacked only now, after the history of the German Jews has come to an end'.[68] The retelling of the story of Rahel not only recovers in memory what has happened, but allows Arendt the possibility of a new beginning. She sought this beginning in the domain of politics, hence her conception of storytelling would have to cross into the dimension in which 'redemptive' powers exercise collective remembrance and judgement. What had happened could then give rise to the narratively reconstructed possibility of a new beginning.

Arendt found herself thinking about storytelling again when she wrote about totalitarianism. She needed a new 'narrative' that would allow her to conceive what had happened when human beings lost their humanity. In my view, there is, then, a direct link between Arendt's initial concern with Rahel's Jewishness and *The Origins of Totalitarianism*: both books salvage the experiences of Jewish Germans that had then been destroyed in Europe. Arendt knew that 'under these conditions one required a story that would once again reorient the mind in its aimless wanderings. For only such a reorientation could reclaim the past so as to build the future. The theorist of totalitarianism as the narrator of the story of totalitarianism was engaged in a moral and political task'.[69] Arendt found herself dealing with what she believed to be an unprecedented moment of history. As she writes in the first chapter of *The Origins of Totalitarianism*: 'There are, to be sure, few guides left through the labyrinth of inarticulate facts if opinions are discarded and tradition is no longer accepted as unquestionable'.[70] She finds this guide in her connection between 'storytelling' and the 'public space'. 'Storytelling' becomes the articulate social weaving of memories, the recovery of fragments of the past, the exercise of collective judgement, the duty to 'go against the grain' and promote, with this retelling, a performative frame for a 'new beginning'.

Benhabib locates Arendt's 'antimodernist modernism' in her political conception of storytelling. This 'antimodernist modernism' has to do with Arendt's connection with the Jewish tradition in storytelling, and with the meaning of 'redemptive power', which she seeks to translate into a secularized modernist frame. It is important to remember that Arendt's sources, as Canovan warns in her essay, came from various cultural traditions. The first and most important source is Walter Benjamin and his conception of storytelling, experience, and the connection between history and memory. Her second source is more literary, ranging from Isak Dinesen to the special cases of Franz Kafka and Hermann Broch.[71] Once Arendt conceives the cultural domain as such, these storytellers serve as examples to formulate the way stories accomplish significant moral and political tasks. The third element, and perhaps the most relevant one, is the connection Arendt establishes between action and narratives in the public sphere, as a result of her concern with the dual role of stories. On the one hand, they must be able to envision the recovery of the past as giving rise to the possibility of a new beginning; on the other hand, such narratives must inform the deepest textures of communication and action. Plurality must be captured in a special space created for that purpose; it must create a worldly space worthy of the collective interest and concerns of all in a display of identities.

I would now like to look more closely at Arendt's connection with

Benjamin. According to Benhabib, 'configuration' and 'crystallization of elements' are categories that resonate more in Walter Benjamin's work than in that of any other thinker with whom she has been associated.[72] Indeed, Arendt not only uses some specific conceptions which Benjamin had been working on in his aesthetic theory, but her whole conceptualization of storytelling comes from him. What is relevant here, however, is Arendt's concern with storytelling in *The Human Condition*: 'Human plurality', she says, is 'the basic condition of both action and speech', and 'has the twofold character of equality and distinction'.[73] Our distinctions can come only through 'communication'. 'Otherness, which [one] shares with everything that is, and distinctness, which [one] shares with everything alive, become uniqueness, and human plurality is the paradoxical plurality of unique beings'.[74] Arendt then defines what she calls the 'beginning' as setting something in motion. Every human being carries a new beginning, because to begin a life is an exercise in human freedom. Thus, the actualization of the human condition is that of 'natality', where speech 'corresponds to the fact of distinctness and is the actualization of the human condition of plurality'.[75] Who somebody is is implicit in words and deeds, but the revelatory character of action is found only in speech: 'the action [one] begins is humanly disclosed by the word'.[76]

The disclosure of the 'who' is implicit in everything one does and says, but 'the revelatory quality of speech and action comes to the fore where people are *with others and neither for nor against them – that is, in sheer human togetherness*'.[77] The disclosure of biographies then acquires a revelatory character. It reveals uniqueness, distinctness, as well as equality 'upon reaching an altogether worldly, material object'.[78] However, the disclosure of the 'who' through speech, argues Arendt, immediately falls into the web of a space 'where [the] immediate consequences can be felt'.[79] This means that, as we are able to grasp what stories enact, as they become part of the symbolic meaning of the social web and are rewoven into a new understanding of what has happened, we are able to exorcize the past. And together with 'human relationships', stories shape our views, capturing, at the same time, the uniqueness of each being, and the equality of our humanness. Thus, there is a special dynamic that makes possible the interplay of collective meanings with individual performances and vice versa.

In his essay 'The Storyteller: Reflections on the Work of Nikolai Leskov', Benjamin maintains that the art of storytelling, in which meaning is immanent and becomes clarified in life itself,[80] is superior to any modern literary genre. For Benjamin, stories are devoid of psychological intentions. He shares with Arendt a scepticism about the pyschological features of the agents, which can be seen from her refusal to draw a psychological portrait in her biography of Rahel Varnhagen.

Benjamin thought that stories were the material richness of life, each story acquiring a new meaning for the community, a role that resembled that of storytelling within the Jewish tradition, which had an 'inexhaustible and lasting' effect upon society.

There is a second connection to Benjamin's thought in his use of a rather unusual methodology, which also figures prominently in Arendt's project. Benhabib put it this way: 'Arendt's work defies categorization while violating a lot of rules. It is too systematically ambitious and overinterpreted to be strictly a historical account; it is too anecdotal, narrative, and ideographic to be considered social science; and although it has the vivacity and the stylistic flair of a work of political journalism, it is too philosophical to be accessible to a broad public'.[81] Arendt's 'crystalline structure through whose binding foci the totalitarian form of domination is revealed'[82] is neither the data nor the fragments that are spread throughout the narrative to give us understanding, but rather the way in which she recovers the experiences of the destruction of humanity as such. 'The death of the juridical subject', the 'murder of the moral person in humanity', the 'disappearance of individuality'[83] are figures[84] of experience. They embody the new narrative that Arendt is seeking through her own understanding of what has happened: 'Under these conditions one required a story that would once again reorient the mind in its aimless wanderings. For only such a reorientation could reclaim the past so as to build the future'.[85] In his essay 'Theses on the Philosophy of History',[86] Benjamin writes: 'The past carries with it a temporal index by which it is referred to redemption. There is a secret agreement between past generations and the present one. Our coming was expected on earth. Like every generation that preceded us, we have been endowed with a weak Messianic power to which the past has a claim. This claim cannot be settled cheaply'.[87] Benjamin's conception of history and possible redemption is taken, as Wolin noted, from the cabbalist tradition.[88] His allegorical mode attempts to make visible the experience of the world, its fragments. Moreover, Benjamin's notion of truth is a religious notion of truth that seeks to establish the importance of 'a pure systematic continuum of experience'.[89] In the same manner, Arendt refers to the importance of experience for Rahel: 'But she could not yet express the essence to which she was referring; only experience could explain that, only experience serves as an example of it'.[90]

For Arendt, action is revealed only through speech, and storytellings, which are told and retold, and which provoke action when one situates oneself on the same plane as the 'doer' and the 'sufferer' (which are 'opposite sides of the same coin', and when one envisions 'the story that an act starts' as 'composed of its consequent deeds and sufferings'.[91] Thus, storytellings can project us into the future through our learning from the past, and provide new meanings that give rise to a beginning. Arendt, then, clarifies how the past is not something fixed and final, but is continually refigured and updated in the present. Once we are able to grasp that 'we have an agreement with the past' – with the 'sufferers'[92] – then our moral task in the political realm becomes clear. Self-understanding, in Arendt's view, involves thematizing our history of recollective acts. It is through recollection that we actively appropriate the past. But this appropriation is always an interpretation of the past, a selective and imaginative retelling of it from the outlook of the present. The past is a tribute to the very meaning of the present. Arendt knew that imagination played an important role in recollection; she grasped the cultural dimension of the meanings that are re-woven within each narrative. But if, for Arendt, 'action reveals itself fully only to the storyteller',[93] it could be argued that the actor can become her own storyteller. What is required is an ability to extricate oneself from embeddedness in the action, perceiving it in the man ner of a plot, a history. If social action is understood as various plots and subplots, many of which have become entangled, then to narrate the figures of the past is an attempt to retrieve ourselves on the plane of self-understanding. And, as Arendt well knew, our stories immediately become the sources of plurality.

Twice Arendt constructed a biographical account of herself, once through the narration of Rahel Varnhagen's biography, and the second time when she experienced the need for a new beginning after the holocaust, with *The Origins of Totalitarianism* and *Eichmann in Jerusalem: A Report on the Banality of Evil*.[94] She exercised her narrative as a moral imperative. Human action is valued action, if only because it involves choice and deliberation, and it is narration that makes explicit and conscious the implicit moral tone of action, and attempts to preserve it. Without narration, the past would sink into an obscurity of forgetfulness. For Arendt, narratives of the past were the vehicles of human aspirations and desires for a possible future. In telling them, we become involved in generating the *value* of a certain state of affairs or course of action, in judging its worthiness. Thus, communication becomes the performative tool by which 'meanings' reveal their fullness.[95] Here Arendt develops her category of action as unfolding on two different levels. On the one hand, there is a 'beginning' made by a single person (the 'hero'); but there is also the achievement, in 'which many join by "bearing" and "finishing" the enterprise'.[96] Telling a person's story invariably defines the type of moral agent she was. As social beings, we are caught up in a network of expectations and obligations. The values embodied in the practices of a society and its individuals are made public and legitimized in the narratives surrounding them. Thus, Arendt's view of language opens onto the past and the future, where social subjects are caught in their own signifying practices, sustained by them and produced by them. Language is not only a way to create a community, it is also a reflection of individual attitudes to the community. With this conceptualization, Arendt gives us a new insight into action. She claims that the 'political realm' arises from our acting together – 'in the sharing of words and deeds' – and that action revealed through speech is the most intimately related to the 'public part of the world common to us all'.[97]

There has been much discussion about Arendt's lack of interest in women. Paradoxically, it is through specific women – Rahel Varnhagen, Isak Dinesen, Rosa Luxemburg – that she developed her most interesting insights into storytelling. She chose Rahel Varnhagen because she embodied the problematic experience of being a Jewish woman, her conscious choice to become a pariah having made her an example of strength and bravery. Arendt chose Rosa Luxemburg, also a Jewish pariah, for her coherent commitment to politics and for her antidogmatic approach to ideologies.[98] Finally, she chose Isak Dinesen as the writer who best reflected the quality of storyteller. She was a 'Scheherazade' who recovered the ancient tradition of storytelling and with it gave new meaning to her life. In her article on Dinesen, Arendt claims that the stories that saved her love are those same stories that saved her life. Stories possess a redemptive power. This is revealed in the epigraph that Arendt chose for chapter 5 of *The Human Condition*: 'All sorrows can be borne if you put them into a story or tell a story about them'. The same kinds of experience are also extensively illustrated in Arendt's biography of Rahel.[99] The connections between the two are not fortuitous. Rahel knew, argued Arendt, that an uninhibited utterance can 'become open indiscretion if it is not addressed to posterity',[100] and that the 'more people there were who understood her, the more real she would become'.[101] Through the biographies of other women, Arendt was able to grasp the importance of her own theory of storytelling, its exploratory and redemptive powers for social transformation.

Women's Autobiographies as Creative Laboratories

The interest of women in women's biographies and autobiographies has had an enormous influence on the way they see themselves, particularly in the late twentieth century. Offering a variety of justifications for their importance, for exactly why it is necessary to recover other stories of women's lives from the past, they can all be understood as vehicles for a new performative level. For women, each new interpretation of an autobiography has been a space in which to perform new meanings of one's own life. Such stories provoke reflexiveness. By renarrating the experiences of other women's past, women have rewoven the textures of communicative praxis into their conceptions of themselves as newly emerging moral agents. These agents, in turn, display new meanings of gender, sexuality, race and ethnicity in terms of understanding the plurality of human beings. The conditions making it necessary to retell those lives have been fully explored. In short, biographies have attracted the attention of women because they have been tools of self-presentation, and they have performed important cultural transformations that have made us aware of the importance of discursive practices aimed at redefining justice on the basis of recognition of life projects.

Feminist historians, for example, understood that 'women' were used as 'specific' moral examples when their confessors wrote their biographies,[102] and have extensively criticized that way of limiting women's own life projects. Feminist political theorists have also analysed philosophical treatises (by Rousseau, for example), written to 'educate' women.[103] However, in the twentieth century, a literature has emerged that is aimed at recovering the history of women from the point of view of women themselves.[104] Since the 1960s, women have begun to work extensively on the recollection, thematization and presentation of women's biographies.[105] If the past presents a challenge for the recovery of women's autobiographies and biographies, the present seems to be an open space where the reweaving of the meanings in such stories makes them the most appropriate vehicles of self-presentation.

It is only in the second half of the twentieth century that autobiographies have become a consistent medium for the public appeal of life projects as narratives. One good example of this is Simone de Beauvoir's multi-volume autobiography.[106] However, the most striking feature of this work is its 'fictitious' character. She invented herself, creating the myth of Simone de Beauvoir as an independent, strong, intellectual woman who could lead a life devoted to her work. The fact that she wrote fiction about herself is revealed through the other works written by her, especially the works that she knew would be 'safely' considered fiction. It is in her novels that we find her 'hidden' contradictions. She accepted Jean-Paul Sartre's offer of an open relationship with him, yet she felt terribly jealous about his lovers, as is revealed in her novel *She Came to Stay* (*L'invitée*), in which she describes an open relationship between two intellectuals, Gerbert and Françoise, obviously based on Sartre and herself. The drama begins when Gerbert falls in love with a young woman and Simone is forced to accept the triangle. In the end, Gerbert's lover Xaviera (the character inspired by the third in Sartre's and Simone's trio, Olga Kosakievicz), is murdered by Françoise. Whatever the possible interpretations of the novel, it is obvious that fiction served de Beauvoir to liberate herself from the myth she herself created.

Those same contradictions play an important role in the basic disagreements between feminists in regard to Beauvoir's views of women in *The Second Sex*.[107] Paradoxically, Simone de Beauvoir's autobiography has been many women's model. Women's images of the 1960s were woven from such performative fabric. It is because of the strong appeal of her autobiography to women's own self-inventions that it can be argued that her own story has played as important a role as her theoretical work in *The Second Sex*. She has become a figure that symbolizes, in many ways, the contradictory aspects of a woman who struggled to be defined on her own terms even while she succumbed to the fascination of Sartre's domination.

The apparent delay in women's conquering the socio-political sphere, compared with the expressive-creative one, is due, in part, to the historical fact that women eventually entered the public sphere through literature. They had to go back and recover the past, retell the stories, in order to recapture the importance of those experiences in the new illocutionary light of performative biographical accounts.[108] Since the 1960s, feminist movements have stopped conditioning their expectations of recognition on left-wing parties, which always relegated feminist struggles to second place, and have adopted a new approach to politics based on the politics of gender. With the conscious assumption of the quest for a path of their own, and the discovery that existing parties would not fight their battles, feminists began systematically to occupy public spaces. Yet, even with this decisive entrance into the socio-political sphere, women's autobiographies and biographies continued to be important, offering scenarios where a plurality of moral agents appeared as models in the public sphere, as actors exercising their skilful imaginative projects of self-fashioning.

This historical explosion of autobiographical products is worth exploring further. Feminist narratives were characterized by their need to expose the concrete nature of personal struggles. These narratives attempted to link moral ends to concrete projects of identity described as articulated choices. For example, Hortense Calisher's autobiographical *Herself*[109] already indicates in its title a personal project linked to a defence of moral values. 'If life is a Minotaur which must find a confessional challenge in the end, then is this his new path to finding it?', she asks herself. Her narrative slowly begins to enter the path of self-reflexiveness. Because Hortense, a Jewish woman, wants to become a writer, she needs to explain how she sees herself as a Jew, how she experiences herself as Hannah Arendt once did. 'I understood what I had done better than they – or earlier. My sin was double. I had expressed some of these tormenting self-doubts which even the most outwardly impregnable Jew – rich, assimilated, cosmopolitan, living an easy life scarcely subject to slurs, much less oppression – may still be born with: Are "we" anything like "they" say we are?'[110] Calisher, then, must retell her mother's story. She was like many, an example of a 'Madame Bovary'. She was after all an *émigrée*. However, Calisher becomes a writer, and, in writing about her journey to become one, she experiences the stories of many women who wanted to become writers: 'As women passed through the expansion of women's rights, they might be expected to take the right to be an artist as one of these: many did, and have, and do'.[111] 'Major art is about the activities of men', says Calisher, 'that's why so much of it is about women. *But not by them. For major art includes where women can't go, or shouldn't or never have'.*[112] Even in serious literature, the rights of women are not granted; male writers can write about the minutiae of everyday life, but when a woman writes like that, Calisher argues, she is classified as being 'domestic'. Calisher's autobiography is an exercise in reflexiveness that gives her the right to become the woman writer she envisioned. 'If sex and politics now cross there, as they do, I take this as hopeful, as a sign of the country's slow recognition that the components of life do cross, and that sex is rarely alone. . . . What is most evident is that the old dictionary distinction between "license" and "freedom" doesn't do anymore. As the Jew had come to know – and the blacks and the queers are now showing us, inside literature and out – "Freedom" is what you are given – and its iron hand often remains on your shoulder – "License" is what you take'.[113]

Like Calisher, Doris Lessing offers a literary autobiographical account of contemporary women in *The Golden Notebook*.[114] Her influence as a prestigious writer in the Anglo-Saxon world allowed her to explore the political, sexual and pyschological revolution made and felt by women themselves. In an elaborate fashion, Lessing sets herself the task of reflecting the experiences of women in the division of her chapters: 'Free Women 1', 'Free Women 2', 'Free Women 3", 'Free Women 4' and 'Free Women 5'. Lessing's technique is to write her autobiographical account as a novel. Each chapter includes sections of what she calls the notebooks (black, red, yellow and blue) of a specific character that she creates. Anna Wulf, the central character, envisions 'The Golden Notebook' as the result of all the fragments from the other notebooks. As Lessing establishes different levels in her writing, supporting the reflexive manner in which 'Anna' thinks of her notebooks – which are based on the experiences of real women – fiction and reality become intertwined. Anna is Doris, and Doris writes about other women. Lessing not only approached the genre of autobiography successfully, but she also allowed herself the freedom to write it as a novel and to play with these levels in an imaginative way.

While in the United States and England autobiographical practices became one of the most admired and popular genres in women's literature,[115] other countries also developed new ways of recovering biographies for the present. Between 1966 and 1976, *The Diary of Anaïs Nin* was published in six volumes.[116] Born in Paris of a Cuban father and a Danish mother, she became a friend and colleague of Henry Miller, a fellow 'American in Paris'. If Henry Miller was the star of the sexual revolution in literature, Anaïs Nin evolved as an erotic writer and a free woman. She understood what she could offer to the public: her best work of art was herself. In the 1970s, her diaries became best-sellers, and other books written by her followed. Philip Kaufman's film *Henry and June* (1990) is evidence of the continuing interest in her relationship with Miller and his wife.

In Latin American countries, since the 1960s, women have also recovered life stories of women from the past and this, too, has been done with a clearly performative strategy. The biographies of Frida Kahlo, Antonieta Rivas Mercado and Tina Modotti, for example, have attracted international attention because of the unconventional nature of these women's struggles. Frida Kahlo is by far the best known of these three, and her life is an excellent illustration of how a path of self-exploration can not only reorder values but also project a new model of a woman. She *painted* her biography, that is, she made herself the object of an aesthetic exploration. Her personal work is now recognized as one of the most important contributions to contemporary painting.[117]

Antonieta Rivas Mercado was the daughter of a well-known architect in Mexico. She grew up in an intellectual elite, becoming a famous contemporary *salonnière*. Later on, she participated openly in a new political project with José Vasconcelos. She wrote plays, poems and political essays, but is remembered primarily for her love letters to the Mexican painter Manuel Rodríguez Lozano, which are generally acknowledged to be literary jewels, filled with passion and intense sadness; her failed love caused her to commit suicide inside the cathedral of Notre Dame in Paris.[118]

The life of the Italian actress, photographer and active political militant Tina Modotti provides another fascinating example. Having worked in Hollywood, she left the United States for Mexico with her mentor Edward Weston, who taught her photographic techniques. Then she met the famous Cuban revolutionary Julio Antonio Mella and became his lover. When he was shot while they were walking together in the street, she was accused of being the murderess; it is more likely that she was imprisoned for being too threatening a figure for Mexican traditional world-views. Diego Rivera and some other intellectuals fought for her freedom; thereafter she worked with Soviet Communists to help get Jews out of Germany and in a hospital during the Spanish Civil War.[119]

The biographies written about these three are among those that clearly show women reconstructing other women's lives as personal projects of identity. Literature for women has begun to be conceived not only as a means of self-expression but as a means of connecting past experiences to a new model of self-fashioning. Everywhere, biographies have become the vehicle of identity projects linking the moral and the aesthetic spheres. This entails a new appraisal of experience and action in the highly imaginative performances of women in the public sphere.

2 Communicative Rationality: Between Spheres of Validity

One of the main criticisms of Habermas' theory of communicative rationality has been his silence regarding the expressivistic aspect of communication. Habermas' work deals sufficiently with the cognitive-instrumental view of rationality, as well as with its normative dimension in the domains of law, politics and morality. However, communicative rationality must account for a crucial aspect of the symbolic meaning and content of communication if one is to consider, as Habermas has, an expansion of subjectivities in the interplay between culture and the public sphere. The problem lies in the breadth of conceptions of knowledge and its communicative mediating forces. In what follows, I would like to recover some of the best arguments offered by Wellmer's theoretical and critical approach to communication between the different validity spheres, specifically between the moral and the aesthetic spheres of validity. I aim to show how the expressive view plays a major role in the creation, expansion and self-understanding of the identities of social actors in the public sphere. My thesis is that it is possible to trace these communicative features of the decentred conception of rationality and their mutual influence to the interactions between social actors and the public sphere. I shall draw on some of the basic criticisms offered by Wellmer to conceptualize how 'expressive' rationality interacts with the moral domain, in order to account for the expansion of subjectivities which plays a major role in the configuration of a new order of moral values and the creation of identity projects of social actors.

A Decentred Conception of Rationality and Spheres of Validity

Albrecht Wellmer provides the missing link in the expressive dimension of Habermas' conception of communicative rationality. Wellmer accounts for the relationship between the aesthetic and the moral spheres, and this brings him closer to the work of Theodor Adorno in more than one regard, for this interrelationship includes the utopian dimensions on which democratic culture is based. Habermas' model of validity spheres has insufficiently shown the dynamics and feedback between them.[1] In his criticism of Adorno's thesis of art, Wellmer finds the interconnection between the moral and the aesthetic spheres, the area in which subjectivities illustrate this interaction or interplay. I find useful his idea that the differentiation of the various discourses on validity in modernity recognizes a decentred conception of rationality, a plurality of modes of manifestation linked only through what Wellmer postulates as 'mediating factors'[2] between the various discourses. This critical stance, which goes against the traditional philosophical idea of the unity of reason, constitutes the main thrust of Wellmer's criticism of _The Dialectic of Enlightenment_, by Adorno and Max Horkheimer.[3] His main objection to Habermas' work is its scientist and restrictive view of communicative rationality.

Wellmer describes the link between aesthetics and morality in his introduction to _The Persistence of Modernity_, which places modernity as a horizon inevitably split into the cognitive, the aesthetic and the moral-political spheres. Wellmer entered this area in answer to the problems he perceived in Adorno and Habermas. He attempts to show through immanent principles the constructive and falsifiable movement of a decentred rationality[4] articulated in modern practices, and defines modernity as a reflexive and critical space in which it is possible to trace new forms of subjectivity[5] that have emerged from social practices and interactions.

The similarity between Wellmer's focus on this interrelationship and Adorno's concern with the aesthetic utopian dimension makes it possible to comprehend the cognitive elements of both spheres of validity and their role in expanding the subjectivities of human agents. While Wellmer thinks that this legacy can be reinterpreted in a form that is potentially different from Adorno's aporetical view, the two authors are united by a common conviction: the aesthetic dimension presupposes a deep transformation in our manner of feeling and living, based on the complexity that only art can explore without fear of oversimplification or banality.

In his _Negative Dialectic_,[6] Adorno tried to argue that the 'mimetic' element converges with rationality in a twist that makes 'mimesis' appear as the other side of rationality. This was an attempt to save the mimetic element from being considered part of the instrumentalization of reason.[7] Adorno was thinking of a much broader and more complex rationality than the rationality of means and ends. The concept of mimesis brings out the sources which nourish expressive rationality. The ideal place for mimesis to be considered meaningful is in art. And if art is a spiritualized mimesis which is only transformed and made objective in reality, philosophy can conceptualize it and provide the rational element that allows the convergence of opposite poles. The 'conciliatory' spirit pursued in Adorno's aesthetics, according to Wellmer, is the common medium of art and philosophy. That reconciliation presupposes not only a 'synthesis without violence of what is scattered', but a no longer violent union of the multiple in reconciled interdependence. By grasping the goals of Adorno's dialectics, Wellmer is able to show that 'his extension of the utopia of reconciliation to nature as a whole is accounted for by the radical character of the antithesis between the instrumental spirit and the spirit that pursues aesthetic reconciliation: both the instrumental and the reconciling spirit signify an order of living nature as a whole'.[8] When Adorno tries to account for the interrelationship of truth, resemblance and reconciliation, he is also attempting to connect the utopian goal of artistic beauty to negativity, and the result is just as aporetical as his view of the interrelationship between art and philosophy. Wellmer reasons that this is just the 'dialectic of aesthetic semblance'.[9]

There is another statement in Wellmer's work which I want to examine, and that is his definition of aesthetic semblance, which plays a major role in the *Dialectic of Enlightenment*. By focusing on the truth of art in Adorno's *Aesthetic Theory*, Wellmer recovers the insight that art shows 'reality, in the light of redemption'.[10] But the truth of works of art is always concrete, always specific; therefore, if one wishes to give a precise account of the validity which reflects the truthfulness of the work of art, one needs to separate analytically the elements that Adorno envisaged in a dialectical manner. That is to say, 'the unity of these two moments would then mean that it is only by virtue of aesthetic synthesis (truth 1) that art can represent cognition of reality (truth 2), and conversely that aesthetic synthesis (truth 1) can only succeed if it helps to make reality (truth 2) manifest'.[11]

With this interpretation of Adorno, Wellmer outlines his own concerns, which are reconstructed under a theoretical recovery of the *Negative Dialectic*. He believes that there ought to be a much broader view that contains even the most expressive and practical aspects of daily life, which allows art and philosophy to be linked, and, at the same time, can express the multiple unity of a decentred form of rationality and the structural element of that interrelated multiplicity. That horizon is none other than the communicative one, derived primarily from Habermas' _Theory of Communicative Action_, as is later shown in the body of Wellmer's work.

Wellmer sheds critical light on Adorno's aporias regarding art and philosophy, while recovering his intuitions about art as the bastion of expressivity and a form of complex rationality. However, while Adorno proposed the concept of mimesis as the 'Other' of rationality, in an attempt to fill the gap in the materialistic theory with 'messianic-utopian' motifs that he considered necessary to conceive a different world, Wellmer discovered fissures in this solution.[12]

Wellmer, therefore, reinterprets the theological aspects of Adorno's work in order to decode his aesthetics in a materialistic fashion. Adorno envisions redemption beyond the reality of this world and, at the same time, articulates a concept of happiness as fulfilment of the senses: 'The theological motif interacts with the sensualist one to produce a utopian perspective in which the hope of redemption is nourished by the yearning for a lost paradise'.[13] Adorno conceives of the aesthetic experience in 'ecstatic terms', argues Wellmer, 'rather than as a real utopia; the happiness that it promises is not of this world'.[14] Wellmer salvages the possibility of a utopian dimension of aesthetic experience within the parameters of this earthly world, and he does so with the help of Habermas' _Theory of Communicative Action_. Wellmer believes that the problem of asymmetry in the cognitive system of the philosophy of consciousness, in terms of subject and object (and which is still evident in Adorno's view), has been overcome.[15] The intersubjective link that the paradigm of language and communication provides for the relationship – of symmetry, of the communicative moment of the spirit – between one subject and another subject[16] thus becomes a necessity. Art ceases to be the opposite of the rational and becomes a specific form of rationality: expressive rationality. Communication and intersubjectivity are conditions for re-dimensionalizing the role of aesthetics as a form of rationality, but also, in order to detect the dynamic flow between the moral and the aesthetic dimensions, as expressed as a form of growing subjectivities.

That is why Wellmer affirms that the 'utopian projection', which is reached by discursive reason based on its own linguistic character, does not outline the profile of the Other, but rather its own ideal based on itself. The interrelationship between both spheres of validity or rationality is the main thrust of Wellmer's critique of Adorno's and Habermas' work. Through the examination of unresolved problems in both authors, he provides a conception of rationality which is completely separate from the instrumentalization of reason, and with a model of rationality[17] that retains neither traces of aporetical views (Adorno) nor scientistic conceptualizations of communicative rationality (Habermas).

Expressive Rationality

As discussed above, Wellmer tried to connect a materialistic theory with a utopian view in order to overcome Adorno's aporetical vision of mimesis as the Other of reason. On this linguistic basis, Wellmer has reached a conception of spheres of validity in which reason unfolds its moments. The interrelation between the cognitive and the normative spheres is excellently described in Habermas' *Theory of Communicative Action*; Wellmer thinks that there is another major relationship – between the normative and the aesthetic – which has not been analysed by Habermas, but which appears as an intuitive insight in the work of Adorno. And again, focusing on Adorno's view that art can also produce knowledge and truth, Wellmer has demystified the connection between semblance and utopia, leaving behind Adorno's dialectical connection between subjectivization and reification.

Adorno contrasted modern art with traditional art, in terms of how the latter represented the fictitious unity that was also a violent 'synthesis of meaning'. He believed that through aesthetic enlightenment, violent features of the inauthentic unity of traditional work had been discovered. He saw open forms of modern art as a response of 'emancipated' aesthetic consciousness to the inauthentic and violent aspect of traditional art, but he also observed that it was through art that a new principle of individuation was achieved.[18] When modern art incorporates those spaces of life which seem senseless or unintegrated to any possible rational account, a much more complex individual organization is required for 'the aesthetic integration of all that is diffuse or has been split off'.[19] According to Wellmer, Adorno believed that a new aesthetic subjectivity should be a precondition for the opening of art that is required to overcome the 'world of appearance'. Adorno related the open forms of art to new processes of subjectivity which somehow long for a different scenario, mainly a 'more flexible organizational form of "communicatively fluid" ego-identity'.[20]

This is the point of departure for Wellmer's original approach. Adorno believed that the unity of reason had been overcome, mainly by the plurality of moments of reason produced by the differentiation of validity spheres. Furthermore, he thought that there was insufficient emphasis being given to open forms of art; an enlightened approach can offer new ways of perceiving reality if one examines the spaces in which modern societies develop their sensibilities. Wellmer argues that 'the extending limits of the subject' are one of the major contributions of art towards suppressing moments of reification, as well as expanding the reflexive boundaries of the 'receiving subject'.[21] The two simultaneous processes that Wellmer points to in this conceptualization of Adorno are particularly relevant to the development of my model of women's narratives. On the one hand, modern art incorporates everything that seems senseless or alien to the subject, the conflictive dimensions of reality. On the other, in order to display this 'opening-up' or to 'expand' these boundaries, the subjects experience an increasing capacity for the aesthetic integration of all that was previously left out or conceived as irrational. In Wellmer's interpretation, Adorno links the open forms of modern art with new subjectivities that leave behind the 'rigid unit of the bourgeois subject'.[22] It is Wellmer's understanding of the importance of Adorno's insight that interests me, in order to make a historical and functional connection between reflexively opened forms of modern art and the 'exploratory' and 'expanding' boundaries of the receiving subjects.

Closely following Gabriele Schwab's examples,[23] Wellmer argues that the genuine expansion of the subjective boundaries of readers has been one of the major achievements of modern literature. Wellmer focuses on a new way of acquiring an aesthetic synthesis, which includes a psychic and a social synthesis. This is possible only if it is perceived in terms of a 'communicative mediation' that simultaneously produces and receives, which would also mean that what occurs is a new process of simultaneous individuation and socialization.

It is no coincidence that Wellmer relates his interpretation of Adorno to Gabriele Schwab's research on the interconnections between expanding boundaries of subjectivities and the aesthetic experience. Schwab carefully selects what she calls 'transitional texts' in order to expose the different elements (psychological, sociological and anthropological) of creative skills displayed in language and its cultural reception. 'New forms of literary subjectivity', she argues, 'relate to the dissolution of subjectivity about schizophrenia, paranoia, or the so-called new narcissism'.[24] In Schwab's narrative, poetic language and the aesthetic experience develop their own conceptualization of subjectivity. Literary subjectivity can then be understood as an effect of poetic language that gains cultural relevance through its differences from other cultural expressions of subjectivity.

Schwab's conception of language allows consideration of the 'asemantic' qualities that highlight presymbolic functions of language. The missing link in Habermas' theory of language – the expressive domain – is traceable through works like Schwab's, which have explored the new interrelationships between language and the subject in order to find traces of the new notions of literary subjectivity in the experimental language innovations of contemporary writers. She rejects the post-structuralist conceptions of language (Jacques Lacan, Jacques Derrida and, at some point, also Julia Kristeva[25]), because she regards the differentiations of subjectivity, not as indications of the fragmentation of the subject, but as the foundation that allows subjectivity to acquire its flexibility and expand its boundaries.

However, what interests me in Wellmer's interpretation of Schwab is that 'the reflexive opening-up of literary forms of representation triggers a playful to and fro between identification and differentiation on the part of the reader, which effectively works toward a genuine expansion of subjective boundaries'.[26] It is here that Wellmer finds the emancipatory 'potential of modernism': 'a new type of "synthesis" comes into view – in an aesthetic, moral-psychological, and social sense – in which that which is diffuse and unintegrated, that which is "meaningless" and split off could be gathered together in an arena for non-violent communication which would encompass the *opened forms of art as well as the open structures of a no longer rigid type of individuation and socialization*'.[27] The challenge for Wellmer, then, is to leave behind the conception that art is a scheme for 'reconciliation', in Adorno's terms, because it can only be considered as a 'medium of communicative mediation', a two-dimensional medium: one dimension is what is produced; the other, what is received. Only then, argues Wellmer, 'can the work of art come to correspond formally to the changing forms of individuation and socialization'.[28]

Wellmer's and Schwab's focus on this dimension of language and the aesthetic experience is helpful in understanding why cultural transformations inspired by new aesthetic practices give rise to new modes of speech, perception, communication and new forms of sensibility. The new envisionings of subjectivity in literary texts become a paradigm that facilitates understanding the changes in the cultural formation of subjectivity. Schwab's selection of texts which she envisions as transgressive works – ones that challenge the existing cultural formations at all levels (psychological, moral and social) – illustrates this viewpoint very clearly.[29]

On the other hand, what emerges as Wellmer's contribution to Adorno's theory of aesthetics is the possibility of a connection between the simultaneous expansion of boundaries in both the works of art and the subject. Wellmer believes that this new form of aesthetic synthesis, provided with the material basis of a communicative theory, will lead to a new scenario for a utopia of 'non-violent communication'. Wellmer defines the new 'cognition' provided by works of art, which affects the subjects' relationship to themselves and to the world, as 'cognitive, affective, and moral and practical aspects in equal measure'.[30] Adorno's concern that philosophy capture the enlightening cognitive function of works of art in conceptual terms is no longer necessary; rather, from this new outlook, 'cognition' becomes an 'ability' that allow us to speak, judge, feel and perceive in new ways.[31]

With the affirmation that art provides a new synthesis, Wellmer finds that the aesthetic realm and the cognitive sphere are interrelated and through a discussion of this he leads to the interrelation of the spheres of validity and their reciprocal communicative feedbacks.[32] Wellmer makes clear that his interpretation of the truth or validity of art cannot be conceived as one-dimensional. He believes there are three different dimensions of validity: the 'apophantic' truth (related to cognitive content and relation to reality), the 'endeetic' truth (truthfulness), and the moral and practical truth. Works of art, argues Wellmer, cannot be conceived as containing the literal sense of any of these conceptions. Art's enigmatic character comes from the way it relates to truth in a very peculiar and complex way: 'not only does art open up the _experience of reality and correct and expand it_; it is also the case that aesthetic "validity" (i.e. the "rightness" of a work of art) _touches on_ questions of truth, truthfulness, and moral and practical correctness in an intricate fashion without _being attributable to any of the three dimensions of truth, or even to all three together_'.[33] Wellmer is interested in the consequences of his linguistic pragmatic reformulation of the involvement of the various dimensions of truth in the truth of art. He clearly differentiates between two relations – the functional and the substantial – between the work of art and 'reconciliation'. Wellmer thinks that Adorno integrated two different notions of art in his concept of reconciliation, aesthetic rightness and the objective truth, which play an important role in the 'truth content of art'. It was for this reason, argues Wellmer, that Adorno needed philosophy to put the aesthetic experience into a conceptual form. Adorno's 'apophantic' conception of aesthetic cognition, then, links the truth of art to philosophical truth. However, Wellmer believes that viewing art in this way may lead to the idea that art merely 'represents' a potential for truth, while he believes that works of art can be conceived as directly connected to an aesthetic validity.

Through an analysis that plays with the misconceptions regarding the truth of works of art in an apophantic sense, Wellmer criticizes our use of metaphors such as 'disclosure' or 'revealing', which imply that works of art show 'reality in an outstanding fashion'.[34] The problem here, argues Wellmer, is in linking the truth of art with a 'mirror-image', to use one of Richard Rorty's most illuminating metaphors. Rather, according to Wellmer, the aesthetic sense of rightness is grasped only as it is perceived: 'When we "recognize" reality in an aesthetic experience, then what we have known diffusely, experienced vaguely and apprehended implicitly, acquires the firm outlines of a _sensual experience for the first time_'.[35] It should now be clear how this pragmatic conclusion links Wellmer's best insights with Schwab's research, for Wellmer emphasizes that art can be 'grasped' or 'comprehended' when what was 'diffuse' or 'pre-conscious' or 'sub-conscious' becomes experienceable knowledge.[36] Thus conceived, art is not only a disclosure of reality but a trigger that opens our eyes. Such transforming moments are captured in Schwab's model of the emergence of new forms of subjectivity and the boundaries that are transformed through these new limits.[37]

Wellmer concludes that the truth-claim of art, which corresponds to the truth-potential of works of art, can be seen only when the inseparable aesthetic validity-claim attached to the latter is understood. Following Martin Seel, Wellmer argues that the connection between aesthetic validity-claims and truth-claims can be grasped only through an aesthetic discourse that focuses on the interrelation between 'authenticity' and 'aesthetic rightness'.[38] The aesthetic discourse substitutes Adorno's 'conceptual' explanation of art through philosophy. Participants in the discussion about the aesthetic quality of truth or falsehood of any work of art need to bring their own experiences into the discourse. They also need to mobilize their experience into arguments simultaneously dealing with the three dimensions of truth: cognition, truthfulness and moral and practical rightness. In aesthetic discourse, the truth-potential of art and its truth-claims are understood only when we appeal to the various dimensions of truth in the experiences of individuals, in their transformations and in their changing ways of perceiving and interpreting themselves. It then becomes apparent that the truth of art can be grasped only in a metaphorical sense, for it is in 'the metaphorical interweaving of the dimensions of truth' that art reveals its eloquence and expressive character. Wellmer warns about the dangers of using metaphors such as 'saying' and 'expressing', because that involves moving from the initially criticized apophantic conception of truth to an endeetic truth. This was Habermas' main problem in his conceptualization of the 'expressive sphere'. Adherents to the apophantic and the endeetic conceptions of truth can interpret works of art only through analogies with specific speech-acts. The notion of truthfulness that Wellmer wants to develop, on the other hand, conceives it as showing the authenticity of the model – construct – that captures the symbolic experiences of the subjects, or, as Wellmer says, 'as a symbolical construct that carries an *aesthetic* validity-claim [that] is at the same time the object of an *aesthetic experience* that refers back to our ordinary experience in which the three dimensions of truth are interwoven in a *non-metaphorical* sense'.[39]

It is precisely the expansion of the faculties resulting from the different moments of the aesthetic experience – the imagination relating to intellectual reflexivity – that is expressed in this reconceptualization of the notion of truth. Only then can Wellmer recover the notion of 'potentiality', for the idea of truth is conceived in the same terms as 'faculties' that allow entry into a dimension of a moment of utopia, 'the point of entry for forces which, in their non-aesthetic usage, might restore a continuity between art and living praxis'.[40] 'Communicative rationality' adds a new dimension to Adorno's concept of rationality and allows Wellmer to expand his aesthetics of truth in a pragmatic way. This new conceptualization reveals the interrelationships between receiving, communicating and acting subjects and art, reality and utopia.

I believe that Wellmer's criticism of Adorno's aesthetics takes a pragmatic view of the truth of art that envisions utopian moments of transformation. I consider this a very important first step in developing my thesis. Wellmer's work and Schwab's research into the expansion of subjectivities through literary works of art are closely connected. Schwab illustrates Wellmer's conception of the aesthetic validity-claim and the truth of works of art. In my analysis of women's narratives, I take these two approaches to focus on the performative dialogue that takes place simultaneously in the public sphere and in the individual's reception of literary works, which are inextricably fused in the cultural domain. I find Schwab's own narrative a very useful tool, for she explains how the transformation of works of art can help create a specific language which is also related to a transformation of literary subjectivity. It is this aesthetic experience – as a mediating force – which I need in order to show the dynamics of the interrelated performative forces between a new narrative and the reception given to this narrative.[41] My thesis, developed in the following chapters, is that women first had to focus on the works of art that narrated their lives, their biographies, in order to envision the need for political discourses or political narratives that allowed them to adopt the viewpoint of moral subjects challenging a narrow conception of justice. In other words, women needed a clear connection with the aesthetic realm, because, as discussed above, the expressive sphere allows new experiences to be presented in the very act of describing them. Women's narratives grasped the potential of a utopian horizon that created a critical space in which they could become authentic subjects. Through this transformation, women perceived the need to generate other kinds of discourse that better articulated their claims for recognition explicitly on normative grounds. However, the historical transformation of women's self-conception first entered the public sphere through the literary public that became the arena for the performative illocutionary forces displayed in those new texts and for creating new ways of living.

Women used works of art because presenting themselves within the realm of aesthetics allowed them to express themselves without the impediments of liberal theories that excluded women from the public sphere. Aesthetic expressions acted as protection for a certain kind of anonymity. As Schwab has rightly argued, 'Literature allows for a cultural communication of "tacit knowledge", which can be seen as equivalent to its communication about the personal core'.[42]

However, the intersubjective negotiations involved in tacit know-

ledge take place within the dynamics of the boundaries between communication and silence. Schwab saw that this tacit knowledge is made
explicit when translated into indirect symbols that, rather than defining
what is known, are evocative. This is the reason why so many feminist
theorists have been concerned with a psychoanalytical understanding
of culture. This is also evident in the enormous importance of the
cultural and symbolic aspects of the new feminist political and moral
discourses. For example, Drucilla Cornell has developed a theory of the
transformation of subjects dealing with the interrelations between the
materialistic and the utopian dimensions. Her feminism focuses 'on
precisely why we can only truly rethink performative possibility if we
also confront what kind of subject could be open to the creation of new
worlds'.[43] In doing so, Cornell argues that imagination plays a crucial
role in envisioning the self and setting up new patterns for living and
transforming oneself, 'in the act of imagining and enacting a new story
in which our uniqueness as persons is celebrated in a living-out persona
beyond the meaning imposed on all of us by gender hierarchy'.[44]

The Interpenetration between the Aesthetic and the Moral Spheres

Wellmer believes that the differentiation of spheres of validity (science,
law, morality and art) is the modern expression of an 'irreversible
cultural learning process'.[45] Thus, Wellmer is concerned with elucidat-
ing how these spheres of validity can still be connected through a
dynamic of influences. He is aware that it is not possible to keep the
unifying concept of rationality that previously permeated the whole
philosophical tradition. It is at this point that Habermas comes to the
fore.

In his extensive essay 'Ethics and Dialogue: Elements of Moral Judgement in Kant and Discourse Ethics',[46] Wellmer criticizes Habermas'
concept of rationality for being based on a criterion of consensus, but at
the same time establishes a connection between this criticism and what
he has recovered from Adorno's work, namely the possibility of linking
Habermas' concept of rationality with the moment of utopia through
the interrelation of the spheres of validity. Many of the important issues
developed in Wellmer's essay are explored elsewhere.[47] I want to relate
some of the main theses in these criticisms to the ideas discussed above,
that is, to the idea that Wellmer has offered an original way of connecting the spheres of validity, and to the idea that the contemporary
discussion of the relation between autonomy and authenticity could
find new grounding in the elements that Wellmer provided in his
cricitism of Adorno and Habermas.

Based on the hypothesis that Habermas' discourse ethics (bound as it was by formal principles) has not been able to solve the problems posed by Kant, Wellmer builds a paradoxical structure. Not only does discourse ethics leave the problems that Hegel posed to Kant unresolved, but the virtues of Kant's system are not understood by Habermas' theory, despite its closeness to Kant.[48] Wellmer believes that, without the mediating factor of moral consciousness, it is hard to recover the best of Kant. To reintroduce it into discourse ethics requires substantial corrections. Instead of a consensual and universalist theory of dialogical ethics, Wellmer argues for a fallibilist interpretation. Similarly, instead of proposing a strong uni-dimensional definition of moral justification, discourse ethics can start from a weak idea of moral justification, which would be necessarily multi-dimensional.[49] In the third place, Wellmer claims that judgement plays a major role in his recovery of Kant's best insights.

Just as Wellmer articulated his immanent critique of Adorno's texts to defend a decentred notion of rationality without the need to rely on final justifications, this proposal removes the element of anticipation from the state of reconciliation of reason (similar to Kant's kingdom of ends), and affirms the recognition of the postmetaphysical stage, which forces the quest for an ultimate fundamental principle of philosophy to be abandoned.[50] Both the argument of plural moments of reason and that of postmetaphysical conscience, which avoids the great fundamental principle, are structured in Hegel's critical shadow. Wellmer thinks that these two corrections are the only ones that allow the vulnerability of Kant's system to Hegel's criticism to be avoided. Thus, in his analysis of discourse ethics, one of Wellmer's central considerations is reflected, namely that the various discourses of validity do not need to share a final agreement about their basis. And it is here that discourse ethics appears 'not Kantian enough' to Wellmer, since Kant did differentiate between the issues of moral concern and those relating to law. The fact that Kant tried to link them is understandable in view of the concerns shown throughout his work; however, the analytical difference has repercussions, mainly for the relationship between the legitimation of norms and morally correct action.

Wellmer's criticism of Habermas' theory of truth reveals the tension between truth and justification. His main concern is to demonstrate the fallibilism inherent in the 'cautionary use'[51] of the concept of truth, which means that the opposition between justification and truth depends on the specificity of the one when confronted with the other, or, in other words, on the impossibility of reducing one to the other. He shows that warranted assertability is specific to this theory, and differs from that of justification (or rational assertability).

Habermas has come to distance himself from the interpretation of consensus theory as providing a criterion of truth. Wellmer's criticism led to a broader understanding of truth and the specific interpretations of validity that were possible in each sphere of human knowledge. Wellmer's first step was to separate the moral sphere from a scientistic model, showing that the consensus theory of truth cannot provide a criterion for truth based on the quasi-circular argument that makes consensus constitutive of validity. Thus, Wellmer argued, it is not possible to deduce a criterion for moral discourse from this pattern, because consensus should be the result of a valid choice, not simultaneously the starting-point and the result. The second step was to point out the 'fallibilistic nature' of his model. Even if conditions for discourse are ideal, there is no guarantee of the truth of consensuses as long as they are 'particular', that is, 'finite' and 'empirical'. Thus, if we must judge the rationality of consensuses according to the reasons upon which they are founded, it seemed to Wellmer that the notion of an ideal 'communication community' contributed nothing to our understanding of 'what a rationally grounded consensus is'.[52] Wellmer concludes that Habermas' 'pragmatic reinterpretation of transcendental philosophy' becomes 'indistinguishable from the pragmatic reinterpretation of Adorno's theory of reconciliation'.[53] According to Wellmer, 'in the notion of an ideal communication community, theoretical and practical reason converge in the ultimate goal of an ideal situation for communication'.[54]

The most important implication of this criticism is that the ideal communication community would suppress the plurality of sign-users. The transcendental subject would then replace such a plurality with a singularity situated 'in the truth'[55]. The connection with Adorno's theory of reconciliation becomes apparent: both attempt to identify the idea of the absolute – the 'highest point' – within this world, or, to put it differently, the 'common element' between them is the notion of a reconciled humanity.[56]

A second important element now appears in Wellmer's main criticism of the conflation of rationality and truth within the moral sphere. Wellmer thinks that unavoidable presuppositions of an argument do not in themselves become moral obligations. He claims that 'it is questionable whether the "must" entailed in the norms of an argument can be meaningfully understood as a *moral* "must" ',[57] for the obligations to rationality refer to the acknowledgement of arguments, whereas the moral arguments refer to the acknowledgement of *persons*. Thus, even if the rationality obligations and the moral ones are found to be interwoven in complex ways, it cannot be claimed that both would ultimately coincide (or be reconciled on the highest level). It is only when Wellmer separates these two notions analytically that it becomes clear that it is in 'public dialogues' that the tests of the moral dimension of language can be understood and differentiated from the rationality of the arguments.

Public dialogue offers the possibility of dealing with the 'obligation' not to suppress any relevant arguments and their possible objections. But this obligation, as Wellmer argues, is not identical in 'meaning' with the obligation to achieve a rational consensus. Neither is it identical in meaning with the obligation to co-operate morally speaking. Thus, Wellmer insists that there can be a different conception of 'ideal communication community' only when it is considered as an ideal that emphasizes – in solitary reflection – all possible arguments by members of an unlimited community. Then, 'ideal' appears as a space that envisions all possible arguments which might be articulated by real persons from a multiplicity of viewpoints. The ideal community as 'regulative' is also evident when communication is conceived as unlimited, the course of dialogue being reinitiated only when better arguments are stressed. Thus, the ideal communicative community can play an important role in real situations, in which idealization becomes a precondition for rational arguments or rational reflections. It is an abstraction of empirical persons who can imagine and articulate arguments, but this idealizing assumption of arguments can neither contain an ultimate foundation for morality nor the promissory glance of reconciliation.

In his reconstruction and reinterpretation of discourse ethics, Wellmer has claimed that Habermas' universalizing principle insufficiently differentiates moral and legal questions.[58] According to Wellmer, Kant had already differentiated between them, though not in a satisfactory way. Wellmer's thesis is that both Kant's and Habermas' philosophical structures are based on an *ideal*: the kingdom of ends in Kant's case, the 'ideal speech situation' in the case of Habermas (and Apel). To ground morality from the point of view of the kingdom of ends presupposes that there are no disagreements, exceptions or conflicts. Therefore, Kant has no real place for the role of judgements. On the other hand, for Hegel, the important thing was to decide what mediating element could play a significant role between the particular and the universal. Wellmer argues that Habermas fails to do this because his discourse ethics 'describes morality *sub specie aeternitatis*'.[59] Wellmer believes that he can interpret Kant fallibilistically; the norm for dialogue must remain unspecific and assume certain contents in the context of specific interpretations, which themselves must always remain subject to revision due to their fallibilistic nature. Thus, Wellmer defines his universal moral principle not as an empirical assumption, but as a methodical one. We are 'limited' in what we feel we should be discussing – 'we are thus limiting ourselves to moral arguments in which the generalizability of ways of acting is presupposed as a criterion of what is morally correct or as a measure of moral value'.[60] Wellmer defines moral arguments as concerned with the interpretation of actions and needs as much as with those who act and those who suffer the consequences of actions and the way they see themselves. The shift occurs when Wellmer places moral discourses in a position in which *narratives* become the central element for interpretations of the subjects themselves. My understanding of situations, and the way I see myself, are now posed in an argumentative form and must be displayed in order to gain recognition. Wellmer argues that he can illustrate this conception on two levels, which he calls 'the collective matrix of interpretations' and 'the place of moral judgement in complex situations'.

There are thus some similarities between Wellmer's moral discursive arguments and Hannah Arendt's conception of dialogue in the public sphere. Wellmer believes that the collective matrix of interpretations can best represent the changes in traditional views of the role of women, sexual differences and other related issues.[61] In this way, 'socially prevailing moral orientations' that determine behaviour are anchored in collective matrices of interpretation. According to Wellmer, collective moral learning processes are stimulated when reasons are brought into the public discourse and challenge former views, claiming the need to revise them. This definite stance, however, occurs in the public sphere when a group's struggle for recognition is directed towards the need to reinterpret and configure a new understanding of things. 'Such learning processes result in a new way of talking about and behaving towards homosexuals, women and children', argues Wellmer; 'they also result in those affected seeing themselves and behaving towards themselves in a new way'.[62] Thus, Wellmer conceives of collective moral learning processes as 'the extension of relationships of mutual recognition through the critical undermining of socially inherited attitudes and matrices of interpretation'.[63] With this vision of discursive ethics, Wellmer defines the concept of 'specific negation'. Rather than presupposing some ideal community, this stresses the arguments and narratives of those that feel they have suffered inequalities as human beings, arguments triggered by convictions about what they have not yet accomplished or by the belief that they are no longer accorded an equal possibility of factual self-determination. This principle, which Wellmer recovers from Kant, is called 'the principle of moral progress' aimed at the elimination of nonsense.

The second level that Wellmer suggests is also related to Hannah Arendt's view of the major roles played by deliberations and judgements. Wellmer distinguishes between what he calls morally complex, morally inscrutable and practically inscrutable moral judgements. The first category refers to various moral demands that collide with each other and make it difficult to choose between them. The morally inscrutable ones are those in which the moral significance is not clear enough. This obscurity could be the result of agents being mistaken about their own motives, or of problems of distorted communication. Finally, practically inscrutable judgements are those in which the consequences of actions are not at all clear. Wellmer holds that moral arguments have significance insofar as they are appropriate and complete descriptions – narratives – that give a full account of possible alternatives. Thus, moral discourse would be a correct way of understanding reality from a moral point of view.[64] Wellmer thinks that moral controversies are dissolved when a new interpretation gains the general acceptance of the actors in the social dimension. 'This also explains', he argues, 'how the question of what we – as rational beings – are collectively able to will is reduced in practice to the question of how we – the persons affected – can achieve an adequate understanding of the situations in which we act.'[65]

Therefore, Wellmer believes that a separation of discourses concerning the justifications of norms and discourses concerning the application of norms is not possible. If this is evident, he says, we can then consider moral judgement in concrete situations to be meaningful only as a problem of the 'application of moral norms'. Wellmer sees the discursive clarification of situations and the way we see ourelves as two levels on which we find a demand to be rational with a moral dimension attached to it, once we grant others the possibility to speak for themselves. And, if the medium of mutual recognition is language, then it is possible to think of mutual recognition in terms of validity-claims. Reciprocity now appears as the real power inherent in the different processes of individuation and socialization. Interpretations as narratives are the ways in which language crystallizes its reciprocal demands in terms of rationality and in terms of moral duty to the others.

One must recognize the importance of the relationships moral subjects establish with their needs and interpretations, and the role the aesthetic realm plays in the possibility of achieving self-understanding and recognition. Wellmer believes Habermas' model of 'consensus theory' to be tied to the ideas of reconciliation and the unity of reason, an ideal final situation in which understanding has been reached and the different moments of reason are ultimately brought together. In his criticisms of the scientistic model of reason, Wellmer points out that the modes of validity are differentiated, but that no adequate answer to the moral 'ought' is offered. According to Wellmer, the differentiation model of validity spheres can lead to 'sharper contours to the internal connection between differentiated modes of validity'.[66] His model, based on the notion of the appriopriateness and completeness of the interpretations of moral subjects, can be seen as a 'discourse of facts', or, in my terms, as 'narratives'.[67] With this model, Wellmer supplies a possible grounding horizon for subjects, where the transition from 'is' to 'ought' is clarified from the moral point of view of the subjects themselves. However, in the interpretations of the facts that are relevant to moral judgements, argues Wellmer, 'aesthetic experiences' are always brought to bear, for 'there is a fluid boundary also between moral discourse and aesthetic discourse'.[68] He believes that through the application of reason, which does not withhold any validity-claim from critical scrutiny, it is possible to develop criticisms in the light of new experiences already stressed in the narratives claiming recognition.

In the interconnections between the technical, moral and aesthetic spheres, rationality has a special place insofar as reason is differentiated into specific moments which correspond to specific validity-claims, and insofar as it is also connected with each other in the right way. Wellmer envisions the possibility of drawing a connection between truth, semblance and utopia, not as a reconciled unity of reason, but rather as an indication of the interpenetration of different validity-claims, which allow the possibility of designing new ways of life through 'narrative' performances, the consideration of human needs and possible new ways of interpreting them, and, finally, through the building of a democratic culture based on recognition and fully realized self-identities.

I believe that Wellmer's account of the dynamics and interdependence of validity spheres, Martin Seel's criticism of Habermas' communicative theory of language,[69] and Gabriele Schwab's empirical research on the cultural and symbolic content of poetic and literary language provide the justifications for me to focus on a theory of the symbolic and cultural content of language. It is because of the need for different validity spheres of language to interact, to influence each other and to provide arguments which translate meanings back and forth that an understanding can be sought of the spaces where the 'arguments' of different discourses do not exhaust their content solely in cognitive terms. This, for example, is the case of 'moral arguments', when their content is not only cognitive but also affective. It is also true for 'aesthetic arguments', where the cognitive and affective elements are intertwined with visions of life, value judgements, and a specific understanding of experience. As Wellmer has argued, discourses about 'facts', when seen as 'moral discourse', are not impervious to moral and aesthetic viewpoints. Language here appears not only as impregnated by value judgements, but facts themselves are differently comprehended in terms of the various possible orientations of lifeworld views. Empirical convictions and moral attitudes are already interwined in these same orientations. Martin Seel is, therefore, right in pointing out the difficulty of seeing that the meaning of validity – the intrinsic logic – of forms of argumentation is 'not reflected linearly in the validity that may be claimed with various utterances'.[70] Seel argues that it is not speech-acts, *'but only modes of justification'*, which are paradigmatic for the intended differentiation between types of rationality.

The aid provided by metaphorical tools in the explanation of scientific theories is already an accepted fact.[71] We can also understand Kant's interest in couching the important intuitions of his *Critique of Pure Reason* in practical terms when, for example, he translated the concept of 'causality' from speculative to practical reason, and transformed it from a concept that synthesized the interrelation between empirical and rational elements of scientific knowledge into an idea of 'causality' as 'freedom', which reappeared as the transcendental condition of practical reason.[72] Similarly, Seel has focused on the concepts of 'expressive truthfulness' and 'expressive rationality' to demonstrate that, in the validity of truthfulness, both the justification of principles with regard to the values of the individual, and collective ideas of the good life, play an important role, along with the justification of aesthetic judgement. Furthermore, Seel has rightly argued that, when aesthetic statements are asserted as *reasons* for adopting world-shaping views, the justification of aesthetic judgements elevates the object of these judgements to the 'status of an explication of lifeworld experiences'.[73] Thus, the arguments for their truth are significant when the experiences provided come to be seen as appropriate ways of seeing. This is the thesis found in the different cases provided by Schwab in referring to modern subjectivity and in the texts she chooses to show how the social symbolic meanings of the expansion and experience of those subjectivities are best understood.[74]

3 Feminism as an Illocutionary Model

In this chapter, I begin to develop a model of recognition that will provide for a philosophical insight into how to relate the cultural and the symbolic order to a communicative paradigm. I take feminism as my empirical reference in developing this model, arguing that this movement exemplifies the interpenetration of aesthetic and moral spheres in a historically unprecedented way. I define my model on the grounds that the discourses produced by feminism have conquered the public space in a rather original way. The success of these efforts is what I will call their 'illocutionary force', which is now illustrated empirically through texts (having been theoretically defined in the Introduction above). As I already explained, I conceive of language as an internal mediation of action, and more precisely, as an intervention by means of which agents take the initiative to produce new meanings into the public sphere. In the move to narratives, I proceed to another level and a broader context in which figures of discourse interrelate speech and language to produce and exchange meanings. Therefore, the methodological device of this chapter is to travel through those linguistic mediations – narratives – that make 'new beginnings' into meaningful actions. This is where the effort to communicate something relates necessarily to the question 'Who is speaking?', and becomes the starting-point of my theory. As Paul Ricoeur claimed in *Time and Narrative*, it is in narrating experiences that time shades the agent's viewpoint and the process of understanding itself through the simultaneous moments of discourse and narration. Because this is where discourse and narrative intermingle, it develops into a twofold task, that of 'meaning making' and that of 'organizing human experiences into meaningful episodes' through the coherent grasping of an agent who acquires a 'cognitive role'. As Calvin O. Schrag has claimed, 'Cognition unfolds as a pre-objective understanding of self and world within discursive practices'.[1] In this sense, the 'who' of a discourse 'as a narrating self' understands herself in the simultaneous act of grasping the coherence of her view and transmitting it in a narrative fashion.

I will consider the specific relation between history and fiction that has produced women's narrative identities continuously displaying them in the public sphere throughout this century. 'Identity' here has to be understood in the practical sense to which Hannah Arendt refers in her statement that 'this disclosure of [the] who is implicit in everything somebody says and does'.[2] Therefore, narrative identities escape the 'dilemmas' of essentialism, both the total fragmentation derived from 'multiple' experiences and total Otherness – because their ontological and cognitive structure reshapes facts into performative discourses.[3] Paul Ricoeur has called these dynamics reflexive 'narrative configurations'.[4] These configurations pertain to no one in particular and to everybody, because 'the disclosure of the "who's" through speech, and the setting of a new beginning through action, always fall into an already existing web where their immediate consequences can be felt. Together they start a new process which eventually emerges as the unique life story of the newcomer, affecting uniquely the life stories of all those with whom he comes in contact'.[5] I will show how agency plays an important role in the possibility of an 'emergent' self. As Arendt claims, the narratives in which we are immersed, and with which it is possible for all individuals to struggle to write their own agenda, provide the space both for contingency and initiatives.[6] Narrative efforts are therefore not nearly as thin and weak as they have sometimes been conceived by some postmodern thinkers. They can permeate, erode, and transform our self-conceptions in the act of stepping into the public arena. Thus, feminist narratives of identity will be my exploratory example of 'agency' and 'transformative' discourses in the public sphere.

Narratives of Recognition

Diversity, plurality, multiplicity and uniqueness do not lead necessarily to incommensurability. For this reason, it is my aim to show that the multiple selves emplotted in narrative performances not only use a variety of semiotic rules and institutional forms, but also a variety of semantic tools and discursive strategies that together configure new spaces for experiencing an expansion of subjectivities. Those efforts are grouped as performances which combine semiotic and semantic possibilities into narratives which configure new ways of seeing the world.

It is my aim to point out the shared elements of 'universalism' in this highly variegated movement to characterize women's moral identity.

In illuminating this shared universalism, I situate as my goal the definition of the term 'recognition' as an 'illocutionary force', a process mediating between institutions and public opinion. This public linguistic
force has been built up through different discourses which have re-
trieved and reconstructed narratives from the past and projected them
into the future, thus envisioning a utopian culture that allows for a
better way of life. In doing so, feminist narratives have also invented
metaphors that provide new ways to symbolize self-understanding and
self-interpretation.

My claim, however, is that these narratives are not only a construction of the aesthetic sphere, but that they have opened a broader spectrum of participative democratic channels in which public opinion
plays a major role and configures greater interconnections between
justice and the good, a dynamic and not an a priori differentiation
between private and public, and an enlarged conception of moral agents
and human capabilities linked to autonomy and authenticity as their
moral textures.

I refer to the diverse feminist struggles in the academic, societal and
cultural levels, and to the many different theories that have helped
establish the revisions and questionings of our historical traditions, as a
more or less coherent effort that can be collectively understood as an
'illocutionary force'. I am well aware of the unorthodox appearance of
this position, for feminists themselves have often rightly insisted on the
particularistic views of actors, specifically males, and this insistence
prompted considerable research into the anti-universalist impact not
only of gender, but of factors like race, class and sexual orientation.
Nevertheless, I find enough evidence to convince me that despite this
overt concentration on particularity, and despite many ideological differences between the variety of points of view, feminism has succeeded
precisely because it has new definitions and a new understanding of
shared notions of justice and the good. Its struggle has been built by
thematizing equality and difference so as to construct a much more
textured space in which all persons can be considered worthy of respect
and valuable as human beings. In other words, recognition must be
conceived much more broadly than just as a claim for respect, or as an
anthropological need immanently linked to moral development. Recognition is an important struggle within the dynamics of civil societies
and the cultures derived from their public spaces. It contributes to these
discourses and is empowered by them, as it finds institutional support
for a wider claim that provides new self-conceptions of a larger 'we'.

In making this demonstration, I draw upon a new emphasis in narrative studies that is especially relevant to understanding how identities
are constituted, namely, the shift from a focus on representational to
ontological narrativity.[7] With this approach, I wish to suggest that

social life is itself 'storied', and that as a result of women's efforts to grasp it in narrative terms attention has been focused on the ontological conditions of their struggles in social life. However, I would like to show how these new stories have guided action and how women have constructed their identities (however multiple and changing) by locating themselves, or being located, within this new repertoire of plotted stories[8] that have struggled to transform the injustices derived from theoretical viewpoints that limited the institutional frames. It is those experiences, constituting themselves as narratives, that led women to act in certain ways, for they did so on the basis of the projections, expectations and memories derived from a multiple repertoire of available social, public and cultural narratives. The basic claim here is then that women's projects of identity are seen as achievements, accomplishments, performances that have helped transform notions of the public sphere. Contrary to those who focus on narratives as explosions of desire or effects of power, I claim that precisely because narrative identities are achievements, they are guided by a cognitive role – a 'praxis-oriented' discernment and understanding of the agents of action in becoming selves through narrative clarification and grasping for coherence in one's own life.[9] In this way, it becomes possible to understand that narrative agents, the 'who's' of action and deeds, are empowered by their own choices articulated in the agency of an enactment – 'the self as an implicate of action exhibits the power to become an effective agent of social change and cultural transformation'.[10]

The model of 'illocutionary force' I wish to describe here, then, arises from the narratives that feminists have written in order to reconstruct their historical, political and cultural 'roots', and, in doing so, to provide recovered images of 'women'. My implicit claim is that women achieved knowledge through narrative, but these narratives in turn have transformed our notions of justice and democracy. This knowledge is developed first in what is now known as the 'counterpublics'; second, in the varieties of different roles played by women in the public sphere; and, third, by the projections of new narratives about the past into a utopian future which, above all, recovers a self-reflexive process: the act of telling the story is also one of projecting it into the future.[11] This is what Paul Ricoeur has called 'refiguration.'[12]

Historical Reconfigurations of Women's Struggles

In situating these narrative efforts in the shift that occurred in France, England and Germany during and after the French Revolution, I draw not only upon new developments in narrative theory but, of course, upon Habermas' notion of the public sphere[13] as a web of cultural, literary and political interactions, in which literature and the written word, as well as graphics and symbolic sources, are considered very important aspects of a specific public because they create a feedback between readers and authors, the public and its artists. From this view-point, writers create new trends of thinking by creating the mediations between private and public claims. In receiving first the attention and then the understanding of other groups, feminists have succeeded in making their claims into 'illocutionary forces'. Feminism built up a narrative that reconfigures the new values and the imagery of the Enlightenment, the so-called new ideals of 'man' as citizen, the sym-bolic representation of universalism and reason, and 'woman' as the 'guardian of the household', symbolically representing the particular. Feminists have drawn attention to how these diverse images and con-ceptions actually led to constructing conceptions of the 'Other', to conceiving of 'humanity', the 'individual', the 'reasonable', the 'sub-ject', not as representations of the universal, but paradoxically in a one-sided male way. A particular group – men – appropriated a whole set of categories that were supposed to designate new moral and epistemo-logical virtues of universal reason. In narrating the partiality of this approach to enlightment, *feminist historians* had to construct 'breaking points', finding the hidden moments when women had some kind of power or participated in some important way in configuring the new cultural spaces. *Feminist political theorists* had to deconstruct the conceptualizations used as categories of liberalism and democracy, and to question the partiality of the normative grounds on which political theory was conceived. They had to invent new terms to designate what these narratives meant by 'universalism', hypostatizing the particular hidden at the core of this view. *Feminist philosophers* had to question the very enterprise of 'democracy' as such, where women were never part of justice. And they argued that the separation between justice and the good implied a strategy to relegate women to the private. *Feminist lawyers* had to construct a new hermeneutical interpretation of constitu-tional law and redefine the terms that in everyday life designated 'individual' and 'citizen' rights. They introduced new ways to address the public and alert them about the need to consider the political and the ideological harm done when the written law marginalizes women's problems by failing to acknowledge unequal power. *Literary critics* then developed feminist narratives by finding women writers who, in spite of their dependence on the private realm, managed to find a way to address the public and transform notions of subjectivity. *Feminist psy-chologists* had to do research on how differently women thought of the moral domain as a source of relational care for the others. Women's narratives thus situated 'differences' as a public issue.

At some point, all these efforts gathered around some very specific features that implied a still larger narrative. Autobiographies, political representations of the moral order in the public sphere, reinterpretations of all the important authors of the Enlightenment and, finally, a whole set of new metaphors like 'body politics' and 'ethics of care' created a new story about 'gender'. It showed how the Enlightenment's theories failed in their definitions of justice and equality, for the aim of universality was never accomplished. This new narrative about the Enlightenment has transformed Western culture. That different layers of inequality are no longer seen as 'truths', but rather as partial accounts that led to injustice in practices of various kinds, is due to the illocutionary force that has brought recognition to the feminist narrative of women's lives. The many theories that feminists have elaborated constitute a 'body narrative' of levels, a powerful discourse and a hermeneutic and deconstructive lens that has been displayed in the techniques of storytelling, in novels and books in general, in films and television shows, in the news and printed media. These performative constructions of women's identity have succeeded because they have been skilful and imaginative in addressing symbolic and linguistic structures in the fragmented public sphere. They have stimulated the appearance of new subaltern publics that have given positive feedback to these narrative claims demanding that 'general interest' be focused on new stories about justice and solidarity. The performative way of generating spaces for women's demands for recognition was acquired in a daily struggle to redefine 'our' habits and to transform our institutions and culture at the same time. Metaphorically, these narratives have occupied every single space where there has been a woman present, every aspect of daily problems seen through a woman's eye, every corner of society from which women were formerly left out. The broader impact of this regained consciousness gives more than enough evidence to show that the problematics of justice and the good life are deeply interwoven.

In historical terms, I wish to locate the beginning of this effort to build up a new theory of recognition in the novel ways women started participating in symbolic and written language.[14] In contemporary feminist narratives about this early participation, it is not coincidental that the focus is on the 'universal male citizenship' achieved through the French Revolution, for it was then that the word 'equality' first acquired political significance. One of the most important of these contemporary illocutionary interventions is exemplified in the work of Joan B. Landes, which can be conceived not only as important historical research, but as a forceful re-narration that inserts women into the public sphere during the age of the French Revolution.[15] The first chapter of her book _Women and the Public Sphere in the Age of the French Revolution_[16] focuses on the _salonnières_, the women who, during a breaking point in history and a major political struggle, found a way to become genuine creators of a more universalizing culture and education. These efforts created new forms of mobility and social interactions for men and women while allowing, at the same time, the creation of a whole symbolic order that conceived of women as a very special 'otherness'.[17] Landes takes an unprecedented step by considering the importance of the performative and vocalizing roles women played in the salon society in much broader terms than had earlier historians. In her new feminist narrative, the 'salons and their hostesses' became the schools and the teachers that imparted the appropriate style for socializing in the Enlightenment. Landes describes how philosophers of that time, when referring to women's skills and virtues, always pointed out their ability to converse and socialize. In her narrative reconfiguration, however, she frames those same abilities – that were considered the very specific 'differences' that made women a particular 'species' – into a new story that suggests they were not in any way a frivolous feature of women but, rather, a very important 'social force that abetted the integration of new individuals into the elite'.[18] As Landes tells her new story, salon women created the channels for acknowledging the relevance of a specific author, allowing women to enter into a social elite where they could be considered interesting and valuable. The characteristics that drove philosophers to think of women as a different kind[19] are thus reinterpreted here as the mastering skills of cultivated women. This new competence gave them a complex way of structuring language, history, mythology and drama, such that their claims for recognition relied on their power to articulate two validity spheres in hitherto unimagined ways: the aesthetic and the moral. Indeed, 'verisimilitude', says Landes, was the core of this interaction, and she insists on the importance of literature becoming a part of life and vice versa: 'Verbal portraits originating as salon games made their way into novels, while novels and other printed materials were read aloud inside the salon'.[20] Because of this interpenetration of validity spheres, these *salonnières* were 'public women'. They were part of the new 'ethos' of sociability, not the domestic space to which women were assigned then. Landes shows that such salons were a 'unique phenomenon', where the lines drawn between public and private were temporarily erased for specific historical reasons. Hannah Arendt gave a very similar interpretation of the Berlin salons in 1932. In spite of her later overt resistance to feminism, she herself made an important illocutionary intervention on behalf of women, tracing the same temporary disappearance of the differentiation between the public and the private to German salon culture. These historical and philosophical efforts, then, can both be seen as new narrations that contribute to reconstructing and recovering the exceptional role women played in expanding the universal in these earlier times.

It is worth drawing attention to the double reflexivity of this situation. The fact is that these women of the salon were already involved in creating a new process of self-understanding. And it is this new way that is rewoven today into a new historical storytelling that itself becomes a performative discourse of recognition. Women had first to consider themselves as subjects of interest and their lives as worth living and writing about for the performative structure of contemporary feminist discourse to discover that the possibility of recognition is in the public's interest, and can succeed, therefore, by using stories recovered from the past to re-narrate the female space of silence and oblivion.[21]

In that critical breaking point of the late eighteenth century, literature became the most important source of a dynamic new feedback between the public and the private in the reconfiguration of values. Women had access to reading, but most importantly, women themselves found the opportunity to write, and they wrote primarily about themselves.[22] Some did it through the path of novels, and others, for the first time, stopped being the model for male authors and became their own subjects. Women's lives were then displayed as moral autobiographies demanding recognition on the basis of erasing boundaries between the private and the public. Private autobiographies interrelating intimacy and public life became interesting and novel, just as earlier epic dramas had been vital to building up the identity of the nation. As important history-changing narratives, there are the examples of Rousseau writing his _Confessions,_ Goethe claiming that between his life and his work there was no difference, and, much later, Kierkegaard making the public confession a specifically moral way to understand one's own limitations. These cases are well known. What is new is the reconstructed narrative that points to women as the actors that led such new and modern self-understanding towards a 'new beginning'. Authors and readers are now engaged in giving new meanings to a conceptualization of women's lives.

For these early feminist writers, life itself, life as a potential whole, became the focus of investigation, for they created narratives against such dichotomies as the universal versus the particular, reason as opposed to feelings, natural as differentiated from the artificial, and finally, male as representing the 'equal' and female as the representation of the 'other'. Because the imposed dichotomous discourse limited women's access to the public, these first feminist narratives, for the first time in modernity, offer a whole new approach that strives for a more complex way to conceptualize human beings.[23] By reconstructing this effort, contemporary historians create a narrative that provides a new reflexivity and allows contemporary women, and men, to possess a more creative understanding of life and its relation to building moral identities.[24]

The new curiosity about intimacy,[25] privateness, singularity and, most of all, about the invaluable discovery of one's own narrative voice, was created by historical situations that broke down the strict barrier imposed between private and public. This breaking out was not only lived through imaginative literature, in other words, but also socially and interactionally through participation of women in the configuration of the salons.[26] Hannah Arendt, for example, regarded the Berlin 'salons' as follows: 'Because the salon was socially neutral ground', she explains, women, and especially Jewish women, had special access to them because 'they stood outside society to begin with'.[27] Arendt shows that by separating herself from Romanticism, Rahel Varnhagen was the first to establish the Goethe cult, bringing Goethe forward as one of the first authors to cultivate people's interest in the intimacy of life. This coincided, of course, with Goethe's own view of himself, for he saw no differentiation in the unfolding of his life story and the evolution of his skill as an artist. Literature thus became the source of self-education, especially, says Arendt, for those 'whose social traditions had been shaken'. At the same time, literature more than anything else became the channel to seek the acceptance of others for the 'fate' of one's particular life. This did not happen 'naturally', Arendt reminds us; rather, it was the result of 'taking private life seriously, a reality that appears more congenial to women by nature than to men – and which was revealed to the public in almost shameless fashion in Schlegel's *Lucinde*'.[28]

It is well known that Rousseau was aware of the connection between people's interest in intimacy and literature as self-education and self-reflection, and that he therefore specifically addressed women on how they should be educated and how their worthiness was to be preserved.[29] But Landes situates him in a new narrative, for the first time describing him as the 'literary heir of Mme de Sévigné'.[30] Landes claims that it was Sévigné who opened up the interior space where the personal self became worthy of attention and of self-creation. Arendt agrees, suggesting that in the 1790s 'everything intimate thus acquired public character; everything public, an intimate one'.[31] Because private life could escape the ban that would be imposed again later, an objective quality was granted to the intimate and the personal, the realm of 'real life': 'From this attitude arises that personal historicity that makes one's own life, the data of which can be recorded, into a sequence of objective events, whatever those events may be'.[32] This narration becomes part of a new, collective *Ausbildung*. This extraordinary insight of Arendt's about the validity of storytelling asserts that it didn't really matter if 'those data' were fictitious. They appeared to the public as 'authentic', or, to repeat Landes, what mattered was 'verisimilitude'. The tone became more one of authenticity than real empirical evidence, which is why women could force the barrier with their imaginations and create different profiles of what was interesting about their struggle to be women. Women thought of 'communication' as a way of bearing pain, discrimination, isolation, lack of understanding; but in return, as 'bearers of life', they received public solidarity, consolation and sympathy. Most of all, they empowered themselves by the performative effectiveness of their claim to recognition[33] and, in doing so, they reversed the self-defeating images of women as 'victims'. By presenting themselves as strong women they became validated.[34] This was accomplished through the crucial interconnection between the creation of fictions and the moral demand that was implicit in them. By relating aesthetic and normative spheres, women writers expanded the boundaries of subjectivity and recovered ways of being perceived that in the male world were considered purely 'feminine'. In representing life as an authentic struggle, they were capable of making effective claims for recognition.

The Berlin salons had disappeared by 1806, and women and Jews were drawn back into the private sphere. In France these public interventions by women also ended, because, as Landes puts it, men feared the 'feminized atmosphere'[35] produced in the preceding years. In her contemporary feminist narrative, Landes documents the ideological battle against the salons. Refashioned in a masculine way, the salons resembled male forms, such as clubs and patriotic leagues, rather than the tradition-breaking social configurations that introduced 'equality-levelling'. But as the salons disappeared, the literature that had been the major arena for women publicly to display their struggles continued powerfully to draw upon sources from the most private spheres. Nineteenth-century women's literature provided ways of communicating that transformed the image women had of themselves.

I believe that while these new narratives are being created, promoting a different interpretation of the identity of women and expanding the gendered conception of humanity, 'illocutionary forces' are at work in the public sphere. These forces consist of new ways of conceiving political forms which have to be imagined before they can be achieved. By 'recovering' the role women played in the past, by taking seriously the way they conceived their lives as struggles for self-clarification, contemporary narratives gain the 'illocutionary force' not only to increase women's self-esteem, but to alter the conception of who women are. However, although they are a real public force, these new arguments must be understood as texts. These texts have gained power because they can be broadcast within the institutional framework in the very same space produced by the normative ideals of the Enlightenment, with its dialogical character. The combination of reconfigured narrative texts, public institutional space and dialogical normative standards has remodelled the habits not only of women but of men, and has promoted the creation of a whole different language.

Illocutionary Effects of Women's Historical Reconstructions

The responsive, dialogical understanding produced by these claims has begun to occupy the spaces of other narratives and allowed an integration of the insights regarding the value of women. This can be demonstrated by comparing two narrations about Mme de Staël, first in the interpretation of David J. Denby, a literary critic writing in the 1990s about the new 'sentimental order' of the late eighteenth and early nineteenth centuries, and then from the feminist viewpoint of Madelyn Gutwirth, writing in the 1970s. I wish to show how feminist visions are integrated into the work of a male author, how he needs these resources to develop his own argument that a new general understanding of feelings played a major role in deepening the subjectivity of human beings. Denby argues, for example, that Mme de Staël's essay *De l'influence des passions sur le bonheur des individus et des nations*, published in 1792, 'points to a shift away from sentimentalism in the private sphere, conceived as unreliable and a source of unhappiness, towards a cultivation of sentimentalism in the public sphere, where it can be the basis of civilized liberal values'.[36] The most interesting claim that Denby makes is that Mme de Staël was getting away from values that the contemporary school of ideologists had about structuring the private/public split, and that in her work of fiction she was able to take 'the dominant sentimental rhetoric, [and] push this inheritance harder and further in the direction of innovation and renewal'.[37] Denby focuses also on the currently fashionable genres of epistolary novels, and letters themselves, showing how they became a vital source for new values. Diderot's praise for the community of readers made France one of the first countries to have an idea of the importance of the 'special public'. By drawing upon her experience as a writer, Mme de Staël provides the best illustrations of what these communities are: '[she] puts a very precise gloss on the notion of community', Denby explains, 'which she extends from the level of personal relations outwards through *public opinion* to the nation and perhaps metaphorically, to a wider sense of *patrie*. . . . Madame de Staël's view of eloquence is linked to the notion of community, for eloquence, too, is an eminently social, communicative form of activity'.[38] In this concept of 'eloquence' Denby is highlighting a feature related to building up a discourse in the public. Using the medium of 'eloquence', Mme de Staël bridges the gap between inner spaces, between speaker and listener, expanding the boundaries of community and promoting the empowerment of women within it. With a strategy that develops from the power of sentiment, she seeks a kind of rational consent.[39] When she refers to the epistolary novel, and she asserts that its specificity is to 'observe the human heart', something transcendent is already at stake there, something that relates to the way the truth comes to the public. When one reads about the hearts and troubles of others, one forms a community with them in the very act of reading. Reciprocal understanding and recognition thus become the basis of the community in a much more powerful way.

However, it is not simply Denby's defence of the sentimental order in the work of Mme de Staël to which I want to draw attention, but the source on which he draws. Denby's own new appraisal is derived from the feminist reading of de Staël's *Delphine* by Madelyn Gutwirth, who writes that the 'suffering of a woman, who wishes to be more than society allows her' is what brought the novel its public attention. Mme de Staël's response to these feelings, in Gutwirth's view, is to challenge the sentimental model based on domesticity and the ideal of self-sacrifice and devotion: 'If this is your image of real femininity, I will show how splendid it can be, but how little it is wanted by your society if it is taken seriously as an ideal'.[40] Gutwirth adds: 'This work consecrates her post-Revolutionary understanding that she may not present herself or any woman resembling herself as a heroine'.[41] For Mme de Staël, to go beyond degrading sentimentalism was to achieve a much fuller expression, á more real empowerment.[42]

Patrick Joyce, in his book *Democratic Subjects: The Self and the Social in Nineteenth-century England*,[43] similarly draws his major thesis about narratives from the work of various feminists. Joyce pays careful attention to the importance of gender in Lynn Hunt's *The Family Romance of the French Revolution*,[44] and, particularly, to how she conceptualized it in narrative terms. In putting the symbolic order in the form of narrative at the centre of her analysis, and at the centre of politics, that book points the way forward for the sort of work undertaken here. Hunt shows how it was necessary for political forms in the Revolution to be imagined before they could be realized – precisely in the spirit of the treatment of 'democracy' in this study. She suggests how the family romance at work in the Revolution set its own dynamic, and that a narrative of the Revolution needs in turn to be written around this romance, a narrative allowing narrative its own autonomous role.[45] Joyce also incorporates into his analysis of democracy the use by Judith R. Walkowitz of narratives 'of sexual gender' in late Victorian London.[46] In other words, Joyce grounds his own, more subjective and symbolic approach to democracy in feminist narratives about gender. 'The political culture I describe below was profoundly gendered, as was the public realm in which it operated'.[47] Joyce's book, like Denby's, illustrates the kind of dialogical responses that have emerged from the reconstructed narratives developed by feminists.

Similar reactions in other fields of science and humanities can be cited as examples of this dialogue, and it is evident that the 'illocutionary force', derived via the transformation of gender narratives, has made a substantial impact on the values and categories which are now employed to deal with the social, political and moral dimensions of life. In the historical and literary disciplines devoted to the French Revolution, the feminist works discussed above have influenced historiography by critically questioning the 'commonplaces' of the past.[48]

The various academic efforts I have discussed here can be seen as a web of feminist storytelling that imaginatively develops new ways of understanding women and the role gender has played in the historical and cultural traditions of thinking about equality, democracy and recognition. In becoming aware of the empowerment provided by these narratives, women have not only succeeded in presenting themselves as eminently worthy of recognition, but in crystallizing the model that I have here called 'illocutionary'.

4 Autonomy and Authenticity as Textures of the Moral Subject

Among the discussions within contemporary ethics is one that involves a critical reflection on the concept of moral autonomy derived from Enlightenment traditions, specifically, the Kantian one.[1] The communitarians claim that this category of autonomy reflects an abstract and formal approach to moral agents[2] that reveals an emptiness in its conception. Thus, Charles Taylor has focused on authenticity as an alternative basis for the configuration of moral agents and their self-conceptions.[3] However, within this controversy, the aesthetic dimension underlying the conception of 'authenticity' as a substitute for the moral category of 'autonomy' becomes problematic in at least two senses. On the one hand, the aestheticization of the moral domain distorts and confuses two different validity-claims (one moral and the other aesthetic), and this analytical confusion reflects upon questions regarding justice.[4] On the other, the relation between justice and the good is not clarified by replacing the category of 'autonomy' with an aesthetic category. I believe that this issue can be reframed if 'authenticity' is conceived not as a substitute for the formalistic approach to the self but as a means of focusing on the interconnections between the two different validity spheres and the interdependence established by the flow of information regarding the good, the realm of justice and self-conceptions. If one considers the interrelation between autonomy and authenticity, one will be able to grasp the dynamics of identity processes and to illuminate the moral textures of the self. After demonstrating this argument, I will show how these issues are interwoven in women's narratives.

Moral autonomy is a key concept in modern ethics. However, it has undergone a profound revision in terms of the problems implied by conceiving autonomy as self-determination.[5] In the moral domain, autonomy has been viewed as the category that includes the task of justifying our actions through reasons, the ability and willingness to assume a reflexive role-distance, to take the opinions of other parties involved in controversies into account, and to reason from their point of view. Yet, it remains impossible to avoid the expressive perception that humans are unique and singular beings, and that our life decisions and moral identities confront us with two different goals derived from two different categories. Autonomy strives for self-determination, whereas authenticity is directed towards self-realization.

The controversy surrounding the role played by authenticity in projects of the moral life must be clarified. Charles Taylor, for example, derives his conception of authenticity from a romantic vision of a moral ideal trying to reach the inner truths of the self.[6] On the other hand, Alessandro Ferrara tries to give a more reconstructive view of what he calls the 'metaphorical sense' of the tradition of authenticity, suggesting that it is based on three ideas: first, the 'capacity for being oneself'; second, a position that allows authors a critical glance at Western modernity; and third, the sceptical and critical insight of all the authors within this tradition towards modern processes of differentiation, which they see as having undermined 'the individual's capacity to become him- or herself'.[7] Ferrara, like Taylor, conceives authenticity as a task that involves a self-reflexive being capable of recognizing needs and feelings that are at the heart of our identities. Both authors argue that authenticity is a category that suits conceptions of moral agents because it links justice and the good.

My conception of authenticity differs from both of these. First, I regard authenticity as a category that belongs to the aesthetic domain and which, therefore, cannot become itself a moral 'ideal' or a 'paradigm' for thematizing moral identities. The role played by authenticity in the moral realm is seen in terms of self-realization, and in that sense, of moral identity. But, as discussed in chapter 1, when referring to autobiographies as self-presentations, an expressive validity-claim is displayed only when there is a 'dialogue' between the author and the public that is interwoven with the moral domain. A specific discourse developing a project that claims recognition is complete only when the acceptance of the public has taken place, which is to say that authenticity relates to the performative way in which a discourse engages the other ('alter') in an understanding of the 'ego'. Thus, my conception of authenticity is related to the acts of 'disclosure' of the 'who's' of action. On the other hand, authenticity is linked to processes of self-realization through responsibility and self-reflexive consciousness, and this is where it connects specifically with the dimensions of autonomy and self-determination. It is this process of self-consciousness as a capacity that is crystallized in narrative as a moral project. My conception of authenticity is also linked to the idea that individuality is a simultaneous process of intersubjective acknowledgement of others, and inter-subjectively mediating self-understanding. Therefore, it is in defining the 'authenticity' of one's own moral project, as an expressive and moral validity-claim, that self-determination becomes linked with self-realization. An individual subject acquires an identity by situating herself in a performative act of disclosure. We connect authenticity with self-realization in order to find recognition from others, and, at the same time, to stress the uniqueness of our identity claims.

While Taylor and Ferrara are right in recovering Rousseau as the first author who conceived of authenticity as part of his moral project, they do not thematize the 'performative' characteristic which, by linking autonomy with authenticity, unfolds the specifically modern process that Rousseau understood as the basis for his being accepted by the public opinion of his time. Rousseau was trying to achieve a certain kind of recognition, one that links together two different dimensions of a moral goal: the right to be considered a unique human being, and the moral worthiness inherent in the struggle to become a moral person occupying a place in the symbolic and cultural order as a result of her acceptance by public opinion.

I believe that in order to understand authenticity one should approach it through a four-stage historical reconstruction. Rousseau's initial claim of submitting his life to the public as an identity project must be connected with Kierkegaard's notion of 'life history' as the principle of individuation as self-choice. Mead's interactive account of a simultaneous process of socialization and individuation leads us to the third stage, which evolves into the fourth in Habermas' reinterpretation of it in his own linguistic paradigm. This fourth stage, however, can be clarified only if recognition is conceived as 'mirrored' in the mutual attribution of rights that emerges from a struggle for recognition, one which centrally involves an act of disclosure in Arendt's terms. Whereas Habermas addressed these interconnections only briefly, I want to explore their interplay fully by further developing my earlier discussions of the concrete example of women's narratives. I aim to show how the struggle to achieve an equal right to an autonomous life was waged through forms of political communication that revolved around women's narratives of identity projects.

In what follows, I would like to present the thesis that the categories of autonomy and authenticity are essential for the constitution of moral subjects. Contrary to those who defend authenticity as the sole basis for projects of moral identity, I will show that each category involves the interrelatedness between the two spheres of validity and their respective rationalities, which, as discussed in chapter 2, are continuously engaged in feedback and exchange. This assertion of interpenetration depends, however, on maintaining the analytical distinction between the categories. Only by avoiding the charge of aestheticizing the moral domain is it possible to illustrate the interconnections between reflexiveness and sensitivity, experience and self-understanding, capacity and imagination, and the interplay between the uniqueness of the moral agent and the universality of the claim for recognition when related to disclosive performances. In developing the relationship between both categories and their mutual dependence in moral agents, I will show that women's autobiographies are new illocutionary forms that demonstrate the mutual dependency of autonomy and authenticity as moral textures.

The Reconfiguration of the Concept of Autonomy

Kant's ideal of autonomy still has a great deal to offer. From the philosophical point of view, Habermas has argued that the right to equal liberties 'is grounded in the autonomous will of individuals who, as moral persons, have at their prior disposal the social perspective of a practical reason that tests laws'.[8] Thus, he takes the connection between the human right to equal liberties and the social contract that sustains its political and moral contents as his basis for defining 'private and public autonomy'. From the sociological point of view, David Held takes a similar stance, saying that 'the cluster of rights and obligations which allow the principle of autonomy to be effective – that is, which delimit and generate a common structure of political action – can be referred to as the set of "empowering" or "participatory" entitlement capacities'.[9] And in terms of 'capacities', such political theorists as Joseph Raz argue that 'a person's life is (in part) his own making. It is a normative creation, a creation of new values and reasons'.[10]

However, it was Habermas who widened the scope of the relationship that subjects must establish in order to claim recognition of one's identity project in a dialogically performative fashion. With this thematization in his historical reconstruction of autobiographies, he stressed that it was not enough for individuals to place themselves in another's position through imagination, but that it was also necessary for their point of view to be subjected to the analysis and consideration of the others in the public arena. This process shows that the moral autonomy of individuals requires a social channel to bridge the spectrum of the merely singular – once it enters into the public domain and strives to gain the recognition of others. Two fundamental values support the intersubjectivization of the concept of autonomy derived from Kant's tradition: liberty and equality. We must be free to choose how to live our lives, but we can only be free if we are equal. For persons to become free and equal, furthermore, they must have 'a common structure of political action', as Held put it.[11] Kant introduced the moral principle that considered people as 'ends' in themselves, thus providing the institutional basis for considering respect from others a condition for the autonomy of moral subjects. If everyone is obliged to consider others as ends, and if everyone must make explicit how this goal is to be achieved, then political agencies and democratic institutions should foster the plurality of life choices. The dialogical performance of an autonomous life is linked to models of the good life, which stimulate, at the same time, an increasing 'demand that one responsibly take possession of one's own individual, irreplaceable, and contingent life history'.[12] This radicalized interiority, which has been manifest in autobiographical models ever since the eighteenth century, displays a specific social and individual dynamic in which self-understanding and self-knowledge intermingle within existential decisions. 'Through the extent that this constellation has an even broader impact on society', argues Habermas, 'through prevailing patterns of socialization, ethical existential or clinical discourses become not only possible but in a certain sense unavoidable'.[13] The result is that reflections on life histories and cultural traditions have fostered 'individualism' in personal life projects, and 'pluralism' in collective forms of life.

But, if it is agreed that the principle of autonomy is not only an individual principle of self-determination but 'a structural principle of self-determination', as Held calls it, then the possibility of exercising our right to self-determination must be protected by democratic institutions.[14] Along with the task of achieving self-understanding and self-knowledge, the reflexive manner in which the norms of interaction are submitted to public scrutiny must be considered. This process links moral autonomy in the sphere of personal life to the legal interpretations of political freedom, 'interpretations of democratic self-legislation in the constitution of a just society'.[15]

But what appears to be a simultaneous process of self-reflexiveness has two distinct origins. On the one hand, autonomy – as a moral principle – gave place to a critical self-reflexive process of interiorization of one's own goals as a self-determining agent. However, in the individual's process of self-consciousness, there comes a moment at which she finds herself dealing with the 'expressivist' standards of possible ideals of self-realization. At the same time, when norms become reflexive, and are questioned through understanding and interpreting the legal system, self-determination is the normative standard of this process. There is a twofold meaning of autonomy that interconnects with the self-reflexive process: a collective and a personal one. Autonomy and authenticity are thus interrelated processes that simultaneously intertwine self-determination with self-realization.[16]

How, then, can I argue that autonomy cannot be replaced by authenticity, if, as shown above, they are so closely connected? The answer lies in interrelating the two dimensions of self-realization and self-determination with a reconceptualization of a specific interaction between validity spheres. The moral sphere is defined in terms of rights. The moral imagination is linked to the aesthetic sphere when it relates to the future possibilities of who one wants to be, and to one's need to have available models from which to choose one's own way. On the other hand, the protection of rights, of the dignity of being, belongs to the moral domain. Both are intertwined in that one cannot be self-determining unless one is capable of envisioning a self-realizing project. Both need to be articulated as the 'normative content' of the exercise of political autonomy, or 'democratic autonomy', as Held calls it. These exercises in political autonomy are displayed in the communicative form of discourses and in their impact on public opinion. A cultural understanding of this interrelationship comes through the mediation of the public sphere between civil society and the system of law.

The 'normative content' that is at the core of the exercise of political autonomy can be related to Kant's moral principle of human beings as ends in themselves. A person can achieve the quality of 'dignity' only if that person is autonomous. But autonomy can be expressed only in a self-conscious choice of how to lead a good life through others' recognition of who one is. Communicative freedom depends on an inter-subjective relationship, which is why this freedom is coupled with 'illocutionary' obligations. In a 'democratic autonomy', self-legislation by citizens requires that those subjects who are the recipients of the law also understand themselves to be the authors of the law. Hence, the principle of democracy must be at the heart of a system of rights.

Intersubjective, dialogically defined autonomy is the only means of achieving a balance between the idea of freedom of choice and the necessary appeal for collective recognition. To the extent to which projects of moral identity become demands for the discussion of rights, one is also under an obligation to create public spaces for collective participation. Only thus is it possible for the individual and the citizen to be seen as two necessary dimensions of a project of moral identity.

Authenticity as a Complement to Autonomy

The notion of authenticity discussed above is the product of the transformation of experiencing art and of the idea of individuals as original beings derived from moral struggles now conceived as disclosures. The ideal of authenticity is a product of the eighteenth century, which brought with it the suggestion of a personal model.[17] Turning modern subjectivity towards a reflexive internalization of who we are implies the task of self-knowledge, of critically determining what is original about ourselves.

The author most often cited as an example of this expressivist shift is Rousseau.[18] In fact, as discussed above, Rousseau brought to light what was already a new form of modern sensitivity. He created a specific link between autonomy and authenticity through his struggle to achieve the moral worthiness of his ethical and moral choices; and he knew that he depended on the judgement of the public. As Habermas aptly put it: 'Once the vertical axis of the prayer has tipped into the horizontal axis of interhuman communication, the individual can no longer redeem the emphatic claim to individuality solely through the reconstructive appropriation of his life history; now the positions taken by others decide whether this reconstruction succeeds'.[19] Rousseau exemplified a secular point of view in which the concept of individuality was performatively displayed and detached from its descriptive function. In justificatory self-presentations, a totally 'new meaning' was revealed in claims for individuality put by a first person to a second person in a dialogue. It was an act of disclosure. Such confessions raised the validity claim of authentification. Only others could accept the project as authentic. Hence, the shift to what I have called the 'illocutionary' performance of life projects.

It is this historical shift that produced a different conception of individuals. The performative usage of an individual is related to the self-understandable subject who is capable of speech and action, and as such, engages in a dialogue to justify herself as an irreplaceable being. Thus, no matter how diffuse or multiple the self-understanding process may be, it lays the groundwork for the identity of the 'ego'. The acceptance of the life projects of others articulates self-conscious understanding with an ethical self-assurance. Individuality is explained through an ethical understanding of a second person.

The recognition that autonomy is not achieved by the rightness of one's decisions, but is subject to public recognition, allows one to relate the idea of authenticity directly to the process of autonomy, now linked to the dimension of disclosure. It is also what Charles Taylor calls 'Self-determining Freedom'.[20] It is obvious that more than external impositions regarding the exercise of freedom (in the negative sense) is involved. In a self-reflexive exercise of authenticity, one often has to break with conventions and external prejudices to be able to self-determine an identity through self-knowledge. What Rousseau shows in his *Confessions* is that both the exposition of the struggle for autonomy and the performative characteristics that relate it to authenticity as self-disclosure entail a new way of conceiving individuals. Thus, he placed his own project in a new light. He suggested that because human beings have distinctive and unique characteristics, the dynamics of respect and the struggle for recognition acquire significant moral dimensions. When one is able to articulate the originality of one's own project of identity, one is also able to define oneself. Self-determination is thus linked to self-realization. Projects of authenticity, then, have two conditions. The first is that one must possess sufficient autonomy to decide one's own life; the second is that self-determination and self-realization must be brought together into a public claim for recognition in a disclosive fashion.

Kierkegaard also cast new light on the process of self-understanding when he situated himself as an individual entangled in history, and appropriated his own history by choosing who he wanted to be.[21] He created himself through the public and responsible choice of who he wanted to become. 'The person who wants to decide his life task ethically does not ordinarily have such a wide range; the act of choosing, however, is much more meaningful to him. Now, if you are to understand me properly, I may very well say that what is important in choosing is not so much to choose the right thing as the energy, the earnestness, and the pathos with which one chooses. In choosing the personality declares itself in its inner infinity and in turn the personality is thereby consolidated'.[22] Kierkegaard was well aware that his narration functioned as a performative tool, adding with great clarity: 'What takes precedence in my *Either/Or* is, then, the ethical. Therefore, the point is still not that of choosing something; the point is not the reality of what is chosen but *the reality of choosing*. This, however, is what is crucial, and it is to this that I shall strive to awaken you. Up to that point, one person can help another; when he has reached that point, the significance the person can have for the other becomes more subordinate'.[23] With his self-positing, Kierkegaard was able to relate himself to the Other on 'whom this relation depends'. He consciously describes the contingencies of life, the impossibility of disentangling himself from history, yet, as a historicized self, through his own narration, he is able to recover himself by showing himself to others.

Because performative knowledge is expressed by the very act of disclosing it – that is, narratively – confirmation from others is what grants it validity. When that identity reaches the public scenario, in a performative fashion, it becomes part of the community. But identities are not static, and no one is obliged to remain identical with herself. Identity narratives are fragmentary and, as historical textures, they are woven into the cultural and symbolic orders. This creation of individualities contains an intersubjective core born of the networks of linguistically mediated interactions.

When the concept of authenticity is interrelated with its moral content, the ability to communicate takes on new shadings. No one can establish an identity project without the help of others, without recognition from others, without exercising the rights to freedom and justice. When one attempts to define a specific, original human being, in justifying the ideals towards which one strives, one appeals to the right to be authentic. The dialogical configuration of this quest for identity shows the relationship between autonomy and authenticity.

Autonomy and Authenticity as a Dialogue Between the Normative and the Aesthetic Realms in Women's Autobiographies

According to Martin Seel, in order to speak of the 'autonomy' of validity spheres one must first address their 'interrelative terms'; once one is engaged in an argumentational portrayal, one needs to thematize these terms as being 'tuned in to a different form of validity'.[24] This is what I have tried to illustrate by focusing on autonomy and authenticity as two interrelated validity spheres in need of each other to be fully understood, at least in terms of identity projects.

In order to influence the public realm, women over the centuries have had to resort to many imaginative strategies. The historian Richard L. Kagan has documented the example of Lucrecia in sixteenth-century Spain.[25] Lucrecia was a young woman who had no money and did not come from a noble family. Her social life consisted of religious gatherings and meetings with her confessors. One day, encouraged by her religious advisers, she decided to make her dreams 'public'. However, her dreams were all forceful criticisms of the monarchy, which the advisers copied down as valuable documents. Lucrecia's dreams had such an impact that Philip II, King of Spain, and his priests decided to submit her to the Inquisition. She was put on trial but, as soon as she promised not to continue to make her dreams public, she was released. Her example shows one way in which women strove to participate in public opinion. Because she had no money or institutional influence, the only way she found to enter into the public sphere was to say that she had terrible 'nightmares' – prophecies – which portrayed the decadence of the political order.

Autobiographies and biographies became an indicator of the change in the interests and sensibilities of the modern world. However, there were women who were already preparing to emerge as public figures by using existing genres, transformed to suit their purposes. Elisa von der Recke is a case in point.[26] She was a Prussian artist who lived from 1756 to 1833. She wrote her autobiography in 1793, but asked that it be published after her death. The autobiography is divided into two parts: her childhood and her life after her marriage. The part dealing with her mature life is written in the form of letters. This apparently trivial fact is very relevant. It seems that the letters were not written to her friend Caroline Stoltz, as the author wishes us to believe, but that she kept a record of certain events and people in notes, which she later converted into epistles. This is typical of the period in novels and autobiographies.

Elisa von der Recke, in other words, chose a known genre to convert her life into literary form. She was forced to marry, and the boredom of her marriage turned her into a sentimental heroine who had to fight adversity to obtain her autonomy. In the construction of her autobiographical tale, however, Elisa's relations with the realm of literature played an important role. There is evidence that Sophie von la Roche's novel *Geschichte des Fraüleins von Sternheim* (1771) was used as a model. Elisa von der Recke read it in 1772, and there are many similarities between the two texts. Elisa saw her own experience through the interpretative lens of her reading of Sophie von Sternheim.[27] The use of the aesthetic realm to attain ethical consciousness allows Elisa to construct her own discourse of self-presentation.

In the tradition of Samuel Richardson, whose works were a fundamental influence on la Roche, the sentimental heroine suffers passively. She was essentially a 'virtuous woman', and her family was responsible in part for her unhappiness. But Sophie von Sternheim was a woman of considerable inner strength with many resources. Even in the worst moments of her life, she acts with great dignity. It is this model, which Elisa adopts in her portrayal of herself, that transforms the formal aspects of the 'virtuous' passive woman into an active self-portrayal, and allows her to overcome her own miseries. Elisa noticed similarities between Sophie and herself as she read Sophie's novel, a projection that illustrates how fiction becomes reality, and how real life produces heroines. Here it becomes possible to illustrate the power of fiction to model self-images which are highly valued. In Elisa's narrative, we have a sense of her loneliness, but also of her great desire for the respect of others and herself. Her project clearly traces an interrelation between autonomy and authenticity in the way she connects the literature which influenced her with her attempt to give a new moral dimension to the narration of her own life. However, Elisa's main goal in telling her story was self-determination as she found her way towards self-realization.

Elisa von der Recke made history. She became famous among her contemporaries, the Rationalists and the Pietists. Even Catherine the Great thanked her for having written such a brave autobiography. After her divorce, she wrote religious poems and songs. The support she received from the Rationalists and Pietists of her time allowed her to break with the traditional restrictions on decent women and to become a much read author with public recognition. Elisa, through her autobiography, obtained her divorce and the possibility of self-determination and self-realization.

This story resembles many others from the period. In earlier chapters I have highlighted various aspects of these retellings. For Katherine R. Goodman, the feminist writer who recovered Elisa's struggle as an identity process, the important point is how 'women fashioned the stories of their lives from the ready-made images at their disposal'.[28] Goodman argues that Elisa fuelled her strength through her readings, finding legitimation and authority. But her project, once made public, allowed her to 'express thoughts and feelings more appropriate to contemporary novels of domestic affairs than to the more objective forms of autobiographical writing about professions of the time'.[29] Elisa became her own creative self-presentation.

Not all cultural examples are drawn from literature. Studies of the autobiographies written by African-American women from the eighteenth and nineteenth centuries, for example, show how they used a particular recovery of religious claims in order to force attention towards the moral domain.[30] These autobiographical narratives appeared as spiritual conversions that 'pictured' sufferings in much the same fashion as 'blue' rhythms and songs. The autobiographies were a sort of sung spiritual; they were connected to individual selves that strove to present themselves as part of the collective human existence.[31] There is evidence that they omitted all the routine details of their lives in order to keep the attention of their readers.[32] Like the music that African-Americans connected to their specific reinterpretation of religion, black women's narratives appropriated the religious legacy to give it a new voice as a 'consciousness of the black narrator as bearer of the Word'.[33]

Many other women also wrote about themselves, presenting their lives as authentic moral struggles of various kinds. The articulation of the search for personal autonomy was an authentic validity-claim, demonstrating that life acquired its meaning through the personal choices narrated. Choices for women mean something quite different from Kierkegaard's explicit existential demand. Women always portrayed themselves as choosing between competing values that left one dimension of their lives subordinated to another. They presented the link between autonomy and authenticity as a reconsideration of complex choices. The right to be considered a human being was displayed along with a vision of how one wanted to live a good life.

This new link between autonomy and authenticity shows a historically specific connection between self-realization and self-determination. One is autonomous, in this sense, when one can determine one's life and when one's ethical project finds recognition. This view allows authenticity to be conceived as a performative claim for recognition that grants the autonomy of the moral agent. With this reconceptualization of individuals, women gained a new sense of agency.

5 Narrative Cultural Interweavings: Between Facts and Fiction

I would now like to concentrate on the complex historical processes of re-reading and reinterpreting women's views of themselves which have constituted the different levels of the symbolic order. As discussed above, women have dealt extensively with a whole range of new interpretations of the symbolic order and the cultural interweavings of subjects' own self-conceptions.[1] Feminists have developed a new hermeneutics for dealing with the past while embarking on a critical study of the present, thus discovering a new level of interconnectedness between the moral and the aesthetic spheres. Through genealogical research, they have narrated plots allowing women to expose power struggles and to question the narrowness of the so-called universal claims of reason. Women have recharted the dimension in which the political and literary spheres intersect and exchange, offering public opinion a whole new conception of 'human being' and 'human capabilities'. Women developed their claim for recognition on the new grounds of a shift to a cultural paradigm. This new paradigm has allowed them to find a new language. As should be clear from the previous chapters, I consider literature and cultural readings very important tools in developing my thesis.

In this chapter, I want to focus on how women have used fiction as a cultural strategy for performing identity claims, once they became aware of the huge impact that literary works can have on public opinion. Jane Austen's novels, in particular, have influenced the public sphere as a result of the recent recovery of her fiction in feminist reinterpretations, films and scholarly analysis. I examine the philosophical approach that uses fiction to delve further into the categorical reweaving that is necessary to acknowledge the transformation that has taken place in contemporary societies because of the new public of women. I address particularly Martha Nussbaum's insistence on an

Aristotelian reframing of human capabilities and moral agents through fiction and literature.

I believe that women's identity formation has been more a process of invention than a recovery of something lost, hidden or forgotten. This viewpoint takes into consideration the importance of language and shows the changes that occur through its use in outlook and life styles. Another relevant issue here is the creation of identities. By narrating a past that best generates a sense of personal identity, women have developed a pattern in which the present is the source of future possibilities. Women have used the word 'personal ' because emplotment has been their tool to create individual meaning through other stories – of women of the past – in order to tie into a historical understanding the ongoing content of women's lives within narratives that offer a wider conception of 'agents' as moral subjects. In this sense, individuals do not simply have memories in the historical sense, but, by adopting everchanging attitudes towards them, continuously reconstructing them, they can develop new interpretations. That is why there are constant changes in public opinion. Identity is conceived differently in narratives not only because past experiences are rewoven through time, but also because each new and broader narrative gives new meaning to society's own larger narrative.

As discussed above, Hannah Arendt's most important insight into the public sphere lies in her idea that 'disclosive' qualities are attached to the 'who's' through speech: 'Only the actors and speakers who re-enact the story's plot can convey the full meaning, not so much of the story itself, but of the "heroes" who reveal themselves in it'.[2] For Arendt, 'action reveals itself fully only to the storyteller'.[3] In this case, the storytellers are women themselves becoming the subjects configuring a new conception of 'moral agents'.

This cultural paradigm is based partly on Paul Ricoeur's theory of narratives in his book *Time and Narrative*.[4] The different symbolic meanings that are woven and rewoven in the public sphere can be grouped into three stages of 'mimetic representation':[5] 'mimesis 1' is the stage in which life is experienced and conceived linguistically in the everyday world of action; 'mimesis 2' is the authorial stage of creative narrative configuration; and 'mimesis 3' is the appropriation of 'mimesis 2' by the world of the readers.[6] Narratives draw on the materials of everyday life, but, as the stories unfold in the public sphere, they return to and reconfigure life itself. In this way, complex webs of narratives emplot action, experience and speech, and stimulate further levels of those same categories in the subsequent readings and self-understandings of the subjects. Anthony Paul Kerby, for example, says:

The level of mimesis 1 already has a considerable degree of narrative structuring that allows actions to be viewed within a purposive and historical dimension. This structuring becomes even more apparent if we consider . . . that mimesis 3 feeds back into the life-world of the reader, for structuring at the level of mimesis 1 is very much the product of earlier configurative acts that have been appropriated by the individual or taken by society in general.[7]

Jane Austen's Narratives as a Moral Source

This reading of Jane Austen must begin in the present, bearing in mind the current explosion of attention paid to her works as a result of the several films based on her novels. Films are narratives in our contemporary societies. The cinematic versions of *Sense and Sensibility, Persuasion, Pride and Prejudice, Mansfield Park* and *Emma* have all attracted a huge public following. The sudden interest in Austen's narratives can be traced to her vision of the roles of men and women in society and, what is more important, the fact that all her stories are portrayals of moral agents with a very specific view of justice and the good.[8] The present is a critical scenario where abstract and formal models of moral agents are increasingly questioned. Both communitarians and feminists agree on this point.

However, the notion of 'mimesis 1'[9] leads to an understanding that Austen portrayed women as very different from the women of her times.[10] Her heroines cut a different kind of moral figure, one that broadened the moral scope of deliberation, judgement and understanding. Allison G. Sulloway writes that:

The decade of the 1790s was characterized by a legacy of the Enlightenment, which for a brief few decades was almost as volatile as the international debates over 'the Rights of Man'. All over Europe, and especially in England, France, and Germany, pre-Revolutionary women had already begun to think that the injustices imposed upon women of all classes were as legitimate a subject for rational debate as the wrongs of any other disenfranchised groups. But when Austen began her mature work, champions of women's rights were considered as insurrectionary as those other restless reformers whom Trevelyan described. As a member of a clerical family, she was anxious to spare herself and her family any ugly notoriety, and so she adopted policies of thematic and rhetorical caution and hid behind the anonymity of authorship. Even possibilities of finding a publisher at all depended not only on what she said but how she said what she said.[11]

With this strategy, Austen can be interpreted as having stepped into 'mimesis 2',[12] a process of creating her own world, and a new reordering of moral virtues – in a combination of Aristotelian and Kantian senses – to offer a specific outlook on women's sphere of life.[13] 'Rather than inverting private and public', says John Ely, 'Austen tends to ignore (at least, superficially) the latter (understood in traditional terms) and reconstructs the former as an intellectual and morally congealed community of friends, one composing her own concept of the "good life" '.[14] Moral subjects were incarnated in her works by women, their qualities were displayed within a series of what were considered devalued features of women's behaviour; at the same time, she combined these features with 'impartiality' and reasonableness. In Austen's view, these women portrayed a new possibility for moral learning through a revalorization of feelings by reason, and a new conception of the capacity for 'judgement' and 'deliberation' as moral learning tools.

While such philosophers as Gilbert Ryle[15] and Alasdair MacIntyre[16] linked Austen's views to Aristotle, some later authors have begun to offer more original versions of what is distinctive about her 'Aristotelianism' in terms of 'mimesis 3'.[17] According to Ely, for example, 'this community, as she portrays it, allows her to transform the traditional Aristotelian order of the virtues, giving "feminine" dispositions and attitudes a more significant role'.[18] In my opinion, however, Austen does this without giving up the valuable tools of reason in its Kantian sense. That is why the experience of Austen presupposes a moral and intellectual equality between women and men.[19] The possible influence on Austen of the Scottish Enlightenment should be considered here.[20] However, as a moralist, she needed to overcome the limits in which this 'equality' was conceived in her time.[21] She used Aristotle in a discourse that recaptured experiences of 'perception', 'impressions', 'sensations', 'sensibility', 'judgement' and 'feelings' within a broader conception of 'moral reasoning'. John Ely has suggested,[22] for example, that while Austen came from a Tory tradition, her moral vision seemed already to be pointing to a new interrelation between justice and the good. As opposed to Ely, MacIntyre and others, however, I believe that Austen shared some basic features with the Scottish Enlightenment, with philosophers such as David Hume[23] and Adam Smith,[24] who regarded feelings as important elements of moral life. As I see it, the most striking feature of Austen's narratives is that she portrayed feelings as morally relevant, not as opposed to reason but as complementary to it.[25] This is shown by the fact that she thought of feelings as 'ethically rationalized'.[26] They were character traits to be cultivated, not to be subordinated to the 'rational will' but integrated with it. In *Sense and Sensibility*, for example, Elinor Dashwood cultivates feelings along with reason. Marianne Dashwood, on the contrary, suffers because she has not yet learned to cultivate her feelings as a source of knowledge and kindness. Austen describes Elinor as possessing 'strength for understanding, and coolness of judgement, which qualified her frequently to counteract. . . . She had an excellent heart; her disposition was affectionate, and her feelings strong; but she *knew how to govern them*: it was a knowledge which her mother had yet to learn, and which one of her sisters had resolved never to be taught'.[27] Marianne, by contrast, 'was sensible and clever; but eager in every thing; her sorrows, her joys, could have no moderation. She was generous, amiable, interesting: she was everything but prudent'.[28] Throughout the novel, Elinor displays that combination of reason and feelings, becoming the only member of the Dashwood family to cope with the complexities of their life. Marianne, on the contrary, learns through her mistakes and prejudices, and her disappointment in the one she first chooses to love.

Another intriguing element of 'mimesis 2' in Austen's work is that, while most of her heroines are portrayed as cultivated individuals, their learning is described in a very original fashion. In *Mansfield Park*, for example, Fanny Price's cousins were educated by their aunt, who taught them merely by rote. Fanny, however, learned mostly from her close contact with Edmund Bertram. As Ely puts it, 'Fanny is anything but a model of Calvinist repression of desire through Christian law and conscience. She has rather "pity and kindheartedness" '.[29] Fanny Price is the only one who possesses enough judgement not to participate in the theatre play, not to violate the dignity and status of Mansfield Park, her uncle's home where she is lodging. She does not, Austen emphasizes, because she knew about 'respect'. This knowledge and sincerity, this cultivated heart and reasonableness, gives her access to a different level of moral reasoning. In the end, she has learned more than her cousins, and knows that her reading and her daily life are two interrelated ways of cultivating herself.

In *Persuasion*, Anne Elliot engages in conversation with Captain Benwick, who has lost his love and mourns her. Anne suggests that he read more prose than poetry, allowing the experiences of human complexity and the different characters of human experiences to teach him a less romanticized view of life.[30] Austen describes the scene as follows:

> And having talked of poetry, the richness of the present age, and gone through a brief comparison of opinion as to the first rate poets . . . she ventured to hope he did not always read only poetry; and to say, that she thought it was the misfortune of poetry, to be seldom safely enjoyed by those who enjoyed it completely; and that the strong feelings which alone could estimate it truly, were the very feelings which ought to taste it but sparingly . . . She ventured to recommend a larger allowance of prose in his daily study; and on being requested to particularize, mentioned such works of our best moralists, such collections of the finest letters, such memoirs of characters of worth and suffering, as occurred to her at the moment as calculated to rouse and fortify the mind by the highest precepts, and the strongest examples of moral and religious endurances.[31]

The third aspect of 'mimesis 2' that Austen can be interpreted as developing is the idea of friendship and love. A theme in all her novels is that the best relations are the product of lasting friendship. In *Sense and Sensibility* Elinor chooses Edward Ferrars because 'his behaviour gave every indication of an open affectionate heart'.[32] When Marianne questions his worthiness, Elinor replies, 'I have seen a great deal of him, have studied his sentiments and heard his opinions on subjects of literature and taste; and, upon the whole, I venture to pronounce that his mind is well informed, his enjoyment of books exceedingly great, his imagination is lively, his observation just and correct, and his taste delicate and pure'.[33] As the novel develops, Elinor will prove that her respect, her friendship with Edward, remains untouched even when she thinks that he is going to marry someone else (Miss Lucy Steele). As proof of the sincerity of her friendship with Edward Ferrars, Elinor passes on Colonel Brandon's offer for him to become parish priest.

In *Mansfield Park*, Fanny Price has two great friends, her brother William and her cousin Edmund Bertram. It is through Edmund that she learns to live a good life in Mansfield Park. He is the first and only person to show his concern for her longings, her needs, her pleasures. He seeks comfort in conversations with her and trusts her judgement when he thinks he is in love with Miss Mary Crawford. Both learn the meaning of friendship as the plot develops. It is this friendship that becomes the best example of true love.

Even Emma, the only heroine of Austen's who is totally confused and has no idea of the meaning of life and love, establishes a true friendship with Mr Knightley. And in spite of the fact that he 'was one of the few people who could see the faults in Emma Woodhouse',[34] his conversations with her, his critical judgements towards her stubbornness, his loyalty towards her are the signs of his real love. Emma will realize this only at the end of the novel, once she has learned to see her mistakes, and she acknowledges her lack of judgement in conversation with him. However, contrary to the opinion of many critics who have considered Mr Knightley to be the 'idealized English gentleman', and *Emma* to be a conventional novel about the heroine's education being provided by the hero, Margaret Kirkham argues that 'Mr Knightley is as ignorant as Emma about the state of his own feelings and, though many of his criticisms of her are just in themselves, he is often motivated by unconscious jealousy and envy of Frank Churchill. If Emma is unjust to Jane Fairfax, he is unjust to Churchill'.[35] It is through real friendship that both will learn about themselves.

Thus Austen subverts tradition and provides a new conceptualization of moral agents. For her, the heart is not an appetite or a passion; on the contrary, it is governed by a combination of reason and judgement, of feelings and responsibility. Both Anne Elliot and Elinor Dashwood show signs of a permanent reflection on human complexity. They are not moved by abstract rules, but rather find forms in which to link deliberations about sensibility, to explain why things happen in one way and not another.[36] One might be tempted to think that Jane Austen's view of women was influenced only by Aristotle, as Ryle and Ely have argued. In fact, however, her women are moral characters who coherently combine reason with feelings in a non-traditional way.[37] The virtues of Anne Elliot and Elinor Dashwood are intellectual and moral, those of culture and experience.

I would now like to focus on the stage of 'mimesis 3', where readers and critics have begun to reinterpret Austen's legacy. In my opinion, the modern side of Austen's moral conception lies mainly in the concept of 'moral learning'. The way she portrays her characters in successive stages of moral reasoning and deliberation presupposes a 'reflexive', 'critical' attitude on the part of the moral agent. That is why, again and again, she recommends the reading of literature as a reflexive exercise. Anne Elliot's injunction to Captain Benwick to read more prose, quoted above, is an excellent example. Marianne Dashwood, on the other hand, is the perfect example of bad reading habits. She needs to learn how to use 'reason' as an 'antidote' to her outbursts of feelings. She has been 'alienated' by her readings. Emma Woodhouse is a character that needs explicit instruction concerning her lack of moral sense and judgements, as the reader discovers in the very first pages.

This 'reflexivity' is characteristic of Austen. As Wayne Booth puts it:

> The resulting 'reading assignment' given by our teacher, Jane Austen, is complex indeed. We must learn to read as I am quite sure Austen herself wrote: both remembering and forgetting what we know about real life. We all know, or should know, that no union can possibly produce perfect happiness; we know it as surely as we know that geese do not lay golden eggs. We know that no man can possibly provide for Emma all that the novel in its conventional form suggests. We can be sure, once we think about it, that Austen did not believe in the existence of such a paragon as Knightley, and she tells us in many ways that she does not see the whole of a woman's life as the pursuit of a single moment of perfect happiness in a perfect union, all past and future qualifications ignored. Again and again she makes absolutely clear that she could never swallow such nonsense. But her *work* asks us to swallow it, in *some* sense, if we are to savor it to the full. And *unless we know how to read, and to criticize what we read*, first thing we know we'll be thinking about love and marriage and life itself with about as little sense as is shown by Sir Edward.[38]

Thus, the 'antidote' that Austen brings to her narratives is the 'reflexive criticism' of the modern reader, a fact that has not escaped some of the new feminist readings of Austen.[39] The reader must have some of the basic characteristics of an 'impartial' judge, allowing for a 'double vision'. As Booth puts it: 'Our journey from page to page is not for the most part focused on some future convention of good fortune but rather on the way people behave here and now. To *be* in a certain way in the world, to behave in a certain way, is its own justification or damnation'.[40]

Feminist readers and critics of Austen's work have found her satire and critical exposure of problems to be indicators of an awareness of her task as a modern moralist. As Allison G. Sulloway has suggested, 'that women from Mary Astell to Jane Austen revenged themselves, sometimes with equal fierceness and persistence and with the very weapons of *satire* that had been inflicted upon them, may surprise even some scholars who are now unearthing the social history of women'.[41] For Sulloway, 'satire' performs an exclusively reflexive political task, as a way of exposing the social distress of injustices. In the same tone, Margaret Kirkham argues 'Jane Austen learned to tell the truth through a riddling irony which "dull elves" might misread, but which she hoped readers of sense and ingenuity would not'.[42] It is worth comparing this conclusion with Wayne Booth's:

> We are asked to embrace standards according to which the ending can only be viewed as a fairy tale or fantasy. The author has been teaching us all along what it means to keep our wits about us, to maintain a steady vision of the follies and meannesses in our world. . . . All is not well, either for their kind (if any such exist) or for those less fortunate men and women who surround them. Every fully engaged reader will discover, in that 'realer' world aggressively insisted on in the midst of all the subtle pleasures, that *the circumstances of women are considerably more chancy and often more threatening than those surrounding men.*[43]

Thus, it is possible to understand that a reading public on the stage of 'mimesis 3' is prepared to enjoy the double level of Austen's work. That is also among the reasons for the great success of the film versions of her novels. The case of *Sense and Sensibility* is particularly interesting: the script was adapted by the English actress Emma Thompson, who even transformed certain aspects of Austen's original. For example, the role of Margaret, the youngest of the Dashwood sisters, is considerably enlarged: Thompson added the scene in which the little girl, knowing that the family will have to leave the house after their father's death, runs off to hide under the table. It is Edward Ferrars who eventually persuades her to accept the family's new circumstances. Elinor watches this scene and is then convinced about Edward's worthiness as a moral human being. This departure from the original adds a new dimension to Elinor as a wise and rational person whose love for Edward brings out his kindness, generosity and understanding. The revival of Austen's fiction in the public sphere has attracted extraordinary attention from the media because it seems to fit so well with contemporary views of women as moral agents, thus revealing the complex interrelation between moral and personal themes.

From Philosophy to Literature

In a manner that offers striking parallels with the above-mentioned interpretations of Austen, and with Austen herself, a philosophical approach can offer a new vision of 'mimesis 3'. Martha Nussbaum moved from 'mimesis 3' to 'mimesis 2' through the creation of a female character, Nikidion,[44] who learns the key concepts of moral philosophy in Aristotle's school. Her recovery of emotions serves, however, as more than a critical element opposing the prejudices inherited from the Enlightenment. This recovery of Aristotle through the figure of Nikidion is actually a device to discover a *different* view of emotions. 'Emotions are forms of *intentional awareness*', Nussbaum argues: 'That is (since no ancient term corresponds precisely to these terms), they are forms of awareness *directed at* or *about* an object, in which the object figures as it is seen from the creature's point of view'.[45] Nussbaum's point is that these emotions are not irrational, as many theorists of the Enlightenment believed, because they are clearly linked to beliefs, and beliefs can be modified. Therefore, a moral education nurtured by emotions is possible.[46]

The second element that Nussbaum shares with Austen is her recovery of Aristotle's concept of love as *philia*,[47] which means mutual affection, reciprocity in the desire for the wellbeing of the other, mutual recognition of the other as a person for her sake. Emotions – as cognitive elements of our textures as moral agents – and the recognition of the importance of others for one's own sake are the central elements of the feminist interpretation of a moral agent.[48]

Further, Nussbaum joins Austen in viewing literature as a source of moral learning.[49] After the success of her book *The Fragility of Goodness*, her contribution to an Aristotelian feminism became increasingly original in its discussion of literature as an especially important tool for moral deliberation. Nussbaum establishes the theoretical importance of expressive and normative relations in this double dimension of validity in her book *Love's Knowledge*. The aesthetic vision offered here is that form and content are inseparable in literary expression, just as certain truths about human life can be expressed only in a narrative, that is, by means of the specific language of literary forms.[50] Novels use a language that not only shows the complexity of life itself, but also encourages the reader to develop perception, weigh problems in the light of several contexts and, through identification with certain characters, to acquire their most admirable qualities.[51] This is the most relevant aspect derived from 'mimesis 3' and going back to 'mimesis 1'.

By making these connections in Austen's and Nussbaum's works, between literature and moral life, and between the aesthetic and the moral dimensions, it is possible to trace the conceptualization of women in the public sphere through the definition of 'moral persons' or 'moral agents' in 'mimesis 3'. This reconceptualization also follows a path that deals more directly and empirically with the interpretation and development of moral stages and post-traditional agents. In the field of social science, this is exemplified by Carol Gilligan, whose work bears similarities to Austen's and Nussbaum's discussion of 'moral agents' and is based on her empirical research regarding women and moral deliberation.

The Pattern of New Voices

Although Carol Gilligan's book *In a Different Voice* has been adversely criticized, the importance of her empirical work cannot be denied.[52] In the first place, she shows the weakness of Lawrence Kohlberg's theory that human beings deliberate best when relating to moral issues from the standpoint of rules and procedures (when the basic concepts are believed to be based on the idea of impartiality, of depersonalized subjects, of justice and rationality as unconnected to feelings and emotions). To Gilligan, one of the main attributes of moral subjects is that they are not divorced from their affective ties and relationships. Moral characteristics are defined in terms of emotional support for other human beings. Her differences with Kohlberg consist, primarily, in the fact that she envisions moral subjects as radically contextualized with specific characteristics. In addition, the moral agent must understand other people as specific beings, not only in terms of formal features that configure them as 'individuals'. In the third place, Gilligan believes that gaining specific knowledge about another person with whom one is to interact is a complex and difficult moral task, one for which certain moral skills must be nurtured on ethical grounds. The role of responsibility, she has found, implies a specific 'relationship' which is achieved through care, empathy, compassion and emotional sensibility. The final characteristic separating her from the Kantian views of Kohlberg is her belief that moral subjects are also defined by their affective relationships with others. Morality, for her, implies emotional, cognitive and affective active relationships that cannot be easily separated. Gilligan, like Austen and Nussbaum, has challenged the separation of form and content in the evaluation of moral judgements.

Some discussions of Gilligan's work imply that it is women, with their specific way of relating to others, who gave rise to the ethics of care.[53] Although Gilligan did not originally stress such female exclusivity, her data were, indeed, based on (white middle-class) women. In her later works, however, she does seem to consider the differences between men and women as differences in the ways they perceive moral deliberation.[54] Yet Gilligan challenges the public to relate universalist approaches to justice with an ethics of care by considering problems of human lives in the moral domain. Her women developed new patterns of thinking about moral agents and moral deliberation, I believe, not because of 'gender characteristics',[55] but because they discover that issues of the good life and justice do have a specific link. Previous models of moral deliberation were, in fact, reductionist, despite their claim to be the universal model for the behaviour of moral agents. What is valuable in Gilligan's formulation is the idea that the development of sensibility and the emotions – of that 'special voice' which is more human, more complex, and in which the cognitive and the emotional interrelate – is a better way of conceiving moral deliberation.

If this definition of an ethics of care is seen as characteristic of women, if the difference is attributed to the condition of being female as such, then the radical criticism of Kohlberg's model of impartiality loses its relevance. Access to this very particular form of deliberation becomes limited. The characteristic of care appears as a gender-related trait which tends to differentiate and classify human beings as being better when they are women and worse when they are men. Thus, instead of promoting ideas in which morality opens its dimensions to specific interactions with the sphere of the good life, morality is reduced to the women's sphere and thus becomes a dichotomous area that loses its universality.

It must be emphasized that Gilligan's research is done from the viewpoint of psychological theory, which not only inserts itself into wider discussions of moral evolution, but also challenges previous normative conceptions by generating a 'disclosive' pattern of self-understanding. If her work is understood in this way, then the normative criticism towards previous conceptions calls for a transformation of ideas about moral agency.[56] Gilligan's work should be viewed as highlighting a pattern in which questions of care become moral issues and, therefore, are related to the universalist conception of justice. She provides the connection between empirical data and the normative and aesthetic dimensions in which reflexive and theoretical horizons can thematize moral subjects as agents of moral deliberation.

This view emerges from consideration of the three stages of 'mimetic representation', allowing the model of moral agents and their human capabilities in an interrelation of justice and the good to be completed.

I must now turn to a discussion of a new outlook on human agents linked to human capabilities.

Moral Concepts as Concrete Universals

The 'mimetic' stages of representation in the public sphere can be understood as learning processes. Narratives can be seen as instruments and expressions of learning. The learning to which I am referring takes place when narratives are used in the context of particular acts of attention. Narratives also have spatio-temporal and conceptual contexts. Through the above discussion of Austen's fiction and Nussbaum's reweaving of her themes, it should be clear how these issues are exposed as processes in the construction of the symbolic order. Gilligan's research also shows how these issues can be viewed in the context of the social sciences. However, if one considers how these processes are interwoven, how continuous they are, and how imperceptibly they build up structures of value, it will not be surprising to find oneself in a whole new realm of moral thinking.

This conception of moral agents and their capabilities thus connects the will and reason as faculties. Our will continually influences our beliefs, and it does so in the perception of moral complexity. Nussbaum's redefinitions of 'human capabilities' summarize the shift in understanding of moral learning processes within women's narratives.[57] She begins by acknowledging that life should be lived for a normal span, that is, not be subject to the contingencies of illness, famine and war, which ravage many countries throughout the world. In an ideal world, life should be lived in good health, with good nutrition and more than adequate shelter, without any form of violence. It should be possible to prevent unnecessary pain, to make use of human senses, imagination and reason through good education. The ability to love other people and things should thus support all human forms of association. Reflexive conceptions of the good and happiness need to be developed. This implies that everyone should be able to plan their lives at work, at home, and politically; to develop solidarity towards others as a capacity for being sensitive to justice and friendship; and, in doing so, to become socially responsible for maintaining and transforming the institutions which help make these processes and abilities possible. It is also important to have the opportunity to develop affection and care for animals and plants, for the world of nature placed in each generation's charge for future generations; the freedom to enjoy recreational activities, to be able to laugh and play. Everybody needs to live an individual life, not that of others, which is to say that everybody must have the right to choose what he or she wants to be, with due self-recognition. And, finally, all individuals should be able to live in their own context, in their own historical and social situation, without the risk of losing their integrity as human beings. These are the ideals associated with this view of moral agents.

This list of ideals might sound unduly facile. But perhaps not everybody has considered that each one of these points substantially affects the life content or capabilities of a person in any given situation. These conditions are fundamental for describing what makes a human being human. However, they do not stem from a theory of needs, and they do not need to subscribe to any metaphysical or anthropological paradigm. They are the products of the 'reweavings' of 'shared experiences of human beings within history'[58] in conceiving life within a specific interactive view that includes feedback between the aesthetic and the moral domains. I do not believe that this list could have been compiled if there had not been, on the one hand, a serious reflexive process – a public debate – on what it has meant for women to inhabit a world in which it was continuously questioned whether women are as human as men. Nor could this list have been conceived without detecting the flaws in those discourses that have attempted to embrace the world of justice and equality while turning their back on half of humanity. Both these critical processes, simultaneously linked in the historical reappraisal of experience, action and speech, have made it possible to present a project of moral subjects in which the image of woman has been connected to the very roots of definitions of capabilities and potentialities[59]. As Iris Murdoch puts it: 'The area of morals, and ergo of moral philosophy, can now be seen, not as a hole-and-corner matter of debts and promises, but as covering the whole of our mode of living and the quality of our relations with the world'.[60]

Part II

From the Moral to the
Political Sphere

6 Justice and Solidarity: Women in the Public Sphere

Political theorists, philosophers and sociologists are engaged in a debate about deliberative democracy as a source of political legitimation and about the recovery of the 'agency' of citizenship in different terms from those of the contractualist theorists of the Enlightenment.[1] At the heart of this debate lies the concept of the public use of reason,[2] and the legitimacy provided by the critical judgements of agents as free and equal citizens.[3] At the same time, there are a number of social scientists[4] and political theorists[5] who consider deliberative democracy idealistic and impractical. Their scepticism is based on the belief that pluralism undermines the possibility of reaching any kind of agreement and produces, on the contrary, arguments that seem intractable and conflicting. In my view, there is a response to the sceptics regarding deliberative democracy, and it can be found in the historical and social struggles of various groups to become part of the 'public use' of reason in different parts of the world. In this chapter, I argue that feminism is the empirical example that best illustrates a correlation between these new social facts and a new conceptualization of the ideals of deliberative democracy. This approach emphasizes the agents' participatory processes and the institutions that allow them to become part of a 'public use of reason'. I intend to show that the interdependence between social institutions and publics is the most important basis for rethinking deliberative democracy under conditions of plurality and social complexity.

As discussed in chapter 1, Habermas developed a model in which 'civil society with the opinion- and will-formation institutionalized in parliamentary bodies and courts offers a good starting point for translating the concept of deliberative politics into sociological terms'.[6] He explains how such civil, or public processes influence 'democratic opinion- and will-formation', which produces issues that enter parliamentary debates and transform and legitimate lawmaking. Nancy Fraser, in a similar vein, addresses the concept of deliberative democracy by differentiating between what she calls the 'weak' publics (various groups) and the 'strong' publics (the parliament).[7] Sociologists such as Jeffrey C. Alexander and others[8] have developed a theory of 'civil society' in which informal associations produce channels of communication with other social spheres and create specific sources of cultural and symbolic content.[9] James Bohman has formulated a model of deliberative democracy[10] that shows how 'robust institutions of a "dualist democracy"' play a major role in transforming the law, and how this has been achieved mainly by 'the People'. My aim in this chapter is to show that the cultural transformations that take place in public opinion can shape and transform public institutions as well as the public's self-understandings. In so doing, they are able to reinterpret and conceive new ways of understanding the interrelations between justice and solidarity.

I offer my model of the public sphere and women's narratives, therefore, as a new conceptualization of the relation of deliberative democracy to the culture of civil society. The latter concept has been much debated, and I wish to follow here Alexander's interpretation, which defines civil society as the 'arena in which social solidarity is defined in universalistic terms',[11] an independent civil sphere, differentiated from the state, religion and the market, linked to an inwardly experienced solidarity that is defined as a simultaneous recognition of the individual and collective obligations by means of symbolic communication and deliberation. It is here that the political dimension can be related to the moral. I argue that the public sphere is where justice is defined and interpreted, where exchanges are pursued with others to redefine and enlarge the 'we'. There are continual discussions about the need to change institutions, to make them more supportive of those democratic processes that relate justice with solidarity.[12] My thesis, then, is that as one transforms one's self-conceptions regarding justice, so also are institutions transformed. This mutual transformation is accomplished by deepening the basic cultural paradigm promoting ever 'more' universalistic conceptions of civil solidarity. I then focus on the relevance of solidarity as the interactive mediator between different discourses of civil society, particularly in women's claims for recognition in the public sphere.

Because justice and solidarity are related to one's cognitive and emotional selves, and recognition of identities can be demanded only through an appeal to justice, these demands must be displayed in the public sphere. However, deliberative democracy, as Bohman has argued, needs a periodic renewal of its institutions when public reason fails to produce agreements between different groups of people. This potential for innovation relates to the problems and needs of individuals in civil society. My argument is that women – emerging as new publics – have developed a new understanding of democratic institutions and citizenship through their innovative understanding of deliberative dialogue. As subjects demanding recognition, they have become the authors of a new definition of justice. If, as Mead and Habermas argue, modern societies have developed simultaneous processes of individuation and socialization, then biographies have played a major role in this task. As discussed in chapters 1 and 3, such biographies link a new conception of solidarity to the problem of justice. Through public discussion of the need for recognition, the moral status of identities interconnects with the political base, and this interrelatedness produces what I have called 'new illocutionary forms'. These forms capture the dynamics of self-presentation, and the impact on public opinion of the acceptance of a new interpretation of justice then generates different kinds of solidarities and institutional transformations.

The Public Domain as a Sphere of Solidarity

The public domain is the centre of self-understanding. Seeing themselves as 'the new emerging public', women have specifically investigated how 'publics' have regarded them historically.[13] Feminists have done a great deal of research on why the public sphere was denied to them. While focusing on the historical and social features of the public sphere, they have themselves entered into that sphere as a new public. Their interpretations reveal the partial accounts offered by previous public opinion. They have exercised what James Bohman characterizes as the 'self-critical and self-reflective' features of public opinion, which have become a source of innovation and change in democracies throughout the twentieth century.

Social arenas provide opportunities for individuals to express their concerns about violations of their normative standards of justice.[14] In contemporary societies, these claims seem always to be related to demands for respect and recognition of individuals and groups.[15] Self-criticism by the public sphere not only contributes to maintaining it, but also, as Bohman has argued, to 'forming and testing the public's attitudes and beliefs'.[16] By gathering new information and making public a variety of experiences, one becomes aware of problems not previously known or fully understood. Women have contested the ideals of 'equality' of participation in issues of common interest. By doing so, they have also focused on the deficits of the institutional filters that provide for real access to public deliberations. As these discourses emerged, new 'female' publics created opportunities for expanding deliberation and for transforming democratic institutions. Active participation in dialogue helps one to develop a reflective attitude and to gain conceptual clarity about others' points of view. This can then become the basis for new interpretations which can reconcile normative standards of justice with divergent conceptions regarding 'facts and norms'. In this way, public deliberations lead to moral learning. They provide the contrast one needs in order to clarify one's views reflexively. Through active participation in dialogue, one can become regarded as a 'special' human being, or as belonging to a group entitled to attention. Dealing publicly with matters that one cares about involves a learning process whereby one comes to acknowledge and respect other people's unique, different and multiple ways of being. In this way, more complex conceptualizations of individuals as heterogeneous and diverse public citizens can be developed. Public discussions are thus an important factor in deepening the democratic culture of civil society; they provide an arena for communication and the self-reflexive critical tools to examine the legitimacy of 'social integration'.

As an emerging public, women have introduced new topics and themes by focusing attention on pressing problems and needs. Offering new interpretations of these issues and demanding the reconceptualization and factual transformation of current institutions, their efforts have provided a whole new agenda for political deliberations. Women have activated the criticism inherent in public speech. Their aim has been not only to acquire 'self-consciousness', but also, by raising their voices as part of public debate, to challenge the implicit and interpretative assumptions and understandings of the public. The public sphere is the arena where the interpretation of needs and rights, together with the contextualizations of needed institutional changes, interweave justice with claims for solidarity. This connection between justice and solidarity is captured in the term that best defines the dynamics between the emerging public and public opinion itself, that is, 'illocutionary force'. Women's claims for justice can succeed only through a responsive acceptance that reframes their claim, taking it not only as a new understanding of a particular issue, but as a newly broadened collective self-understanding of the daily life of civil society. Thus, a whole set of cultural, social and political problems are included in discussions of 'gender identity'. The communicative notion of 'we' – the public – is an ongoing process of engagement and critique that establishes a connection between justice and solidarity based on the insight that moral norms are aspects of a shared form of life. Solidarity is our shared expectation. As Jodi Dean has rightly noted:

> we must institutionalize processes of greater inclusion and communication. We must avoid saddling those who come after us with debts, pains, and obligations that will simply repeat hierarchies of domination and

subordination benefiting few. Finally solidarity toward present generations is expressed in our willingness to recognize and strengthen the ties
connecting all of us, to let others know that they are neither forgotten nor
alone. Here solidarity requires us to speak out against oppression and
exclusion.[17]

These dialogues take the form of new interpretations or revisions of
law aimed at assuring their institutional acceptance. The legitimacy of
deliberative democracy depends on people being able to construct new
interpretations of justice which include the needs and rights of emerging publics. 'Cultural innovations by critics', argues Bohman, 'change
understandings by creating new patterns of relevance. Such changes in
assumptions about what is relevant in a problematic situation can
clarify why it is effective to introduce new frames into public deliberation, since they _disclose new possibilities of interpretation and action_'.[18]
Bohman has found a novel use for Heidegger's term 'disclosure' – or
'world disclosure' – that captures the 'illocutionary' dynamic that 'designates radical change in the ordinary interpretation of the world – just
what is needed for innovation in public deliberation'.[19]

In my opinion, Bohman describes a way in which 'critics' and 'collective actors' _perform_ innovations – 'innovations as _changes in public
understandings_'[20] – which they do 'in the free and effective exercise of
capacities of understanding and cognition, as when ordinary communication with others can sometimes make us change even deeply en-
trenched understandings and assumptions'.[21] Despite the aestheticized
way in which the notion of 'disclosure' has been used since Heidegger,[22]
Bohman insists – rightly, in my view – that the concept can also be
related to changes in moral codes and understandings. Poetic language,
for example, is considered a disclosure of the world in the sense that
new metaphors connect to disparate experiences or objects that are
brought together in an expressive connection.[23] As discussed in chapter
2, Wellmer was referring to this kind of experience when he argued that
sometimes it is only possible to illuminate the meaning of moral or
practical experience through another realm of validity. What Bohman
argues is that this should be considered only as 'disclosure' 1, whereas
'disclosure' 2 refers to moments in which political or moral ideals are
put in such a way as to suggest a new way of conceiving the social
world. Bohman argues that 'it is precisely because the world is disclosed in the first sense, that we need disclosure in the second sense:
innovation rearranges such cultural frameworks in order to make new
experiences and different meanings possible [for the] world that is
disclosed in this sense is a whole new set of possibilities for thinking
and acting'.[24] In Bohman's conception artists and critics can perform
discourses that disclose new possibilities of action and thought, as long

as the artist is also a critic, for it is criticism that allows her to envision possible new ways of thinking and doing. The novel ways in which social criticism is performed offer some important elements in the apprehension and perception of reality in its aesthetic dimension.[25] This does not necessarily mean that criticism is elitist; it simply means that, when one wants to call attention to some specific problem and frames such a vision in an appealing and original way, one is more likely to obtain the interest and understanding of others. In any case, Bohman relates 'disclosure' to the dynamics of criticism in provoking a reconceptualization of things that were previously considered normal. Bohman has captured much of the social dynamics of one cultural paradigm replacing a previous one, just as the American philosopher of science Thomas Samuel Kuhn did in terms of scientific revolutions. In my opinion, however, the correlation between moral and aesthetic spheres is what makes the use of the term 'disclosure' particularly relevant in illuminating the implication of poetic language and providing new metaphors to describe reality.[26] In the social dynamics of a 'critical group' confronting public opinion, a positive or negative response is what validates the successful performance of the 'disclosive' criticism. What Bohman calls 'criticism' can also be seen in works of art that 'perform' a new way of conceiving life, such as the examples offered by Gabriele Schwab that I have cited in chapter 2. One need not restrict dialogue between two spheres of validity, as long as one clearly understands that there are utopian visions of the social world that only art can present in an unprecedented way.[27] Once these experiences are made public, they exercise a powerful influence on public opinion and can be integrated into practical or moral discourses as criticism.[28] According to Bohman, 'Critics are thus disclosive in the sense described by one of Kafka's narrators: they don't talk like the rest of us, but they show us things that we cannot fully describe in quite ordinary ways'.[29] Bohman thus shows the need for the aesthetic realm when one attempts to offer a totally new interpretation of the order of things. In that sense, the relation of the aesthetic to the moral is unavoidable.

Disclosure, as Bohman sees it, is related to the 'expressive' effect and the aesthetic dimension of speech. He attempts to show that these 'contextual effects' occur in ordinary language (not only in its poetic use), and uses the notion of 'relevance' to include 'modifications' of the cognitive environment of the hearer, 'such as establishing new synthetic implications, manifesting implicit contradictions, or weakening or strengthening of the beliefs that make up this background set of assumptions'.[30] I agree with Bohman that these transformations occur as collective understandings only within certain contexts: social criticism can be viewed as a 'paradigmatic instance of disclosure' in a dialogically constructed social world. However, social criticism has always taken images, metaphors and visions from expressive language in the same way that art displays a new perception of life. In fact, one can say that it is the expressive aspect of criticism, or of works of art, that gives a specific reordering of things and provides the effect of 'disclosure'. Art, and its reception in the public sphere, are the best examples of these possibilities. However, it is not only artists who provide new frames for social criticism. If one understands the major role of art itself in the dialogically constructed social world, and that there is feedback between different validity spheres, then anyone capable of finding a new way of framing things can attain a disclosive effect that strengthens their arguments through the influence of other validity spheres. What is interesting, then, is that Bohman's concept of 'disclosure' explains the cultural changes that occur when a discourse publicly reorders previous assumptions. According to Bohman, 'the audience is then reoriented to the social world, and it can take up a different attitude toward the world of cultural meanings and possibly a new position in its holistic interpretive field'.[31]

It is in the process of understanding an 'alter' – as opposed to an ego – that the 'hearer' comes 'to see things in a new way'. It is this performative interaction that I call an 'illocutionary act'. Such a performance can be considered successful when these claims or criticisms change the 'context of public assumptions about justification'. In this way, they become 'truth candidates'. Bohman argues that disclosure, then, is 'audience-relative', and that its truth content lies in its verification through further reflection on what is disclosed. Disclosures, in other words, cannot be self-verifying or self-justifying; they can only legitimate themselves through the filter of public opinion.

The importance of Bohman's conceptualization is that he views 'disclosure' as having a pragmatic twist; by doing so, he shows that in disclosing new possibilities, critics are not only announcing a new way of thinking about justice, but also that 'they are addressing an audience and expanding what it considers relevant to deliberation.'[32] With his cultural interpretation of 'disclosure', Bohman envisions new patterns for freedom:

> Such an open relation permits reflective agents to change these conditions, even if one piece at a time. All critics open up fields of meaning and action of a culture by introducing new themes or facts – they change them. The world here is the cultural background and context that informs institutions and their taken-for-granted understandings. Only _a public can create a world, in organizing itself and the larger public around these new understandings. Such innovative publics make democratic deliberation a dynamic and historical process._[33]

Emergent publics in need of new institutional frameworks and new forms of democracy change their own institutions by 'learning processes'. Here the term 'disclosure' relates to performances as 'illocutionary forces' and signifies the 'innovative side of social learning'.

When the suffragists were struggling to be considered human beings, and therefore deserving of the right to vote, public opinion held that women were 'citizens' of a different kind from men. In the United States, for example, the 'Equal Rights Amendment' (ERA) was originally introduced in 1923 by Alice Paul and other feminists. Nevertheless, ERA did not receive congressional approval until March 1972, and in fact, was not ratified before its extended deadline expired on 22 March 1982. What happened in the intervening years, however, was a totally new recontextualization of what 'equality of rights under the law' meant to public opinion. Only when 'gender identity' as a paradigm had permeated every single space of the cultural, social and political heritage was it possible to conceive a new account of what such 'equality' would mean in terms of justice and democratic institutions – beginning with public opinion's own self-conceptions. Thus, the feminists of the 1980s were able to disclose a whole new idea of gender identity and the rights of women as human beings. Catharine MacKinnon's most famous phrase – 'being a woman is not yet a way of being a human'[34] – acquired its full disclosive meaning only after it was realized that women and human beings had been considered totally different species in the past. The meaning of 'disclosure' is clear here, because the different stages of public opinion regarding 'equality of rights' in various historical stages can be compared. MacKinnon's lapidary expression shows how perceptions of justice have changed since the 1970s. Despite the eventual 'defeat' of ERA, public opinion's own transformative learning process led to a better interpretation of deliberative democracy.

Solidarity as the Expression of 'Illocutionary Force'

Habermas has dealt extensively with the relationship between justice and solidarity. In fact, he sees them as two sides of the same coin. I consider this view of great importance for the development of my thesis. Nevertheless, Habermas' interpretation of solidarity has been strongly criticized by many feminists because of his formal and abstract conception of the moral subject and his narrow vision of the possible interrelation between justice and the good. His Kantian approach to solidarity is based on the 'moral point of view' and a universalistic conception of 'solidarity' that seems to lack substance. Feminist theorists have focused on the weakness of his position, and sought new ways in which solidarity could be reframed without attaching it to a universalistic claim.

Women have created a new cultural paradigm that approaches solidarity in a rather different fashion. A very significant step was taken when women social scientists questioned Kohlberg's famous explanation of the stages of postconventional moral agents. As I indicated earlier, this was accomplished through Carol Gilligan's empirical work on women and moral theory in her book _In a Different Voice_.[35] In spite of the controversy generated among feminists themselves, the fact is that this work proved that Kohlberg's 'universalistic' explanation was partial. Gilligan tried to provide a 'different' voice, a voice that said that not everybody had to consider the stages described by Kohlberg when considering maturity in moral reasoning. Despite the claims that Gilligan was an essentialist, or that she was recovering the features that men took as the proof of the inferiority of women, Gilligan shows that Kohlberg's moral reasoning was incomplete because he used only men in his studies, thus treating the resulting 'postconventional stage six' as if it were universal. This is the importance of her findings; they provided a 'disclosure' in the field of moral reasoning when, for the first time, the notions of 'care' and 'responsibility' appeared as complementary sides of the impartial abstract reasoning of moral agents. The 'new emerging public' reaffirmed that 'once women are inserted into the picture, be it as objects of social-scientific research or as subjects conducting such inquiry, established paradigms are unsettled'.[36]

The emerging public of women has revised what moral reasoning meant for the claim for solidarity. It was through another disclosive term – 'difference' – that the need to reconceptualize solidarity became apparent. 'Difference' as opposed to 'sameness' – where 'sameness' hypostatized men's views as synonymous with factual 'equality' – was the tool used to show that 'uniformity' was necessary when it came to conceptualizing postconventional moral agents. In contrast, Gilligan tried to show that the relational, 'care' side of morality need not be considered exclusively in terms of the good life. Good life and justice are interrelated dimensions, and behaviour towards others may not be restricted purely on 'formal' grounds. Women provide an interpretation of personal issues that are not opposed to moral reasons.[37] They have made apparent the need to enlarge the notion of solidarity beyond its 'impartial', 'abstract' and 'formal' aspects.

It was precisely the 'disclosive' element inherent in the vision of an ethics of care that produced a discussion of how this could be understood in light of past definitions of solidarity. Seyla Benhabib, for example, argues that Habermas and Kohlberg 'conflate the standpoint of a universalist morality with a narrow definition of the moral domain as being centered around "issues of justice"'.[38] She has developed a category – 'the concrete other' – to allow a contextualized connection between justice and solidarity. She does not deny the need for a 'universalist approach', where the categories of 'impartiality' and 'respect' are interrelated with moral reasoning. This viewpoint considers the 'dignity of the other' as an acknowledgement of respect for their needs and interests. Benhabib does insist, however, on reframing 'moral respect' as the mediation between a 'generalized other and concrete other', thus bringing a more complex and fruitful insight to moral deliberation. Citing Hannah Arendt's conception of 'enlarged mentality' and her own definition of the 'concrete other', Benhabib writes:

> I am not ready to say that 'callousness, lack of generosity, and concern' are evaluative but not moral categories; that they pertain to the quality of our lives together rather than to the general procedures for regulating intersubjective conflicts of interests. . . . A universalist moral position of enlarged mentality provides us with a procedure for judging the validity of our judgements in this context as well.[39]

Similarly, Martha Nussbaum argues that feelings are not necessarily unreasonable. For her, too, the strict separation between feelings and reason is a narrow view that has prevailed and informed moral deliberations in a prejudiced manner. In her book *Love's Knowledge*, she writes:

> I believed that the Aristotelian ethical stance was inclusive enough to encompass every constituent of the good human life, love included. If one moves from a narrow understanding, with its question about the good human life, one could, I then argued, think and feel about everything that is a plausible part of the answer to the question, passionate love included, asking how it fits with other elements and how one might construct a balanced life out of all of them. (I pointed, here, to the fact that Aristotle's ethical works include many aspects of human life that for Kant and many others would lie outside of morality: joketelling, hospitality, friendship, love itself.)[40]

Nussbaum urges a recovery of the Aristotelian conception of 'perception', for it is a defence of 'the priority of concrete situational judgements' that better allows one to deal with 'ethical vulnerability that arises from the perception of qualitative heterogeneity'.[41] Her Aristotelian approach recovers the 'universal' as differentiated from the 'general', and she claims that her universalism 'may be highly concrete, citing features that are not very likely to be replicated'.[42] Her vision of moral reasoning then becomes a 'practical insight . . . that is noninferential, nondeductive; it is an ability to recognize the salient features of a complex situation'.[43] Her idea of deliberations highlights a connection between the cognitive and the emotive elements; but, as with Gilligan's notion of care, Nussbaum grants a cognitive status to emotions.[44] Thus, she rejects the 'difference' strategy that has preoccupied many feminists when recovering something previously considered typically 'feminine'.

From a totally different angle, Drucilla Cornell's view of 'equality' leads to an understanding of 'individuation' as a 'project of self-transformation' of those individuated beings 'who can participate in public and political life as equal citizens'.[45] Here, solidarity stems from the belief that 'one must be open to each one of us on an equivalent basis'.[46] If each project has the right to be defined through an 'endless process' (manifested in narrative ways), there must be a collective space – the public sphere – in which the right to promote the 'renewal of the imagination' is displayed in order to secure our freedom. Cornell takes John Rawls' notion of 'self-respect' and integrates it into the 'imaginary domain' – her cultural tool – in order to overcome the 'degradation prohibition',[47] which portrays our 'sex' as being 'defined, symbolized and treated as antithetical to equal personhood and citizenship'.[48]

Jodi Dean, similarly, has reconceptualized 'solidarity'. By critically connecting Habermas' discourse ethics with Gilligan's ethics of care, she claims that the 'subject of discourse ethics exists in relation with others'.[49] Our identities take, argues Dean, 'the perspective of those struggling for recognition to show how reflective solidarity emerges out of the problems of recognition exposed in the course of this struggle'.[50] The task of morality is to protect our mutual ties and relationships in which we build up our identities in the same process of socialization and individuation. Justice then, is present when we claim our dignity, yet, at the same time, we are obliged to reconsider the role played by our notions of the good because we need others to become ourselves.[51] Dean defines 'reflective solidarity' as 'the mutual expectation of a responsible orientation to relationships'.[52] She tries to base her conception of solidarity on dissent. As a theorist of the critical emergent public mentioned earlier, she suggests the fruitful potential of a 'permanent risk of disagreement' that lies in moral dialogue which 'must itself become rationally transformed so as to provide a basis for solidarity'.[53] For Dean, the 'we' is always constituted through a permanent effort of the 'I's', in a struggle to transform the boundaries of those who configure the 'we'. When the 'I's' are involved in a performative task of self-presentation, they can be recognized only by the 'alters' of such dialogues: the 'we's'. It is through language that the world together builds up a 'public space'. Dean argues that 'because communicative actions are intimately connected with criticizable validity claims, hearers as well as speakers can be understood as creating the public space of their interrelationship'.[54] Because of its integrative force, the 'we' that Dean claims is the 'bond for recognition' can never be fixed: 'It is constantly recreated and renewed through the very acts of mutual recognition on which individual identities depend'.[55]

Dean has thus developed a conception of 'solidarity' in the public sphere by giving it a linguistic basis which connects action with self-critical reflection. With such a communicative notion of the 'we', she avoids the problems of exclusion of conventional solidarities. Furthermore, she claims that with this notion it is possible to avoid the exclusion of 'individual difference': by 'accentuating the particularity of this perspective we are reminded of the necessity to leave it open. The perspective of a situated, hypothetical third thus enables us to take accountability for others whom we risk excluding'.[56] Dean believes that her notion of 'we' is normative – thus linked to justice – because there is a responsibility of the 'we' permanently to enlarge its boundaries. Responsibility here is understood as a 'potential for omission' which deserves critical reflection. Dean develops the connection of justice and solidarity through her claim that 'inclusion, reciprocity, equal respect, and mutual recognition are requirements not only for the justification of normative claims to validity, but also standards by which we can evaluate solidarity'.[57] With this twist, Dean has argued that identity can be 'reconceived in terms of reflective solidarity'.[58]

As the emerging public, women have defined the correlation between justice and solidarity as necessarily linked to the public sphere. They have integrated reason and feelings as complementary categories. They have reframed notions of 'responsibility' and 'care' as the moral textures that interact, enrich and facilitate the 'impartial', 'autonomous' features of the moral subject. They have performatively defined how 'solidarity', or rather, *solidarities* are created by public dialogue. Differences require a type of solidarity that can deal with plurality. Society would become a better society, a more democratic society, if a way could be found for plurality to be conceived as profoundly enriching the diversity of life projects and their claims – through public discussions on the reordering and interpretations of themes and needs. Public space is the ideal arena in which these plural and different ways of recognizing the other and ourselves become a legitimate way for democracy to comprehend solidarity and the individual as two inter-related parts of the culture of civil society. Participatory discussions are crucial for dealing with conflicts, dissent and heterogeneities, because the normative standards of democratic discourse can only appeal to judgement. Women brought to public attention the need to reconceptualize the complexity of the moral textures of 'agents' as well as the necessity of rebuilding institutions.

The abstractly conceived notion of respect leads only to the possibility of tolerance, or to the first phase of the dynamic in which subjects can be seen as ends in themselves. Tolerance and distant respect are not enough when one has to deal with difference and the experiences of subjects that are in need of being considered equal. The idea of relating processes of recognition and solidarity to the public domain also implies that postconventional identities are formed through the acceptance of differences within a larger 'we'. When those differences make one aware of the possibilities of different world-views, one learns to contrast them, exercising judgement and reinterpreting values and needs. By this process, boundaries can be expanded. In this sense, postconventional identities are neither finished projects nor dogmatic choices, but, rather, open and contingent. Deliberative democracy seems to have the capacity for developing a 'special engagement' with difference. But in addition to this, as various groups and people submit life projects to discussion in the public domain, one exercises the capacity to learn and be transformed through these differences. Recognition, thus, has become a social and individual need. One is no longer dealing only with problems relating to the notion of autonomy and its domain (the normative sphere), from which the two key concepts of this view can be drawn – respect and tolerance. The category of authenticity has now been integrated within visions of the good in the expansion of moral and political agents.

Contemporary democracies are confronted with the challenge of pluralism and multiculturalism. The reflexive and critical insights of feminism – as the 'new emerging public' – have shifted into the paradigm of 'gender identity', where the recognition of differences on all levels has become a primary task of democracies. Women, as the new public, have revealed that 'justice must remain linked to solidarity' in a wider conception of deliberative democracy through the public use of reason.

7 The Moral Foundation of Recognition: A Critical Revision of Three Models

I would now like to consider 'recognition' as a concept that interrelates justice with the good. I wish to provide a critical context for this discussion by examining how 'recognition' has been developed in the history of philosophy by male authors who have not taken into consideration the issues of women's struggles for recognition. Women's narratives provide the clarifying counter-example of how the cultural contents of their struggles relate their voices to a specific new understanding of the public sphere. In this chapter I examine three models, which I call the 'expressivistic' model by Charles Taylor, the 'anthropological' model by Axel Honneth, and the 'hermeneutical' model by Paul Ricoeur. In the theoretical discussions, once again, feminism is my empirical reference point. The theory of recognition has not sufficiently linked itself to the public sphere and to illocutionary attempts to reorient social understandings within it.

The concept of recognition appeared within the moral realm and, although Hegel was not the first philosopher to thematize it, he was certainly one of the few who thought of it as suggesting a complex social and psychological process. The process of recognition he developed was conceived as a struggle between two people. This conflict, however, led to a clarification of the identity of the life-projects of alter and ego. Contemporary philosophers and social scientists have addressed recognition anew, largely because pluralist societies are confronting new challenges concerning the place of otherness, challenges that demand more adequate ways of understanding difference, of how tolerant coexistence among peoples and cultures is possible within post-traditional societies.[1] One can say that many contemporary social movements, and feminism in particular, have been vital in bringing the thematization of such 'old/new' categories to the fore. In what follows, I discuss extensively three major contemporary projects in the recovery of this category, and I examine the wider moral proposals that each model contains. In spite of their insights into the process of recognition, I suggest that the models proposed by Taylor, Honneth and Ricoeur are problematic in ways that are of great relevance to the challenge of finding a model of morality that is adequate for complex societies.

Every social project of recognition must meet two major conditions. First, it must submit its demands to collective opinion in the public sphere. Second, while this claim for public recognition is being pursued, it must devote itself to creating a discourse that eloquently captures a better understanding of the concept of justice. As I have shown with the model of feminism, a project of recognition must enter public spaces as an arena to open up dialogue and to stimulate further democratic institutional transformations. This involves an interaction between institutional and discursive processes, in order to gain acceptance from other members in the public sphere. The success of this project can be understood as the exercise of 'illocutionary force'. As discussed above, feminism was able to achieve such an 'illocutionary force' because it developed a new correlation between two validity spheres, the moral and the aesthetic. This interpenetration is critical to an accurate understanding of recognition.

The problems created by Honneth's model stem from his 'anthropological' approach to needs. I aim to show that, while Ricoeur avoids these problems in his more hermeneutical theory, his approach remains incomplete because the institutional background of recognition is insufficiently thematized. Finally, I show that by over-emphasizing the 'expressive' sphere, Taylor's approach to recognition ignores the vital importance of providing a normative transcontextual frame. In making these criticisms, I will suggest that, while incomplete, Habermas' philosophical intuition in developing a paradigm of communicative action based on his categories of language is basically correct. In my opinion, what Habermas' linguistic paradigm needs is an empirical corrective so that the dynamics of recognition – as struggle and as dialogue – can be understood as an effort to achieve an illocutionary force linked to the content of the broader symbolic order that articulates collective understandings of 'justice' in relation to the 'good'. Successful recognition is achieved through acceptance of redefinitions of justice that embrace a whole new spectrum of cultural and symbolic understandings of life.

Historically, specific contingencies play a major role in this process, which is far from being guaranteed simply by the illocutionary need for agreement. Parties that seek recognition gain success only by showing that theirs is a new project of universalism; in doing so, they have to appropriate – hegemonically, as it were – the public sphere. In facing contingency, imagination, energy and eloquence are critical, as is a sensitivity to the openness and tolerance demanded by the public sphere. Only if a civic culture is thus permanently reinforced in the public sphere – as an integrative and utopian arena – can the kind of equilibrium be established that makes it possible to handle claims of recognition that seek the opposite of openness, that wish to create exclusion. Enlarging notions of justice means including groups, persons or problems that were not contemplated before. 'Polluted discourses', by contrast, narrow justice by demanding exclusion. Only when the claims for recognition persuasively enlarge notions of 'justice and the good' will it be possible to acquire a reflexive critical standard which will counterbalance the emergence of polluted and restricting discourses. Civic culture in a democratic society means being able to exercise a reflexive critical approach towards the different claims for recognition exerted in the public sphere. In the argument that follows, I try to develop the thesis that normative constraints can impose limits on polluted discourses. This is possible when illocutionary efforts are persuasively connected to enlarged notions of justice and the good. Movements for recognition can achieve this enlargement only if they seem able to create greater openness. They must somehow convince others that, by accepting their own point of view, other members of society can, at the same time, enlarge their own notions of who they are. In expanding the limitations of the existing culture of civil society, actors engage in what I would like to call the exercise of moral deliberation. Moral deliberation allows subjects in a social interaction to achieve a better understanding of the complexities and contingencies of life in relation to the conceptions of justice and the good in democratic postconventional societies.

The Expressivistic Model

In 1992 Charles Taylor wrote *The Politics of Recognition*.[2] He believes that his attempt to reconstruct the sources of what he called a struggle for recognition of the unique identity of each human being led him to the source of ambiguity in the foundation of the liberal philosophical tradition. Taylor suggests that it is the understanding of the meaning of our identity as individuals that has historically changed, and this assertion is the basis of his expressivistic model and how he fits it in with modernity. Taylor maintains that it was Rousseau who first made explicit the ideal of authenticity as a form of affirmation of identity. In Herder, this appreciation of the differences between human beings became a significant means of achieving moral recognition. Because our identities are constructed dialogically, argues Taylor, we require the recognition of others. Our perceptions of who we are, mediated through what others mean to us, allow us to define demands for recognition of our identity as historical and social projects which may or may not be successful in their claims for recognition.[3] In his _Sources of the Self: The Making of Modern Identity_, Taylor fully develops the expressivistic model that links the aesthetic with the moral domain, reconstructing the way in which first Rousseau, and then the Romantics, conceived of a differentiated understanding of artistic and natural beauty which relied more on the mode of experience it entailed than on the nature of the object. The term 'aesthetic', says Taylor, points to a mode of experience.[4] The novelty of Taylor's view is that sentiments and feelings are now implicated in notions of what needs to be spoken about publicly; in Habermasian terms, they have been connected to validity truth-claims. But for Taylor, these truths are not categorized according to Kant's procedural approach to morality, that is, as reason separated from passions and desires. Rather, it is through feelings that one connects oneself with conceptions of the quality of life one wants. In finding a way to express oneself, to delineate our projects, it is possible to find the originality and the 'truth' contained in the creation of those identities. The project of expressing oneself to others is here seen as part of the process of defining what needs to be realized.[5] Taylor thinks that this 'expressivistic' turn forms the basis of a new and fuller individuation. Originality here plays a major role, for it is from the standpoint of an irreplaceable self that each individual must live up to what makes that person different from others.

The idea that there is an inner source that lies in the deepest part of us, that each human being has some original measure to develop in a dialogical way, is what Taylor calls 'the cornerstone of our modern culture'. A new understanding of art as something more than mere 'mimesis' is the root that links originality to our vocation to find what it is that makes us unique as human beings. Taylor thinks that this sense of art as an original creation is drawn from our experience of the 'numinous', a feeling that in the past was provided by religiosity and that in modernity is developed through processes of individuation. Once the Romantics replaced metaphysical sources of numinosity with nature as the basic source, art became experienced as something that caught the cosmic significance of human life. Art expresses what is unrevealed; the manifestation of what is invisible requires the creative skill of imagination. This is the power that moderns now possess.

Taylor considers the category of autonomy, as currently conceived in the Kantian tradition, to be different from this expressivistic tradition in that it regards nature as an objectifying and neutral order of things. Although Kant spoke of the significance of life as a self-chosen, he separated reason and its instrumentality from feelings for nature as an inner source.[6] Thinkers like Hegel strove, on the contrary, to find a way out of this separation between nature and reason. Taylor notes with approval their efforts to find unity in a project of radical autonomy with an expressivistic shape.

In *The Ethics of Authenticity*,[7] Taylor fully expresses his separation from the Kantian conception of autonomy as self-determination. Taylor suggests that the consideration of one's own project of recognition comes from the expressivistic model first outlined by the Romantics, with Herder and Humboldt as the most representative figures, and later developed in the changed perception and understanding of the experience of art. These are the new ideas that allow moderns to contemplate a unity between reason and feeling. What is basic to Taylor's conception of authenticity is this idea of one's own originality and irreplaceability as modern human beings. This new ethic of authenticity defines the need for recognition as a moral obligation which can be accomplished only through dialogue.

Before entering into a fuller discussion of how Taylor relates his conception of recognition to the discursive level, I want to focus on the problematic assumptions within his expressivistic point of view. While I think Taylor correctly points out the newly differentiated notions about the experience of art, and is right to suggest that through those experiences an enlargement of subjective horizons has been achieved, some of the conclusions he draws from this claim require further attention.

Taylor suggests that it is in the objectifying mode of reason and nature that problems arise in Kant's conception of autonomy. He also claims that Kant himself was aware of this problem because the idea of choosing one's own life project was necessarily connected to some conception of the good. Taylor thinks that it is possible to replace Kant's limited idea of autonomy by focusing on the expressivistic category of authenticity. In my opinion, this is wrong. Kant's conception of autonomy as a rational way of approaching one's own life project provides the possibility of rationally exercising a critical distancing from one's beliefs and distorted feelings towards others. This rationality is, in part, what allows subjectivity to become a self-reflexive and critical horizon. It is impossible to approach other projects of recognition without the respect that rational human beings should have towards differences. But the ability to exercise a critical distancing towards a sense of who one is leads to the kind of rational self-criticism needed to cope with one's own distortions, the feelings one may have about others' differences. However, the category of autonomy as a purely rational attitude is not enough to result in the real mutuality of recognition that is needed in addressing others. Taylor is right in this regard, and this has also been a major concern of feminist theories when they focus on respect as not being sufficient for recognition. Nevertheless, one cannot get rid of the constraints imposed by autonomy to take others as ends in themselves, as other human beings. That was exactly why Kant thought that respect would suffice if a barrier were imposed between justice and the good.

True originality, as something that must be sought and that becomes a moral obligation, is one of the major transformations in the conception of individuation of modern subjects. My question is whether this process can be achieved on the basis of an _undifferentiated_ mixture of the aesthetic and the moral spheres, as Taylor seems to suggest. Perhaps it is less a question of breakdown and mixture than translation between one validity sphere or another. The aesthetic sphere translates its understandings of life as original, and imagination as the critical source, into moral terms that allow one to expand horizons of belief, values and ways of understanding oneself in relation to others. Is it possible to thematize how such an interrelation of the moral and aesthetic validity spheres can enlarge and deepen our subjectivities in this way?

It is his problematic assumption that the lines between the aesthetic and the moral domains are blurred that produces the greatest objections to Taylor's expressivistic view. In the _Ethics of Authenticity_, he seems to argue in favour of the right to define oneself through dialogue with others, assuming that recognition is a moral obligation. In these terms, some kind of rationalizing antidote would have to be developed to stress the normative nature of such rights, which are to be granted to all of us. Instead, Taylor suggests in his 'Politics of Recognition' that the normative status of such a category is something more like 'religious' respect, which suggests that a non-rational feeling prevents one from denying others equal worth.[8] Taylor thus relies on the aesthetic domain, where originality is the main source of value, ignoring the fact that choosing one's life project and the struggle for its public recognition must be firmly grounded in the normative sphere. It is in this sphere that autonomy – as a rational antidote to 'distorted feelings'[9] – has the possibility of restoring some kind of neutral and critical space that allows one to alter or transform interpretations of needs. The restoration of critical space was, after all, Kant's principal concern when he established autonomy as the category that allows lives to be self-chosen, for he believed that one cannot acquire the right to demand respect for what one is from others without also granting them the very same respect as human beings. Because Kant was also concerned that feelings could distort the possibility of accepting others, he thought that 'respect' could hold as a categorical imperative, a rule or constraint that was grounded in the normative domain. One can agree with Taylor that autonomy seems a narrow way of coping with the problem of recognition. It also seems insufficient when one focuses on the relation between justice and the good; but it is impossible to jump to a category that is grounded only on an aesthetic level. The public definition of the right to choose one's own life presupposes that everyone is capable of giving each other equal treatment within the principle of equal protection and its legal expression. That is what justice is all about. The territory of justice should be one where feelings and rationality are interdependent, for it is only there that normative standards can create and communicate the needed textures of solidarity. That is why it is in the public arena that one claims recognition for one's life projects in order to expand one's own notions of justice and the good. The creation of new vocabularies of needs, the new understandings of values that are presupposed in these new needs, and the wider and deeper interpretations of life and respect for it – these are the really critical elements to be discussed in any model of recognition.

This is why it is vital to consider the interconnection between the aesthetic and the moral spheres. Taylor's expressivistic model fails in *The Politics of Recognition* because it fails to interconnect these two validity spheres and, therefore, fails to articulate the normative grounds needed for accepting an aesthetically grounded category like authenticity.

Taylor devotes the second part of *The Politics of Recognition* to the dimensions of this problem in the public sphere. He argues that the historical change that overthrew honour in favour of an ideal of egalitarian human dignity for each citizen is formulated in a politics based on the universal principle of equality. However, recognition of the specificity and originality of identities gives rise to a politics of difference. Thus, there are two political currents between which contemporary societies are caught. On the one hand, there is the demand for equal treatment of all human beings, a basic equality which entails certain rights. On the other hand, there is the need to recognize the unique way in which identity is defined, that is to say, the need for recognition of differences. Yet, once again, I would argue here that Taylor is unable to develop the necessary mediation between his category of authenticity and the normative links between recognition and solidarity, between solidarity and justice. It seems to me that he has not addressed the reasons for the intertwining of solidarity and justice in a strong, non-metaphysical sense. That others are owed a right to their own life project is a strong claim which needs strong normative grounds, a strong moral constraint. If one works with Taylor's principle alone, one would be incapable of denying racists' and misogynists' claims that they too have a right to recognition. After all, they too are cultures, they too 'have survived'; as persons, they too are 'unique'.

As in his criticism of Kant's conception of autonomy, in his model of liberalism I find that Taylor simplifies democratic societies by taking so-called 'neutral' liberalism as something empty. In fact, something much more complex is going on. Let us look more closely at his arguments. When Taylor says that equality tends to configure a project of homogeneity, he conflates two major problematics. The need for equal recognition of all human beings has been a major argument in feminist criticisms of the liberal model insofar as the liberal claim of equality tended to eliminate gender differences from public discussions. But the problematic liberal treatment of gender difference cannot be equated with a lack of normative judgements about good and bad differences. Post-traditional, modern cultures accept the possibility of relativizing their own horizons, mainly because they can conceive of other values and beliefs that are different from their own and see themselves as others do in a critical fashion. Traditions and cultures can be called modern, precisely inasmuch as they have exercised such a critical self-distance and achieved a self-reflexive horizon. Reflexivity allows some critical distance from oneself.[10] Tolerance is itself the product of these self-critical, self-reflexive horizons; it is very difficult to argue that all cultures, just because they are unique, possess this capacity equally. Not all cultures include the kind of collective reflexivity that forces those socialized into them to exert critical distancing towards their own point of view and to seek to understand the other in a self-critical way. While it is true that liberalism as a model often effaces the acknowledgement of differences even before public discussion begins, it cannot be concluded from this that the ground gained through the neutral stance in post-traditional societies is not the right place to consider the value of different cultures. Otherwise there would be no public discussion of these new insights into differences. Traditional, premodern, and antimodern societies do not even consider the possibility of any kind of critique. In the modern horizon, by contrast, there is always an opening for the challenge of a dialogue between different cultures. These considerations show Taylor's claim that 'liberalism is not a possible meeting ground for all cultures' to be false. Self-critical subjects are, in principle, open to discussion and public deliberation, embedded in a self-reflexive horizon that privileges openness as the most highly regarded moral and epistemological quality. It is not surprising, therefore, that only post-traditional societies have promoted the appearance of public spaces to discuss general topics of concern to the entire community.

The basic issue here is how to make claims for recognition subject to a larger discussion, so that others feel as involved in thematizing these problems as philosophers are in need of understanding them. It is here that Habermas comes to the fore. He correctly criticizes Taylor's view of liberalism on the grounds that it challenges something basic to democracy. Democratic political arenas provide the necessary space for collective discussions to be held and for the participants to struggle over interpretations of legitimate rights that can transform conceptions of needs and interests. Habermas is also right in arguing that the process of individuation is never separate from the process of socialization. Both occur within political struggles for some kind of recognition. As Honneth has also pointed out, these struggles strive for a wider understanding of values and goals as part of a vision of justice and a relationship to the good. Habermas argues that feminism has helped in the transformation of traditional views: 'The classification of gender-specific roles and differences addresses fundamental levels of how society sees itself. Radical feminism has only now made us aware of the fallible nature of this self-conception, which is radically contested and is in need of revision. It insists, and rightfully so, on the public debate over the appropriate interpretation of needs'.[11] Habermas acknowledges that it is in the public sphere where different experiences and life situations are discussed and our world-views are at stake. This is the case not only because one's experiences lack some kind of recognition, but because only in the public sphere is one capable of making demands on the grounds of this need to revise old and traditional interpretations of the law and of notions of justice. It is through the process of the struggle to engage others in discussions in the public arena that one is able to protect one's interests as private autonomous persons and as citizens bearing legal rights. What is at stake is not the abstract level of the procedural notion of justice and autonomy, which Kant and liberalism represent, but one's own understanding of democracy. When one mobilizes to exert influence in the public arena, one seeks the radical transformation and reinterpretation of democratic theories as well as practices, and a more adequate public hermeneutical reading of the laws protecting the rights demanded by citizens. Success depends on the eloquence and persuasiveness of the discourses which are developed as claims that justice must be understood on a much broader basis.

Discursive struggles in the public arena can help to decide when one culture or one group identity defines its claims for respect in a manner that implies the expansion of previous notions of justice and the horizons of who one is. Cultures can cohabit and respect each other only on a shared common ground of tolerance and self-criticism. That is what Habermas has rightly called 'the common horizon of interpretation within which the self-understanding of a political community is publicly disputed for topical reasons'.[12] What is common about this horizon is that, no matter how intense the interpretative dispute, it is always constituted by the 'same' basic rights and principles, those that constitute the cornerstone of liberal democracies. Feminist narratives have contributed to the understanding that not all 'differences' were bad; they have therefore introduced a different perspective from liberalism on the possibility of thematizing about differences as publicly accepted features of human beings. (I focus in more detail on the feminist narratives that have sought to configure this new public understanding in chapter 8.)

The Anthropological Model

In *The Struggle for Recognition: The Moral Grammar of Social Conflicts*,[13] as Habermas had done before, Honneth analyses the young Hegel's philosophy in his Jena period. But, in his historical reconstruction of the Hegelian concept of recognition, Honneth outlines the basis for linking it to the ethical dimension of the moral life. The recognition of the uniqueness of individuals that Hegel saw as the foundation of modern identity – built simultaneously on the levels of socialization and individuation – is reconstructed by Honneth based on a new interpretation of the 'struggles for recognition'.[14] Just as in Taylor's work, Honneth's argument demonstrates that a strong theory of recognition emphasizes its intersubjective nature. The reconstruction of the concept of the struggle for recognition is based on the perception that one's identity is acquired only by means of confrontation and acceptance of who we are through others. According to Honneth, Hegel's achievement lies in having stated that intersubjective recognition of the individual dimension of humanity is a moral act. As in all moral processes, when this is achieved it implies an evolution towards a higher state of ethical relations.

One of the most interesting ideas Honneth develops in his investigation of Hegel's Jena period is the theory that acceptance of what the other means to both parties is the driving force of recognition.[15] It is in the absence of recognition that subjects also experience a lack of the respect necessary to commit themselves to the struggle for recognition. In order to round out his argument that subjects need to affirm their identities and struggle for recognition to be shared, Honneth turns to George Herbert Mead's theory of socialization and individuation. In this he shares many elements with Habermas' recovery of Mead, which attempted to construct a theory of identity based on the dialogical, intersubjective elements which Mead postulated in his social psychology.[16] Within his naturalist explanation of the theory of recognition, Honneth believes that Mead links the normative idea of recognition to a theory of individual development.

Honneth believes that Mead uses the tools of empirical science to invert the relationship between the subject and the external world and develop the idea that the perception of the other is a necessary requisite for self-awareness. Thus, according to Honneth, Mead links the normative idea of recognition to a theory of individual development. Mead's distinction between the subject's 'I' and 'me' provides a structure of evolutionary levels in which the subject seeks recognition by others and confirms the self-worth of her identity in the process. A conception of maturation emerges in Mead's evolutionary emphasis on stages in the development of the subject. In his idea of the 'generalized other', Mead brings together the concept of respect with that of recognition. This joining of the normative with the concept of recognition can be explained only because Mead's model presents the 'I' as the psychological counterpart of the 'me'. The process of identity formation of the 'generalized other' involves a dynamic in which the collective 'me' is confronted by the demands of the individualizing 'I', a process that requires breaking up the collective conventions and prejudices which prevent the 'I' from expanding. It is here that Mead introduces the idea that the tension between the collective will and the demand for individuation brings about a moral conflict between the subject and the social environment. With this approach to the problematics of identity formation, it is possible to explain historically how, in each period, individuals have set out to decrease the limitations imposed by certain rules. Because Mead explains how autonomy necessarily becomes joined with self-realization, Honneth argues, his social psychology broadens the Hegelian view by suggesting that the process of identity development also contains a motivational foundation. This is exactly what Taylor is looking for in his concept of authenticity. The 'me' of individual self-realization requires an understanding of the person as a unique and irreplaceable being.

There is a final strategy used by Honneth to relate recognition to its moral dimension which is worth noting. Thus far, I have shown that Honneth gets the category of recognition from Hegel, and how he takes it to a level on which it is necessary to the very idea of socialization and individuation. I have also shown that his concern with strengthening his hypothesis through scientific methods leads him to Mead's model of socialization, in which it is again possible to frame the struggle for recognition as a dimension encompassing the dynamics of contention between the 'I' and the 'me'. Thus, Honneth comes back to the normative dimension; his model illustrates the constant moral expansion entailed by the social struggles of groups claiming recognition of their needs. He goes on to demonstrate, moreover, the extraordinarily interesting manner in which Mead ontologized individuality: Mead linked the restless and nonconforming 'I' to the self's ability to construct an imaginary world of idealized others who would, in principle, supply psychological and social recognition of the ego's individuating, nonconforming acts.

Honneth justifies his emphasis on recognition empirically, citing common linguistic usage. 'In the self-descriptions of those who see themselves as having been wrongly treated by others', he observes, 'the moral categories that play a dominant role are those – such as "insult" or "humiliation" – that refer to forms of disrespect, that is, to the denial of recognition'.[17]

On the theoretical grounds of classical philosophy and sociology and the empirical grounds of ordinary language, then, Honneth calls for critical theory to focus on a term that has a decidedly subjective, non-economic, psychological and cultural character.[18] He suggests, for example, that denying recognition hurts people 'not simply because it harms subjects or restricts their freedom to act' – the Hobbesian and Kantian claims respectively – but also 'because it injures them with regard to the positive understanding of themselves that they have acquired intersubjectively'.[19] With this Hegelian term, then, Honneth can make the normative ideal of critical social theory more textured: recognition suggests not just abstract justice or equality, but 'self-realization', the 'settled ethos of a particular life world', the 'good life'.[20]

Yet, by putting recognition, rather than communication or equality, at the centre of his philosophical-cum-empirical model, Honneth does not see himself as taking the side of anti-Kantian ideas. On the contrary, he believes that if recognition is theorized appropriately, it can bridge the classical opposition between philosophical and sociological thought. Thus, while Honneth acknowledges that 'our approach departs from the Kantian tradition in that it is concerned not solely with the moral autonomy of human beings but also with the conditions for their self-realization', he insists that:

> in contrast to those movements that distance themselves from Kant, this concept of the good should not be conceived as the expression of substantive values that constitute the ethos of a concrete tradition-based community [but rather] with the structural elements of ethical life, which . . . can be normatively extracted from the plurality of all particular forms of life [thereby leading us to] the most general norms possible.[21]

Honneth believes there is a categorical imperative for recognition. In their desire to achieve recognition for themselves, people must give recognition to others. In this process, actors will, without realizing it, develop general categories that justify recognition and institutions that correspond to them. These categories and institutions will, simultaneously, have a particular, subjective reference and a universal, objective reach. Efforts to achieve happiness and the good life perforce involve movements towards universalization and, vice versa, movements towards universal justice are inevitably rooted in local communities of culturally shared identities and interests.

The problems in Honneth's work emerge when he 'operationalizes' recognition, dividing it into subcategories on the levels of personality ('self-confidence'), social organization ('self-respect'), and culture ('self-esteem'). Each of these categories defines an ideal end-state of social development, a set of equilibrium points for social and moral progress that are anthropological in the sense that they constitute social and moral arguments – like those of Marx's early manuscripts – produced by a theory of human needs. For each level, Honneth points to a set of social restrictions that frustrate a human need, denying recognition and creating social pathology and conflict as a result. In so doing, he also produces theoretically informed suggestions for progressive social action and change.

But linking human needs so closely to social structures and pathologies is too neat. In conceptualizing self-confidence, for example, Honneth employs object relations theories that underline the importance of 'good enough mothering', by parents and other socializing agents, in providing actors with the 'basic trust' necessary for establishing friendship and independence. Being denied the recognition that 'good enough mothering' represents, Honneth writes, results in pathologies such as criminal aggression and violence. It seems to me, however, that this is too simplistic a way of thinking about the motivational aspects even of interpersonal problems. As Anna Freud first pointed out, and as subsequent ego psychology convincingly demonstrated, even 'well brought up' and 'secure' people have complex and fragmented cognitive and affective structures and frequently employ defence mechanisms such as splitting, projection, denial and neutralization.[22] This means that, even in 'healthy' adults, the potential for violent and aggressive interpersonal relations is always present. 'Confident' people can be, and have been, anti-Semitic, racist and misogynist. Equally important, however, is the fact that unconfident, insecure, badly brought up persons can act in ways that give others esteem and recognition. They can be led to do so by structures of the symbolic and organizational environments within which they act. Otherwise it would be very difficult to explain why so many different women struggled to achieve a different kind of recognition, coming, as they did, from backgrounds of terrible problems in their family lives and upbringing.

What is missing from Honneth's model is the concept of mediation. Confidence is a psychological medium, but it should not, for the purposes of social theory, be conceived as an individually or even interactionally generated one. On the contrary, confidence, and the lack thereof, can be articulated *culturally* and regulated *institutionally*; it is not only or even primarily the result of socializing institutions. In her influential book *The Reproduction of Mothering*,[23] for example, Nancy Chodorow demonstrated how misogynist socializing structures created strong and supposedly debilitating dependency needs in girls and women. How then, did it come to pass that these same girls and young women created the active, autonomous and self-confident, often very 'aggressive' women's movement of the 1960s? What Chodorow missed was the mediation *vis-à-vis* female psychological structures provided by surrounding cultural ideals, which increasingly emphasized universal and neutral conceptions of freedom, and the surrounding social structures, such as increased participation in the labour market and extended legal guarantees, which provided opportunities for learning how to transform personal feelings of inadequacy into healthy, confident and assertive *public* behaviour.

As I have argued above, actors in the women's movement found psychological gratification (self-confidence and recognition) in the interactional and cultural structures that were institutionally available in the public sphere. Because they were so gratified, they could act with illocutionary force to redefine those structures in more universal and gender-sensitive ways. The subsequent psychological (confidence-related) effect of the women's movement can be examined in much the same way. Insofar as it succeeded in establishing new normative guidelines for interactional and institutional behaviour, new economic rewards and legal punishments, and new cultural categories of moral human beings, feminism has made it possible for 'insecure' women to be treated in ways that increase their self-confidence and recognition.

Honneth articulates recognition on the level of social organization, defined as self-respect, primarily in terms of the broadening of citizens' rights. Arguing, quite rightly, that self-respect can be produced by legal obligations demanding that others respect one's moral autonomy, Honneth produces a developmental model that concentrates on showing how law has become ever more abstract and generalized, and its normative reach continually extended. He demonstrates that law was integral to the transformation of hierarchically organized states into horizontally defined citizen communities, and that the extension and generalization of law was later central to the kind of political and social enlargement of these earlier civil rights that Marshall and Parsons described.

Despite the importance of drawing attention to the significant role of legal development in these regards, Honneth's argument is seriously weakened by his unmediated, anthropological linkage of self-respect and legal institutions. In historical terms, increasing legal generalization and abstraction does not, necessarily, mean extending recognition of autonomy. This is too evolutionary and developmental. Apartheid laws were imposed during South African modernity, in the 1940s; the Nuremberg laws emerged in the midst of what had been considered an expansion of German modernity in the 1920s and early 1930s; laws severely reducing social benefits of citizenship have been proposed with increasing frequency during the final decade of the twentieth century.

It is clear that legal generality and abstractness do not, in themselves, signal recognition of moral autonomy or the lack thereof. Once again, I would argue the contrary, that the moral capacity of different groups of actors is crystallized by social movements that intervene in the public sphere in an illocutionary way. However, these can be movements of the right just as often as of the left. Once public moral identities are symbolically constructed, the moral majority specifies them in terms of legal codes and enforceable mandates. Honneth has ignored the fact that illocutionary – linguistic and symbolic – forces always mediate the relationship between psychological motivations, interactional gestures and social organizations. Because he has ignored this mediation, he has conflated the recognition of moral capacity with the growth of legal regulation *per se*. This avoids the whole problem of the relation between procedural, universalist law – the only kind Honneth addresses – and legal norms that seek to enforce substantive rationality through category-specific protections. The 'partialist' legal position that some multiculturalists have suggested is necessary if complex societies are to respect differences in gender and ethnicity.

In his discussion of the third, culturally related type of recognition (self-esteem) and of the role that social movements play in the struggle for recognition, as it is generally understood, Honneth moves closer to illuminating the symbolic, illocutionary mediation in complex societies which I have emphasized. Esteem, he writes, comes from the actor's ability to participate in an intersubjectively shared value horizon, in a true community of values. For this reason, he suggests, it is the cultural self-understanding of society that provides the criteria for establishing self-esteem. There is, however, a crucial unacknowledged ambiguity in this discussion. On the one hand, Honneth suggests that mere participation in a shared value or community ethic can provide recognition. On the other, he acknowledges that for this recognition to be moral or just, it must involve, not only symbolic participation in a tightly bonded community, but in the community of society, a relatively universal community. In the latter sense, it is the 'climate of public attention' that becomes critical, not simply the communal sharing of values *per se*. This distinction is not merely academic. The failure to make it explicit, and to relate different forms of communalization systematically to different outcomes in the culturally coded struggle for esteem, would seem to be a significant omission in moral and empirical terms, one leading to the very same kinds of difficulties I have already shown in Taylor's work. The problem presents itself because esteem is, in fact, often provided within the particularistic, self-affirming boundaries of segmented communities which experience themselves as downwardly mobile, as having recently become peripheral to ongoing public concerns. In this kind of situation, demands for recognition that appear subjectively legitimate to social actors, which, indeed, emerge from their concrete forms of ethical life, are highly suspect in moral terms. Since they are based on deep resentments, they can easily become demands for domination, for the subordination of the values of other groups to those that appear 'naturally' to be affirmed in one's own.

Honneth seems theoretically able to avoid such a possibility – to avoid theorizing on the darker possibilities that the search for esteem might imply – because of the ambiguity in the 'community' reference mentioned above. This optimism on his part is due to a new form of categorical imperative, one that predicts mutual valuation from the anthropological force of human need: 'Solidarity can be understood as an interactive relationship in which subjects mutually sympathize with their various ways of life because, among themselves, they esteem each other symmetrically'.[24] Yes, solidarity *can* be understood in this way, but will it be so understood empirically? Honneth simply admonishes, 'only to the degree to which I actively care about the development of the other's characteristics (which seem foreign to me) can our shared goals be realized'.[25] This submerged developmental commitment to an anthropological imperative makes Honneth seem rather optimistic that the struggle for recognition will lead to progressive social change.

It is important to point this out in a carefully balanced way. By emphasizing the particularity and subjectivity of recognition, and by recognizing its sociological contingency, Honneth has gone well beyond the Habermasian formula – which Taylor criticized – that simply describes solidarity as the 'other side of justice'. Drawing from the Hegelian and classical traditions, his model is the first to conceptualize the possibility – which Taylor ignores – of solidarity as a moral criterion, thus avoiding the proceduralism of the neo-Kantian tradition, still evident in Habermas' work, that conceives the impartiality of solidarity in a very abstract way. In my view, however, Honneth does not go far enough. It is important to go beyond saying that solidarity is not an empty space and that groups are included and excluded on the basis of recognition. Recognition must become a more textured term, and it can become so only if it is broadened to include a more illocutionary concept, such as symbolic representation.

Solidarity is never a single possibility. It is always partial, multilayered and incomplete, because recognition in a moral and ethical sense is filtered by the intermingled representational structures of various social groups. In opposition to the partially institutionalized values of 'modernity' or 'postconventional morality', one must recognize, as neither Honneth nor Taylor does, that the core groups in society can and often do establish hierarchical valuations that justify subordinating groups by identifying them as dependent, irrational or libidinous – in other words, as civically incompetent.

These institutionalized languages of disrespect exist in tense relationships with the self-images of excluded groups and with the 'properly civil' normative language of democratic society. For this reason, in order for a group to gain esteem and recognition, it takes a lot more than just demanding it, more than justifying this demand on the basis of an anthropological reciprocity. It requires entering into the convoluted, interlarded language of public life with illocutionary force, with such creative rhetorical power and non-institutionalized resources that one's own and other's identities seem to require a reconstructed narrative of the social, one that is coded in much more democratic, egalitarian and humanitarian terms.

The Hermeneutic Model

I would like now to move to another philosophical angle which bears similarities to the other two. It also attempts to show, on philosophical grounds, how the acquisition of identity is achieved through interactions with others. In this case, it is relevant to look at the work of Paul Ricoeur, who, with the help of hermeneutics and the analytical philosophy of language, envisions recognition among different people in terms similar to those of Axel Honneth. The title of his text, *Oneself as Another*, reveals how deeply his view is linked to that of Hegel, in which the understanding of one's own identity is not possible without the concept of otherness.[26]

In his attempt to develop a hermeneutics of identity, Ricoeur first tries to broaden his discourse from a semantic and pragmatic viewpoint, that of Anglo-Saxon analytical philosophy. In a second section, dealing with the philosophy of action, Ricoeur attempts, rather analytically, to develop a view of identity clearly rooted in linguistic acts; action and language become the main focus. For Ricoeur, it is through the concept of 'narrative identity' that 'action' recovers its link to the Aristotelian conception of praxis. The ethical and moral determinations of subjects in action will be articulated within what Ricoeur calls autonomy, solicitude and justice.

Ricoeur sets himself a twofold task. He illustrates, first, the highest level of dialectics between permanence and identity contained in the notion of 'narrative identity'. Having achieved a particularly insightful view of narratives in contemporary philosophy in his earlier *Time and Narrative*,[27] Ricoeur now tries to use his narrative theory to mediate between a theory of action and a moral theory, thus defining the possibility of moral judgement.

Ricoeur argues that the fact that one constructs one's identity only inasmuch as one can narrate it presupposes a unity or a singular totality. His model, based on permanent change, focuses on the need for coherence in order to regard one's life as a unity, which in turn allows one to recognize oneself as the same person despite change. Here the interpretative view of a particular way of evaluating oneself finds a new order, as do one's evaluative standards. For Ricoeur, literature provides the example of an imaginative laboratory. To narrate a story, according to him, is to unfold an imaginary space for reflexive experimentation in which acts of moral judgement are displayed in a hypothetical way. In *Oneself as Another*, this view has led Ricoeur to argue that morality depends on ethics. The ethical intention corresponds to self-esteem, and the deontological moment to self-respect.[28] As in the case of Honneth's interpretation of identity development in Mead, Ricoeur claims that this evolution of identity depends on the possibility of finding channels for self-esteem, which allow the creation of dimensions of self-respect as a translation from the ethical to a moral domain. His hermeneutical theory presupposes that self-interpretation becomes self-esteem. Thus, the concept of identity is enriched by the relationship between the interpretation of the action-text and self-interpretation. But the adjustment of such ideals and decisions as these requires a different kind of verification from that of the exact sciences. The modification of these interpretations is based on value judgements, which aspire to plausibility in the eyes of others and of oneself on the evidence of experience. On this level, one needs others to give evidence of who one is, and this dimension of mutuality and reciprocity is articulated in the Aristotelian concept of friendship. What interests Ricoeur in Aristotle's view of friendship is that it is located in the territory of justice, for 'we are friends with those we consider our equals'.[29] With the acknowledgement that the other is equal to oneself there appears the reflexive dimension of recognition of otherness. With this twist, Ricoeur refurbishes Hannah Arendt's conception of 'narratives' as storytellings and connects her with her own Aristotelian affinities. His religious approach, however, impedes his understanding the interrelation of the moral, aesthetic and political dimensions that are interconnected in Arendt's view.

Ricoeur believes that what allows one to seek the good life is self-esteem. To make this possible, one needs friends, because only through mutuality and reciprocity can one experience the normative dimensions of equality. This is to say that only within friendship can one fully understand the concept of justice.[30] He adopts the Aristotelian concept of friendship because he feels that it contains the dimension of mutuality and reciprocity that he needs to develop a broader model. This new frame is found in the dimensions that intertwine responsibility towards others and one's need of them. Giving and receiving friendship illustrates the meaning of this relationship of reciprocity linked to responsibility.

Violations of personal integrity evoke the suffering of the other. This level of asymmetry can be transcended only by perceiving the suffering of the other with solicitude. Ricoeur believes that individuals have a 'disposition' to perceive the feelings of the other, and an awareness of the moral dimension to which they pertain. The perception of the other's suffering – the full comprehension of the meaning of this suffering in terms of the fragility of human mortality – is what restores the dimension of equality which is lost when what is perceived is someone else's suffering. To self-esteem, conceived as a reflexive moment of the aspiration towards the good life, solicitude adds the dimension of absence, the fact that one needs friends. Solicitude adds a dimension of value in which each person is irreplaceable in one's affection and estimation. The irreparable loss of the other means also the irreplaceable nature of one's own life to oneself. I am irreplaceable only to others.

Ricoeur provides us a third, interlinked concept which suggests that self-esteem and solicitude are complemented by similarity. Similarity is the product of the exchange between self-esteem and solicitude towards others. This exchange allows one to understand that one cannot have self-esteem for oneself unless one esteems others as oneself.

As one glimpses possibilities of living life well, which also implies exercising a sense of justice, it becomes clear that doing so is represented by an understanding of the other. Living well is no longer seen only in terms of one's immediate others but in terms of any other. Thus, relationships with others become institutionally extended. What is more, since justice presents an ethical dimension with features akin to solicitude, the results become apparent in the way equality is perceived. This is the core of justice and of what Ricoeur calls 'repairing justice', which constitutes the moral legal framework.[31]

Ricoeur believes that Kant's conception of autonomy is unable to develop a real link with solidarity unless it is somehow related to matters of the good life. Unlike Taylor, however, Ricoeur is not trying to develop a new category to fill in the gaps of Kantian formalism, which views moral subjects as acting only in response to duty. Rather, he gives a new twist to the idea of autonomy, which then reappears as irrevocably linked to the search for the good life. Ricoeur argues that respect is self-esteem filtered through the legal dimension. Here, Ricoeur's strategy consists in questioning the idea that there are no affective dimensions in the conception of autonomy. On the contrary, he believes that 'autonomy is not autonomous'.[32] In this sense, respect for people demands an ethical goal, that of solicitude. Or, to put it differently, respect for people, in the moral domain, has the same relation to autonomy as solicitude does to the goals of the good life on an ethical plane. Thus, the interpretation of the Golden Rule – 'do unto others as you would have them do unto you' – becomes an expression connecting solicitude with the norm, a norm that Kant saw as the duty of reciprocity. Here we find the core of Ricoeur's proposal, that this norm presupposes a space of asymmetry that has a grammatical projection in the opposition between doing and being done to, or between inflicting and suffering. The successful undermining of the victim's self-esteem – which has been raised to the category of a norm through the idea of self-respect – becomes humiliation, which is nothing less than the destruction of the ability to act, or the loss of self-respect. Thus, Ricoeur reinterprets Kant's second imperative, which claims that people should be treated as ends in themselves. In Kant, this is achieved through his abstract formulation of the idea of person and his principle of autonomy. Ricoeur places the Golden Rule in an intermediate position, so that the Kantian imperative reappears now as a formalization of such a rule. Respect assumes a new value when humanity is seen not only as the sum of individuals in the abstract, but as the idea of the plurality that constitutes it. The concept of humanity thus has to be broadened to include the particular value of each of the people that make up humanity as such. In this sense, 'humanity' becomes synonymous with 'multiplicity'.[33] Ricoeur believes that both Kant's imperative and the Golden Rule are grounded in an absence of reciprocity, and that the affective mediation of the Golden Rule – which, we have already noted, is legally based on the definition of respect – recaptures the insight inherent in the term solicitude, namely, that otherness is the root of the plurality of people. This view allows Ricoeur to argue that the idea of plurality is unavoidably linked to the idea of a person as an end 'in his or her own right'.[34]

In order to describe the dynamics by which self-esteem is linked to solicitude and in turn to justice, Ricoeur finally decides, as Honneth did, that it is necessary to recover the category of recognition from Hegel's Jena period. Recognition introduces the dyad and plurality within the same constitution of identity. But identity itself becomes a text, and it is only through this new hermeneutical insight that institutions can be presupposed. A text, an action or a life project is irrevocably connected to meaning and interpretation, and meaning and interpretations make sense only when they have meaning for someone else. Thus, Ricoeur believes that self-interpretation becomes self-esteem on the ethical plane, and 'self-esteem follows the fate of interpretation'.[35] This approach to recognition avoids the anthropological problems of Honneth's theory. Ricoeur understands that the 'fate of interpretations' is decided in a public arena through 'controversy', 'rivalry' and 'dispute'. In short, the 'conflict of interpretations' is the empirical stratum where the need for practical judgement sets the limits on whose life projects are worthy of moral recognition.[36] This understanding brings to the fore the central role that deliberation plays in Ricoeur's framework; whether exercised on an individual or collective basis, moral deliberations are conditions for the formation of public opinion.

Although there are striking resemblances to Honneth's project, Ricoeur's more hermeneutic approach shows the progress that has been made in taking actions as texts and therefore revealing struggles for recognition as life stories that demand meaningful interpretation. Both authors are trying to bridge the abstract conception of autonomy, seeking a way to recover it through a means that demonstrates the interactions between ideas of justice and the good life. While Honneth finds the possibility of a reformulation of the categorical imperative in his conception of the need for recognition, Ricoeur sees a new mediation in the Golden Rule, a value taken from his Christian background. This religious notion, Ricoeur believes, links the incomplete achievement of one's own identity – which comes from not being valued by others – to the achievement of self-reflexivity via narrativity. Both authors describe triadic stages through which autonomy is achieved. Humiliation and suffering are the roots of the struggle, says Honneth. For Ricoeur, it is also the humiliation that can now be understood by the linguistic action of a doer and the one done to. However, the notion of narrativity that Ricoeur introduces as a tool of his hermeneutical vision must be regarded as a further, important step towards the recognition that I am interested in exploring here. His notion of narratives as involving the retelling of stories of what has happened, and then a reconstruction in broader terms of the meaning of justice, closely resembles Arendt's conception of storytelling and the public sphere. This is by no means a mere coincidence. In some aspects of his work, Ricoeur has incorporated existentialist notions from Heidegger and Sartre; but in his conception of narrative, he is much nearer to Arendt without much acknowledgement of his debt to her theory.

This argument deserves closer scrutiny. The power of narrating life stories lies in the construction of a 'unity of life' that can project one's ambitions as projects for the good life. But life stories are always entangled with other stories, and the singularity as well as the common elements of each life story are caught up in the 'experience of life'. Ricoeur is interested in showing how those stories form processes of self-understanding and relate to a dialectic which also connects Reinhart Kosselleck's notions of 'spaces of experiences' with the 'horizons of expectations' and 'space of expectation, although there is still some meaning in these expressions. What is at stake here is the demonstration that the presence of the past is distinct to the presence of the future'.[37] Arendt was very much aware of this as well, pointing to this capacity, for example, in her discussion of how the public sphere can be used for the purpose of developing 'new beginnings'. When speaking about the unity of the narrative of a life, Ricoeur says that we find 'the sign of narratives that reach us [in] how to articulate narratively retrospection and prospection. This dialectic reminds us that the narrative is part of life before being exiled from life in writing; it returns to life along the multiple paths of appropriation and at the price of the unavoidable tensions just mentioned'.[38]

Ricoeur connects his concept of narrativity to the ethical dimension through the idea, taken from Benjamin, of the 'exchange of experiences'. For Ricoeur, this is the art of storytelling. The judgements needed here, judgements that have to be made in public, are subject to approval or disapproval, and agents must be blamed or praised. These exercises of evaluation perform their function of discovery or transformation 'in the phase of refiguration of action by the narrative'.[39] As in Arendt's narration of stories, the view Ricoeur recovers is closely related to Benjamin's. Such a concern explicitly acknowledges that everyone is always indebted to people of the past: 'And in certain circumstances – in particular when the historian is confronted with the horrible, the extreme figure of the history of victims – the relation of debt is transformed into the duty never to forget'.[40]

With the hermeneutical tool introduced by Ricoeur in his conception of identity, he steps away from the anthropological or expressivistic views. Furthermore, his notion of storytelling clearly alludes to the need to construct a public space in which judgements can be exercised, thereby reconstructing a narrative whose notions of justice embrace the debt to victims of the past. But this notion of narrativity also includes the unfolding of a capacity to convince others of how the past has to be redescribed and the future constructed. Elements of linguistic force enter into this pattern, as do elements of the symbolic. Nothing is solved *ipso facto*. Moreover, by placing narrative theory at the crossroads of the theory of action and moral theory, Ricoeur is able to consider recognition not as an anthropological need or a new categorical imperative but as a step leading to new understandings of who one is, and as a responsibility to those goals. His idea of 'ethical intention' – the aim of the 'good life' with and for others – is that institutions should provide the basis for a never-ending dialogue.

Ricoeur moves to the territory of 'solicitude' when he tries to connect the 'aims of the good life with and for others' with 'just institutions'. Self-esteem helps him to unfold the category of solicitude, which is the need for others.

To understand the term 'capacity' correctly, we must return to Merlau-Ponty's 'I can' and extend it from the physical to the ethical level. I am that being who can evaluate his actions and, in assessing the goals of some of them to be good, is capable of evaluating himself and judging himself to be good. The discourse of 'I can' is, to be sure, a discourse in I. But the main emphasis is to be placed on the verb, on being-able-to-do, to which corresponds on the ethical plane, being-able-to-judge. The question is then whether the mediation of the other is not required along the route from capacity to realization.[41]

Ricoeur thinks that the bridge between capacity for and realization of an identity can be overcome when the roots of the mediating role that others play are grasped. It is his interpretation of Aristotle's conception of friendship that allows him to connect 'capacity' and 'realization' – 'that is, finally of *power* and act – that a place is made for a *lack*, and through this mediation we give a space for *others*'.[42] This is where reciprocity appears, and it is constitutive of 'mutuality', in Arendtian terms, because Ricoeur thinks that only through friendship can people grasp the domain of mutual respect that will connect them as 'equals'. This, in turn, is what makes Ricoeur's proposal subject to criticism. He is dealing with elements that feminist theorists have considered in their own discussions of respect and equality, discussions which have also focused on the meaning of friendship and whether or not it can be situated within a larger sphere of justice. Despite their efforts to think these problems through, feminists have encountered great difficulties because of traditionalist views of solidarity, and their mediating efforts seem very uncertain. Ricoeur does not take these efforts into consideration, despite the fact that they deal with the kinds of problem he himself is trying to resolve. Indeed, his proposal seems blind to these very difficulties.

Ricoeur thinks that the reflexivity of the self in need of others will suffice to achieve the affectionate feelings of friendship that allow one to consider others as equals. But the very opposite seems empirically more likely, for the plurality and complexity of societies make it difficult to feel friendliness. The otherness of the other is often too great. Recognition is restricted only to the others that are already part of a common world. What Ricoeur's proposal needs is a much stronger role for the public arenas and their mediating role. As I have suggested above, it is the public contest over opinions that can build up the possible 'spaces for friendship' of which Ricoeur speaks. These can be spaces for creative performative discourse. They can generate forms of concrete solidarity by introducing the discourses of others. In this sense, Ricoeur is wrong to link moral solidarity with friendship. As I see it, one is not obliged to be friends with others, yet one does owe them respect. How this respect can develop on an empirical level is one of the difficulties with Kant's categorical imperative, and Kant was well aware of this problem.

Feminism has managed to put it differently. Feminist theories hold that recognition must come first as a struggle over resignifying the spaces of appearance. Then narratives attract the attention of others and play a significant role in disposing them to listen to one another. Once some kind of respect is granted institutionally, through the strengthening of channels to promote respect, then one can ask oneself why it is important to want to listen to other people's claims. Friendship enters in here, but it is conceived as a category that does not automatically grant 'equality'. The normative content of friendship must be firmly grounded in the field of justice, a fact that is not well thought out in Ricoeur's Aristotelian approach. The notion of equality must be strengthened by positive actions developed by 'civil society' groups who try to use the channels of communication to conquer public spaces and to transform institutions. In their concrete performances, they strive to find ways of creating new community bonds that can redefine the meaning of 'equality' as well as the revaluation of each one of the differences that appear as public now. This, in turn, contributes to broadening conceptions of justice. If the idea that one owes respect to others in different and concrete ways is to be reinforced, communities must have recourse to some kind of shared notion of recognition that can be conceived in a larger, transcommunitarian sense. In learning how to listen to those others, one is also able to find something morally valuable for one's own life. That has not been easy to achieve. When one is faced with the different cultures which have now become part of post-traditional societies, one must acknowledge that preconceived ideas of respect are far from providing a real understanding and appreciation of otherness.

Ricoeur's attachment to religious hermeneutics is expressed in his concept of solicitude as the arena where the 'unequal power [that] finds compensation in an authentic reciprocity in exchange' is tested.[43] Solicitude can make one aware of one's fragility and, therefore, can make one realize that one needs others, that these others are irreplaceable beings. However, it is not in his notion of friendship that Ricoeur tries to ground the aim of recognition, but in the conception of power he derives from the works of Arendt.[44] With Arendt's conception of plurality as the core of modernity, Ricoeur thinks that one needs to shift to a model that covers not only the 'I's' and the 'you's', but a third party. With the notion of plurality, dialogue seems insufficient because third parties are not often included in the public. The inclusion of the third party is not yet secured, for it implies that one can act only where those others actually are present. Therefore, it is only in the institutional arenas that the 'span of time' is recovered as a vital element, and power needs this temporal dimension. This dimension or span of time obsessed Benjamin, and made Arendt think of ways of salvaging past experiences as a memory that projects itself by transforming the present into a utopian dimension of the future, a new beginning. Temporality, for Ricoeur, means that 'publicness is more a task to be accomplished than something already given'.[45]

Surprisingly, the twist that Ricoeur gives to his projection of the utopian dimension of the public sphere returns in his notion of the textures of the 'forgotten', those who were left behind and who were always in Benjamin's mind. It is because one forgets that one wants to live together. And in order to act in concert, one needs the public sphere to exist and to force one to recover the forgotten moments in which these aims were destroyed. Thus, the ethical dimension becomes a constitutive element of the public sphere.[46]

Ricoeur has thus moved into a hermeneutical model of recognition that has accomplished at least two major tasks. First, it has succeeded in situating life projects and lives themselves as texts which need to be addressed to others in order to gain meaning for themselves. Because not only references to cultural structures but institutional channels of communication follow from this conceptualization, the dangers of considering recognition on anthropological or aesthetic grounds are avoided. Second, Ricoeur's insistence that 'conflicting interpretations' of these life texts can be resolved only in the public is important in that such resolution demands a third party in order to provide a real expansion of spaces. Ricoeur has managed to preserve the Kantian conception of autonomy, but has done so only by introducing the affective dimensions of self-esteem, which are considered necessary for the self-reflexive and interpreting moral agent. When considering life texts and the imagination as the basic tools for interpretations and for moral judgements, Ricoeur touches the aesthetic sphere. Still, he has not, in my view, gone far enough. He has not explained why, when one 'reads others', the affective and cognitive dimensions are intertwined in the process of creating new understandings of life. Only by seeing the interconnection of these spheres can one understand what a powerful tool reinterpretation is, how it allows one's own values to change when one learns that others can provide new insights about oneself. It is not friendship that makes one believe that one needs to learn more from other worlds, to see oneself enriched by them. It is the creation of public spaces where discourses are constructed and opened as channels for raising the issues of others. By 'conquering' such public spaces, subjects in need of recognition can become part of collective deliberations and discussions. In the end, only this process can lead to an acknowledgement of the possibility of new friendships, although this cannot be guaranteed empirically. By *presuming* the availability of friendship,

Ricoeur too easily adopts Aristotle's conception without realizing that a more complex insight into contemporary political and social realities is necessary if one is to learn how to lead a good life with and for others. The concept of autonomy needs to be strengthened with more and different inputs from the expressive sphere than Ricoeur envisions. How these performative interactions configure this new understanding of values, and of others, is what is at stake when a discourse – a text – is built up, addressing others in an attempt to be understood as a larger, fuller expression of 'us'. If this figurative effort is successful, further steps of reinterpreting self and other are possible, in ever-widening circles. It is this further step that I call 'illocutionary force' and I find its best empirical example in how the feminist model of recognition developed its cultural understanding of the public sphere.

Despite his achievements, I reluctantly conclude that Ricoeur has not fully accomplished his aim of developing a theory of recognition. He has done so only in part. There is a sense in which his work is too purely philosophical. His major insights into the importance of friendship, for example, are not related to the complexities of actual communities, but only to definitions of life projects as texts and the difficulties in their interpretations. If his notion of self-esteem were seen as a part of a much broader interaction between validity spheres – the normative, the expressive and the cognitive – it could be developed in much greater depth. Ricoeur lacks a complex vision of the political. Indeed, the only time he directly addresses institutional problems is when he refers to Rawls' notion of 'distributive justice', which he understands as a possible corrective to notions of equality. Yet, as feminists among others have shown, Rawls' 'veil of ignorance' does not provide for real equality, precisely because it is not sufficiently sensitive to differences in relation to real people and because he already presupposes that democratic institutions are given as such. Ricoeur himself is well aware that the people who are not in the public sphere must remain the silent third parties. Why then, does he seem to agree with the basic notions of liberalism as Rawls understands them? I would point, once again, to the corrections provided by the best feminist criticism, which has made such extensive revisions of the concepts of equality related inextricably to differences, pointing to justice creating public spaces where solidarities can be performed, learned, acknowledged. The significant step in women's narratives was taken in challenging previous interpretations of how each one of these relations was conceived by a particularistic male view that appeared as neutral and undifferentiated.

8 Feminist Models of Recognition: Problems of Multiculturalism

Multiculturalism is now a major concern in democratic societies. This is simply because, in the conditions of globalization, there are few, if any, monocultural societies left. It is, rather, as Bhikhu Parekh suggests, that there has been a deep historical shift in the understanding of plurality, which has given the idea of 'multiculturality' a new meaning.[1] In this final chapter, I would like to address the contributions that feminist narratives have made to this shift in understanding, in the process proposing what I believe to be a more satisfactory concept of recognition than the ones examined in chapter 7. I suggest that women's narratives and their arguments about the absence of 'moral' consensus in Western 'universal' definitions of citizens' 'rights' have led to new ways of perceiving how individuals and groups can demand recognition and respect for their self-chosen ways of life.

I approach these issues by reviewing the narrative of difference developed by Iris Marion Young,[2] the narratives of universalist feminism proposed especially by Seyla Benhabib and Nancy Fraser, and the model of performative agonistic narratives drawn by Bonnie Honig. This provides an opportunity for critical reflection on the challenges faced by plural societies when recognition relates both to equality and difference. This time around, however, I move more deeply into the particular *narrative* forms regarding gender, sexuality, nationality, ethnicity and race, considering them as models of public space in multicultural societies.

The concepts of tolerance and respect seem insufficient for the protection and acceptance of diversity inasmuch as it proves difficult to find a balance that is not refracted in the very societal bonds of collective identities which liberal democratic institutions themselves require. Thus one is confronted by paradoxical structures, or 'practical vicious circles'.[3] These 'practical vicious circles' have made manifest the need to thematize the relationship between the recognition which stems from a horizon of projections of the good life and the channels through which public discourses are generated about how to improve on the reinterpretations of conditions associated with the realm of justice – the recognition of needs, the right of each individual and group to have different life projects, to define their own identities, and to gain recognition for the potential equality of each individual and group in terms of their achievements and goals. In this chapter, I discuss three examples of how the tension inherent in this process may find a release through feminist universalist narratives that generate interpretations of the public sphere and new public performances.

Feminism as the Narrative of a Cultural Revolution

Of all the revolutions originated in the twentieth century, the most relevant, the one that has most changed, and will yet change, habits and culture is feminism. Historically, this fact is unquestionable. The radical transformation that feminist demands brought about in the traditions, beliefs, habits and cultures of post-traditional societies, far from being an already resolved problem, has opened up new horizons of reflection and criticism, in turn giving rise to problems the resolution of which depends on finding the necessary theoretical and conceptual clarity. This is due not only to the great schism brought about by the critical works that feminist theories have systematically deemed incoherent, incomplete or biased, but to the fact that various feminist positions have developed, through their criticism, diverse conceptions of what recognition and equality mean. It is mainly in this area that I would like to approach the issue of multiculturalism, and point out what I consider to be the fundamental theoretical legacy of feminist interventions.

At its inception, a feminism of equality took the Enlightenment's theory of equality, which considered honour a class privilege, and corrected this inherited distortion by linking citizenship much more powerfully to a moral framework of justice. Paradoxical as it may seem, extraordinary efforts, including political struggles, were required to make the partiality of the initial interpretation of equality apparent. The feminist arguments showed that more than half of humanity was not included in this new dimension, demonstrating that earlier versions of civil, private and legal rights were based on the premise that women were not considered subjects of rights.

Therefore, the initial goal of feminist theories was to criticize the classical liberal authors and the concepts they initiated, concepts which today are, in many cases, the cornerstones of the constitutions of democratic countries. Feminist theories dealt extensively with Rousseau[4] and Locke,[5] and pointed out the inconsistencies of concepts which were considered universal. The demand for equality necessarily led to the immediate revision of other concepts: justice, freedom, the respect for civil and private rights, the separation between public and private spheres, etc.[6] This debate, which is not yet over, has led directly to the thematization of the concept of democracy, and with it, the necessary reflection on the category of recognition as the basis for the idea of equality. The reflection on recognition has, of course, not only come from theoretical and academic analysis. Feminism as a political movement has had an equal impact on practice, questioning the conceptual and interpretative elements of the laws in which a lack of legal recognition of the equality of women as citizens has been found, as shown in the preceding chapters. The radical feminist criticism of democracies in developed countries places under intense debate the projects of the 'social welfare state', the concepts of citizenship, salaried work and non-remunerated work, and such issues as health care. Similarly, from a feminist point of view, laws began to be questioned in terms of the same biased interpretation which had been the cornerstone of the defence of human rights in its private and citizen sense.[7] This double work, on the practices that pointed out the inconsistencies in theory, and the global review of the theories which became practices of inequality, made feminism the most significant cultural, political and social revolution in contemporary life. What began as a systematic review of the concepts of liberalism and democracy generated the possibility of translating to various theoretical levels the concepts of recognition and equality, of difference as a cultural and political construct, and generated the very need to theorize the distinction between gender and sexuality.

The various feminist theories have obvious points of convergence, but they have also offered several interpretations of what equality and recognition mean in the social, political and economic life of contemporary democracies and even in countries in which democracy does not fully exist or which may be considered as traditional. I am interested in reflecting on this critical debate over liberalism, in the hope of finding guidelines under which recognition as a category can become a substantial notion, where the struggle for equality is translated into a reflection on the universality of this 'right', and the cultural transformation which this implies.

One of the keys to the convergence of the various feminisms has been a shared political activism, in groups and organizations, in debates and in the formation of public opinion, and in the generation of communicative spaces as a central factor in a necessary democratization. The reason for this is apparent, for without the point of view of women, it is impossible to transform legislation, typify crimes, counter atavisms and prejudices, and confront the politics of injustice. The immediate goal was to achieve systematic and free communication in public spaces. At the same time, theories and systematic interpretations arose seeking historical evidence of public life as a space for masculine privilege from which women were marginalized.[8] The aim was not only to denounce the exclusion of women from public spaces, but to recover those spaces in light of the revolution required to transform concepts and practices in social, political and democratic life.

Yet this story remains incomplete. The historical debate begun by feminism eventually generated a discussion of multiculturalism. The key to what is missing from the story lies, therefore, in the historical reconstruction of different feminist debates, particularly as narrated from the standpoint of a shift that took place in how feminism understood itself within the domain of justice. Different feminist theories from the 1960s to the mid-1980s brought on confrontations between what was then called the feminism of 'equality' and an emerging feminism of 'difference'. The demarcation between these two different versions of feminism was based on how each one understood 'justice' ('gender injustice') and how each one wanted to reintroduce a new meaning of 'equality' ('gender equity'). The feminist discourse of 'equality' held that it was important for women to be considered equal to men, and regarded 'gender difference' as a form of sexism. The discourse of 'difference', on the contrary, considered it to be impossible to use the measure of 'equality' as conceptualized from the male point of view. Therefore, what was needed to overcome this partial view was the recovery of the qualities attached to women's 'difference' that were considered less valuable in men's discourses. 'Gender difference' then became the active selective strategy to cope with revaluing women. This debate, of course, is far from settled. The core of the problem lies in how these different approaches regard 'gender injustice' and 'gender equity'.

In her article 'Multiculturalism and Gender Equity: The U.S. "Difference" Debates Revisited',[9] Nancy Fraser says that this debate has translated itself into a more contemporary framework, yet one that still leaves the problematic unresolved. The two different viewpoints, she believes, offer important criticisms of each other. The feminist egalitarians rightfully seek the goals of equal participation and fair distribution of goods. On the other hand, while the feminism of difference has also discredited the undervalued conception of women, its goal has been to redefine cultural standards so that women can be viewed as their own self-descriptive agents. Fraser thinks that the only way to make this debate more fruitful would be to find a model referring both to socio-economic and cultural injustices within a dual framework of redistribution and recognition. Yet, the debates of the 1990s have done exactly the opposite, Fraser maintains, for the 'equality/difference debate was displaced', and 'the focus on "gender difference" gave way to a focus on "differences among women" inaugurating a new phase of feminist debate'.[10] During the 1990s there has been a new dimension to the thematizing of difference, when women began noticing that others were claiming differences of race, class and/or sexuality. The arena of difference now displayed more fully the multiple layers in which one confronts oneself with or against others. Fraser claims that this was a gain, because 'instead of focusing on gender alone, we focus on its relation to other cross-cutting axes of difference and subordination'.[11] What has happened is that women have thematized so extensively the problem of difference that other, non-gender differences have become important considerations, and are now being fruitfully examined within the various feminist discourses. Feminism has moved into a broader scenario of political struggles where its issues are not only those of gender but also race, ethnicity, nationality and sexuality. In short, because it has conceived a novel language of justice, feminism has become an appropriate model for thinking about all of these problematics.

However, Fraser thinks that the old debate has merely translated itself into new forms, for there remain, even in the 1990s, two opposite accounts of what is being sought. On the one hand, there are the 'anti-essentialists', who are sceptical about identity and difference, considering these to be discursive constructions. On the other hand, the 'multicultural groups' celebrate and promote all kinds of difference and group identity. Fraser is right that both groups fail to provide a model of democratic processes of identity claims that could enable democratic identities to be differentiated from anti-democratic ones. As such, neither approach provides a framework for just differences to be distinguished from unjust ones. Fraser also argues that both models have lost their interest in combining redistribution with recognition, concentrating only on the injustices of cultural valuation. In response, she claims that 'cultural differences can only be freely elaborated and democratically mediated on the basis of social equality'.[12]

In my opinion, however, what Fraser has correctly identified as this 'cultural turn' in feminist discussions does not necessarily lead to the avoidance of fair distribution and justice. On the contrary, the models of universalism (Fraser's included) that I want to propose for thematizing multiculturalism are broadly based on the Habermasian conception of discourse ethics. In my model, power is thematized insofar as institutions are a specific and important site within which cultural discourses of civil society arise. The empirical element supplied by this conception also gives rise to a dynamics of public opinion in which the (cultural) thematization of identities leads to broader notions of justice. It is true that the demands for recognition and fair distribution are always inter-twined, but as long as groups needing to be heard or accepted do not first conquer channels of communication to call attention to the way they have been treated, nothing will be solved.

This model views the subjects of deliberation as one of the most important elements of the process of recognition, for it is their descrip-tions of what is missing in their lives that make their claims meaningful and understandable to others. Therefore, the model has to deal with an institutional element, the public sphere, in order to supply a communi-cative pattern. It must also provide for some kind of theorizing about how the various publics construct their demands and the dynamics involved in the formation of public opinion. From this viewpoint, I believe that some elements from Fraser can be connected with the 'agonistic' dimension of performative claims for recognition drawn from recent readings of Hannah Arendt's work, particularly Bonnie Honig _Feminist Interpretations_, to create what I propose to call the 'femi-nist universal model', one which will provide a new methodology to deal with the issues of multiculturalism.

Fraser is concerned that the 'pluralist version' of feminism becomes problematic because it regards differences uncritically. This model 'balkanizes culture'[13] and offers no insight into the concept of power (as discussed below, in the context of Iris Marion Young's analysis). The theory of feminism I hope to formulate here, by contrast, develops a dynamic model in which power is present in the very struggles to draw the attention of the public to injustice and the lack of recognition. It also admits the possibility of failure to obtain such recognition, for empirical contingencies can lead to the appearance of groups that want to exclude others instead of accepting them.[14] This model also avoids the charge of being inconsistent – which Fraser makes against many theories of the so-called deconstructive antiessentialism[15] – by recognizing that some feminist theories do fail to focus on the dimension of justice, a focus that requires intersubjective agreement as to which feminist narratives best suit a new and wider understanding of democracy.

My claim is that, despite the fact that all these 'differences' between theoretical positions lead to problematic 'crossroads' or even dead ends, the empirical results of such narratives have become illocutionary forces in the public sphere. They have done so by redrawing the understanding of conceptions of justice and the good life. They have also fought to deconstruct the liberal understanding of 'public-private' frontiers be-cause it is there where one asserts the possibility of entering the perfor-mative space of the public. The 'anti-essentialist' narrative of Judith Butler is an important example. She suggests that 'identity categories tend to be instruments of regulatory regimes, whether as the normalizing categories of oppressive structures or as the rallying points for a liberatory contestation of that very oppression'.[16] Yet, Butler's narrative has had a profound impact on the consideration of gender in relation to conceptualizations of heterosexuality, challenging previous misconceptions that the two categories were necessarily linked and could be related to new forms of oppression. Despite her theoretical claims, in other words, Butler's work has opened the door for the possibility of deconstructing such fixed identities as 'women', 'heterosexuals', 'homosexuals'. Her theoretical writings can be viewed as performative interventions in the public sphere, as narratives that have offered wider conceptions of how things can be transformed precisely by such illocutionary 'interventions'.[17] The claim that it is impossible to accept agency and that performances can only be displayed as negative resistances paradoxically turns itself in the direction of an illocutionary intervention promoting positive social transformations. Thus Fraser argues that Butler has transformed conceptions of sexuality: 'much of Butler's subsequent work can be read as an extended answer to this question. She seeks to show how a subject that is "merely" a discursive position can indeed rewrite the script'.[18] In Butler's narrative we can also find traces of the intermingling of ontological and normative domains. Her discourse focuses on 'subjects' as beings through their discursive practices, practices which are, in turn, embedded in a web of power strategies. Through such contestatory performances as Butler's, culturally constructed reflexivity becomes aware of hegemonic power; one is able to rewrite the social script in the moment one publicly captures the attention of others. It is for this reason that Butler's normative conception can be described by Nancy Fraser as an exercise of 'critical capacities'.[19]

Public space is the arena where all discourses have to compete for the acceptance of a new interpretation criticizing previous ways in which people understood themselves. The normative element, therefore, has always to be present in order to overcome the lack of criticism of narrow conceptions of cultural and discursive identities. The cultural dynamics established when a narrative is successful produce a kind of transformational energy that moulds subjectivities and provides collective images that shape the cultural self-understanding of society and the self (including, of course, the unconscious contents of those self-conceptions). This new viewpoint links the cultural function of narratives (storytelling) to its power to affect and change individuals, and to intervene in other cultural practices. As agents of cultural contact, narratives work across the boundaries of their own culture, as well as of those cultures that incorporate them. They engage public opinion in a continual process of dissolving, reshaping, expanding or transgressing boundaries that have been drawn at the various levels of cultural socialization. These transformations of boundaries are determined by the histories of the new self-understandings of cultural communities as well as those of individuals.

The shift towards a cultural paradigm does not necessarily leads to the exclusion of the problematic of 'social equality'. A more normatively sensitive cultural model provides an explanation of the dynamics of communication and the interaction of different groups that strive for recognition of their own notions about what is lacking in order to impart justice. These claims are public, and they are always related to how discourses appeal to justice. Whether these discourses are accepted or not depends on the normative judgements of public opinion and on the power and imagination with which a group calls for the attention of other groups and articulates its need for integration.

In her article 'From Redistribution to Recognition? Dilemmas of Justice in a "Post-Socialist Age" ',[20] Fraser acknowledges that recognition is a term that has now been adopted by virtually any kind of project that deals with justice. She insists, however, that recognition must be coupled with distribution, for 'only by articulating [both, can] we arrive at a critical-theoretical framework that is adequate to the demands of our age'. By thinking of recognition within a narrow conception of cultural and symbolic content, she sees redistribution and recognition as having different goals. Recognition relates to difference, she says, because the injustice that promotes the claim for recognition refers to patterns of representation, interpretation and communication. On the other hand, she argues, redistribution strives for equality, for it is in that universal arena that money and power are the subjects of injustice. Although Fraser claims that the distinction between these two different kinds of injustice is only analytical – for they are always intertwined – she believes that, on an empirical level, claims for difference and equality have arrived at opposing goals, thus making it difficult not to take one side or the other, either the cultural claim for recognition or the institutional claim for equality and redistribution.

In my view, however, the problem is less real than conceptual. Fraser's conception of the cultural and symbolic dimensions of social life is too narrow. While she acknowledges that 'even the most material economic institutions have a constitutive, irreducible cultural dimension',[21] she insists on making an analytical distinction so that she can focus on two very different kinds of solution for two different problems. I would like to argue in exactly the opposite way, that there is no possibility for change in redistributive remedies unless there is an institutional ground where these claims are exposed. This is particularly relevant for the multicultural post-traditional societies that are now dealing with how to integrate the various groups and cultures striving for some kind of recognition.

In my view, the key to overcoming Fraser's false separation of recognition and redistribution lies in the need to define the universal dimension of the grounds for recognition. Only when one accepts that the universality of the claim for recognition lies in seeking the acceptance of others can one finally integrate the issues of redistribution into a much more complex scheme, and create the moral textures – the different kinds of solidarity, for example – that relate to this broader cultural framework. Therefore, the narratives that appeal for recognition can be successful only when the elements that are included in their cultural and symbolic content seem to provide an intersubjective conception of 'we'. However, this conception of the 'we' must not be understood as the homogeneous conception of identity. The normative 'we' that is at the basis of this formulation (which constitutes the act of founding) must be differentiated from the declarative, factual 'we' (the addressee of the obligations to obey the rules, which always stands in relation to others).[22] Between these two dimensions in which the 'we' is understood, there is always a space – a permanent tension – that allows us to thematize what is heterogeneous, other, different, incongruent, unfamiliar.[23] This normative conception of universality is a falsifiable concept that accepts the exclusionary character of given historical articulations of its universality, and that also relates to the possibility of extending and rendering 'substantive' new notions of universality. In providing a better normative understanding of who we are, for example, the historical and critical reframing of 'gender' has been acknowledged as a social construct, not an essence of human beings. 'Race' has also been reinterpreted as a social construct. The relations of 'sex' to heterosexuality have also played as two sides of the same social construct. These issues have now been reinterpreted as historical and social categories: they were created because of specific social arrangements; they have been demonstrated not to be facts of nature.[24]

The term 'universalist' that I wish to develop here, in fact, must be considered in its cultural and symbolic meaning, that is to say, as a code that narrates a wider conception of a 'we' that comprehends various groups, their differences as well as their relatedness and similarities. This symbolic status means that universalism is an open-ended ideal that is falsifiable through the responsive reformulations that challenge, from the outside, its previous, narrower meanings. The normative 'we' functions as a transcendent ethical imperative that is able to produce new meanings. The broader justice that ensues would reside in the ever new appropriation of how the principles of democracy should be understood. This kind of universalistic approach links self-conceptions with competing notions of justice which are clearly connected to a larger interpretation of human beings and their needs. These needs are historically situated, and it is always possible to envision a different viewpoint, a better understanding of how things should be changed and where to expand self-descriptions. Women changed not only themselves, but other groups, other self-understandings. Women's narratives revealed the partiality of the account of how things were when they were 'told' by a previous narrative.

Deconstructive strategies are necessary tools, once one understands the cultural dimension of the construction of historically contingent social and personal identities. They need some kind of normative standard in order to compensate for the ontological weight of the conception of narratives as merely 'fictitious'. This normative and transformative ground should be present when recognition is linked to claims for a better notion of justice and the specific forms of solidarity that are needed to change earlier world-views.[25]

A Multicultural Model of Difference

Contrary to some versions of feminism that consider equality as the cornerstone for the reconfiguration and transformation of the social and political reality of contemporary life, Iris Marion Young believes that the concept of justice derived from these ideas must be transformed, and that this seems possible only from the standpoint of the struggle for difference itself, which offers a fundamentally heterogeneous model of the public sphere.[26] This implies a reconceptualization of the idea of equality. The 'assimilationist' models, with their category of 'equality', believe that everyone can be treated the same, regardless of such distinctions as race, gender and economic situation. Young, on the other hand, believes that both group participation and inclusion require differentiated treatment.

Young shares a concern with other feminists when she states that the assimilationist model of equality, while important for emancipatory movements, has also been a cover for one group's power over others. The assimilationist conception of difference is viewed as discriminatory, for it is seen only as inferiority. Drawing from the experiences of social groups in the United States who have conceived their differences as being valuable, Young concludes that a more political model may combat the hypostatizing atavism of the assimilationist notion of equality. She takes the most concrete experiences of feminism and vindicates the feminism of difference, which has maintained that feminine values are a much more affirmative way to achieve the projection of identity and the struggle for recognition. I shall focus my criticism on this example.

The argument that 'assimilationist' equality is polluted by shades of masculine dominion holds that feminine values, such as caring and relatedness, were purged from the historical culture which wove together the feminine and the masculine. I would argue, however, that considering masculine and feminine as completely differentiated forms oversimplifies these concepts, which are the result of a historical inter-action of social subjects and for this reason cannot be entirely separated, despite the empirical benefits of the many efforts that have been made to extract the feminine from its masculine deformations. In psychologi-cal theories, for example, different functions of the masculine and femi-nine are located in the same subject, and interpretations of these 'voices' in the unconscious have varied a great deal according to theories that give more weight to the masculine (Freud), to the feminine (Jung) or to both (Lacan).[27] This dichotomy also seems reductionist considered on a strictly hermeneutical level, where we can never achieve total interpre-tative 'purity'. Literature provides many examples of characters con-ceived by a man but with the spirit of a woman, among the best known being *Madame Bovary*. Flaubert's famous response on being questioned about the origin of the novel's central character Madame Bovary, 'c'est moi', was meant to shock the literary intelligentsia of his time. But it also reveals the extent to which he identified himself in his portrayal of the depth and sensitivity of a woman. There are many contrasting examples that are equally compelling, such as *Hadrian's Memoirs*, by Marguerite de Yourcenar, who uses a first-person narrative for her forceful account of the Roman emperor and his meditations.

The real problem with the 'difference' outlook, however, goes bey-ond these claims, to the fundamental criticism that this model does not understand the interrelationship between culture, the symbolic order and the interaction of groups on collective political grounds. The value of differences must be asserted in front of others, not only others who are like oneself but others who, precisely because of their difference, matter to one. This is why the quest for identity does not depend simply on showing others one's personal and specific features. This problem-atic was clearly described by Hegel, and Mead has made a vital contri-bution with his theory of simultaneous socialization and individuation. Axel Honneth's book *The Struggle for Recognition* (discussed in chapter 7 above) describes these two efforts and shows how important the other is to the definition of the self. Not only externally, but internally too, one is frequently confronting, rejecting or accepting others, and this perma-nent dialogue with others is what constitutes the basic process of a quest for identity.

The idea that separatism stimulates plurality is also questionable. The separatist practices of some groups do not seem to promote spaces open for dialogue, but rather, enclaves or 'monads that dichotomize the relationship between genders. The affirmative claims of difference have been worked out on a rather different level. Claims for recognition have gained some credibility and acknowledgement from others be-cause everyone is capable of transforming previous ways of thinking, of talking, and of reflecting on who one is. Once one understands how valuable it is to accept those features that once were thought to pertain only to others, one undergoes a reordering of beliefs and world-views. The dominant aesthetic conception of body, dress and hairstyle, for example, changed dramatically in the 1960s, when the affirmative performances of African-Americans provided a powerful discourse of self-presentation – 'black is beautiful' – producing a shift in the projected images of their specific features that became fashionable and provided a compelling new aesthetic pattern for others. The appearance of 'Afro' hairstyles, and the wearing of certain kinds of jewellery and clothes were some of the external features of a generalized and more enriched cultural self-fashioning of 'freedom' in the 1960s.

Transformations entail a 'fusion of horizons', a new and novel way of seeing the other that also becomes a new way of understanding oneself. Recognition is a struggle, a struggle that must be fought in relation to others and in the permanent tension of changing prejudice and transforming the symbolic order. This battle plays a major role in how one uses institutionalized channels of communicating with others, and how one redefines the limits on traditional views, enlarging one's own understanding of values and 'changing the rules'.[28] Dialogue is not only a means of showing what makes one different, but also of showing that those differences are an important part of what should be regarded as worthy. Solidarity enters here because it is through others that one can define one's own identities, and no solidarity is possible if the discourse does not form a bridge to the other's understanding of what are considered to be worthy features and needs of human beings. Recognition, in this sense, is a performative process of acquiring identity.

I also believe that an exclusive emphasis on heterogeneity blurs the complexity of social interaction between groups. Not all differences are good, and a great many separatists are racist, anti-Semitic or xenophobic, portraying their differences as superiorities. A post-traditional view of dialogue between different groups with different traditions should allow one reflexively to select what part of the other world-view would enable one to enhance understanding oneself. One cannot accept the simplified claim that every universalist moral value is suspicious; nor can one accept uncritically the claim that any tradition can be rejected without further examination. A model based only on difference might lead one to believe that any difference is as good as any other; if so, one would deny oneself the means to reach a partial consensus on how everyone can live a better life and be respected by others.[29]

The most difficult part of this critique of a theory of difference is, perhaps, the necessity to break with the refusal, which has become quite common, to accept that moral and ethical evaluations presuppose normative standards, value judgements regarding contrasts, and a non-prejudiced awareness that all cultures possess not only positive but negative aspects. As the notion of transcontextual values of ethical and moral judgement disappears, it is assumed that achievements are morally equal among all cultures and, therefore, that there must be a certain blind respect on the grounds that any value is as good as any other. This can become dangerous. If struggles for recognition attempt to define a broader notion of justice, one must submit one's claims to some kind of public agreement on what needs to be done institutionally and collectively to reconfigure the parts of the 'official story' that are in need of being retold. This cannot be done unless one fully explores the diverse institutional channels of communication and interaction in order to attract the attention of others and explain why a traditional view of justice must be changed.

It is true, of course, that many groups in the United States[30] have had their identities reinforced through the radical vindication of their differences. In these struggles, however, there has been a strong mobilization of public opinion through which other groups have argued against injustice and have done so, not only based on differences, but from the conviction that they themselves have not been treated as real human beings. Frantz Fanon's book *The Wretched of the Earth*[31] brought clearly into focus how oppressed cultures tend to regard themselves as less valuable. The impact of the book on the 1960s (especially on the Black Power Movement) and 1970s was extraordinary, because oppressed groups became aware that their first task was to value their own differences and then to convince others to do so, too. But racially oppressed groups in the United States have also worked not only to reclaim an image of worthiness but also to defend it on a universal basis.[32] Today, Martin Luther King is a hero, not only for African-Americans in the United States but for people the world over. He has become an icon symbolizing the most valuable characteristics of human beings. As an example for all democratic cultures, King's views represent not just the struggle of African-Americans but the best teachings on the struggle for recognition of human rights and equality, and for the full achievement of universal justice. (See also the Conclusion below, in which I discuss King in the context of the relevance of my model to the black public sphere.)

Cultures may co-exist because they are granted respect-as-tolerance, but it is only through public discussion that other kinds of respect can gain general attention and stimulate solidary responses from other groups. I have already discussed what is at stake when one submits interpretations of how to improve on reconfigurations of standards of administration of justice. Standards of value and critical judgements of them must be contrasted. Both Iris Young and Charles Taylor wish to ground their models of difference without elaborating a critical analysis of different kinds of difference. It is not enough for the preservation of one culture just to accept its existence. Rather, I am compelled to suggest that by preserving it one gains a better insight of who one is. Young's theory of difference, like Taylor's position, can be dangerously close to that of some conservative politicians who, arguing in favour of difference, claim that immigrants erode 'native' cultures. There are some groups that claim their difference and do not wish to be integrated, and there are many who want others to be excluded. That is why normative standards are always needed. Justice demands the inclusion of larger groups, not the exclusion or disappearance of some cultures. Because cultures are complex and heterogeneous, moreover, a culture in its totality cannot be accepted without critical examination, for good and bad elements exist side by side. The dynamics between respect as esteem and respect as tolerance are always at issue in a public debate, offering the possibility of openly discussing the contrasts among various cultures. 'Neutrality', which both the feminism of difference and the politics of difference see as a trap concealing privatism, runs the risk of being placed at the opposite pole of the critical liberal tradition, for it is no longer possible to find a transcontextual basis from which to defend the qualities of certain ways of life if they are all equal. Perhaps a clue can be found in the context of 'cultural rights' as individual prerogatives of the citizen, but it is impossible to view this dimension without the acceptance of some normative bases that already exist in contemporary democracies. This is where 'neutral' tolerance becomes a useful tool in providing an acceptance of diversity, without having to impose on others.

Cultures may survive or not, depending on the capacity for transformation which springs from their critical vision and the permanent revision of their legacy, as well as from their utopian projections. It is to this challenge of 'possible horizons of experience' that Ricoeur appeals.[33] However, this challenge, as Habermas points out,[34] cannot come only from the demarcation of an identity of one's own with respect to other identities and cultures. Rather, it must prove itself, as an identity, by undertaking a dialogue of recognition in its interaction with other cultures.

Universalist Feminism

Seyla Benhabib developed her concept of the public sphere from Habermas' idea of discourse ethics. As a feminist, however, she assumed the need to be cautious about the suppositions imposed by liberal theories and procedural ethics regarding public and private spaces and about how the issues of the good can be integrated into the collective space of discussion. Her enlarged conception of public space helps avoid deciding on aprioristic bases which issues are related to the public interest and which are not. Rather, discussion itself guides the contextualized viewpoints of the 'concrete others' into a process of broadening notions of justice, also leading to the possibility that some notions of the good can translate themselves into a political content, as the famous slogan of the women's movement showed by claiming that 'the personal is political'. In her book *Situating the Self: Gender, Community and Postmodernism in Contemporary Ethics*,[35] Benhabib develops a substantive category for the idea of public deliberation and recognition – the 'concrete other'. Her strategy is to use Carol Gilligan's findings that women as moral subjects, rather than relating to an abstract model of deliberation, face moral dilemmas through their concern and sense of the importance of their relation to a concrete other. Through this dimension of the importance of the representativeness of the subject of deliberation, the ideas of recognition and equality are reconfigured in a different sense from that of an abstract autonomy derived from the Kantian tradition, since self-determination is now linked to self-realization. The 'concrete other' may be understood as a criterion that is based simultaneously on normative and expressive validity. That is why, in this interpretation of autonomy and its relationship to the field of expressive validity, issues about the good life are not banned from the public interest; rather, the concrete meanings that allow one to choose ways of self-realization within an interpretative hermeneutics of needs are interwoven. Benhabib shows how universalist feminism argues that recognition is a basic form of solidarity, and that justice cannot come from a strict a priori division between the interests of public life and the projects of private life. Only through the process of public deliberation can one understand why some issues of the good life are linked to public interest, or why there is a need to expose the incongruity of considering some problems only as private dilemmas.

Benhabib also uses Hannah Arendt's theoretical resources to recover her main insights through a feminist reinterpretation. One can say that Benhabib is one of the few feminists who, instead of focusing exclusively on Arendt's lack of interest in issues relating to women, has tried to make use of her legacy to find novel ways of approaching the problematics of women and the public sphere. In this way, Benhabib opens up a new path for feminist hermeneutics, one in which the recognition of theoretical absences opens up the possibility of tracing the needs which any personal and collective struggle entails. This new hermeneutical method – searching through silences and redirecting them towards a new viewpoint – refracts the problems of the private lives of women into a public discourse about the interpretation of needs.

Much criticism has arisen about the Habermasian framework from which Benhabib recovers Arendt. Her critics have acknowledged the originality and creativity of her interpretation. Dana Villa, for example, suggests that Benhabib's recovery of Arendt via Kant's description of the 'specific validity of taste judgements' is 'ingenious insofar as it manages to combine Arendt's emphasis on plurality, deliberation, and exchange of opinion with the normative power of Kantian universalism'.[36] However, argues Villa, 'Benhabib's redemption of the deliberative dimension of Arendt's political theory comes at the expense of the initiatory or performative dimension'.[37] In a similar fashion, Bonnie Honig argues that Benhabib has reduced 'Arendt for feminism by excising agonism from her thought'; by juxtaposing agonism and 'associationism', she suggests, Benhabib has found two alternative 'models of public space'.[38] Both of these criticisms suggest that Benhabib's approach loses sight of what is 'unique' in Arendt's conception of the public sphere as a 'worldly' scenario of performance or agonistic intervention.

I would suggest, in fact, that it is not necessary to rescue Arendt from her agonistic model of the public sphere. Once it is reconnected to her conception of storytelling it can be reinterpreted as a source of plurality and individuality without losing its connection to normative and moral insights. According to Arendt's definition of the heroic narrative, the 'hero the story discloses needs no heroic qualities'.

> The connotation of courage, which we feel to be an indispensable quality of the hero, is in fact already present in a willingness to act and speak at all, to insert one's self into the world and begin a story of one's own. And this courage is not necessarily or even primarily related to a willingness to suffer the consequences; courage and even boldness are already present in leaving one's private place and showing who one is, in disclosing and exposing one's self.[39]

There are, in fact, other feminists, like Honig, who defend Arendt's 'agonistic and performative politics' because 'identity is the performative production not the expressive condition or essence of action'.[40] In this sense, performance in the public sphere is what makes possible an act of producing a 'we', the 'who's' of action. These dynamics, in turn, not only engender identities but tie them to their very action in the public and make them become fluid, renovated, transformed and unstable. In Honig's view, there is no 'self' prior or apart from action.[41] There is a second feature which also seems relevant to me in Honig's defence of Arendt's agonism, namely, her creative interpretation of Arendt's artificial boundaries of 'public/private'. 'What if we took Arendt's own irresistibly lodged public/private distinction to be a line drawn in the sand, itself an illicit constative, a constituting mark or text, calling out agonistically to be contested, augmented and amended?'[42] The 'private realm' would be a cultural space to be redrawn, to be contested, because the distinction of 'public and private is seen as the performative product of political struggle'.[43] And, I may add, this is exactly what feminism has empirically achieved. Honig's narrative rescues Arendt in a cultural frame where action is opened as a site of performances and illocutionary interventions. Her agonistic interpretation of Arendt's politics does not, moreover, lead to the individualistic performances of an aestheticized view, for she stresses that performances are a 'kind of action in concert', of 'shared and public practices', that open up and create 'founding new spaces of politics and individuation'.[44] For Honig, Arendt's agonism reveals the characteristic of performances as struggles for recognition which 'may be read as a struggle for individuation, for emergence as a distinct self'.[45]

However, Honig's theory is not clear on how association and agonism are related.[46] Her agonism does not explain how 'resistance' can lead to institutional transformation. Her model fails to provide a criterion for judging what kinds of identities are emancipatory and what kinds are exclusionary.[47]

I would like to return to Benhabib's defence of Arendt's associationism, to what Benhabib calls her 'new reading of the salons' as a model of the public sphere. As discussed in chapter 3 above, the salons were possible not, as Honig argues, because of a permissive 'patriarchal power', or because 'the salons hosted by women were owned by temporarily absent fathers and husbands',[48] but rather, as Arendt herself claimed, because within salons the boundaries between public/private were erased. Evidence for this can be found in the stories of how salons appeared as spaces crowded with women's interventions that eroded dramatically 'patriarchal power'. The story of Rahel Varnhagen recounted by Arendt herself is the best example. Indeed, men felt so threatened by salon socialites that they sought to close those spaces, and typically they succeeded. Joan Landes clearly exposes the attacks on these eroding spaces.

> Disgruntled members of the traditional aristocracy accused the salons of being merely brothels. They linked illicit love, the reign of women, and the breakdown of traditional social stratification. . . . The public role of women, and the ideal of leisure it represented, was thought to corrupt society. . . . Antifeminists denounced the effeminates (of their own class) who adopted the refinement and leisure ethic of women, abandoning their military professions and thus weakening the state. . . . The metaphor of 'the reign of women' signified the corruption of society at its heights. . . . The isolation of woman in the home was offered as a way to preserve the world from feminization and a way of saving individual women from the corruptions of *le monde*.[49]

To make Benhabib's associationist model of the salons a target of adverse criticism does not acknowledge that salons were not only places of contestation but also of emancipation. Therefore, Honig is mistaken to ignore the salons' emancipatory potential as emerging public places designed by women. The idea that salons were only sites of uncontested patriarchal power contradicts the fact that they were also places of new forms of socialization. Benhabib is right in recovering the concerted dimension of action, which relates to the public sphere as being also a space of emancipation. Thus, if Honig is right in accusing Benhabib of erasing the agonistic dimension of action, her failure is that she does not provide an account of how individual and collective performances stimulate institutional transformation in the public sphere.

Benhabib is right when she focuses on Arendt's conception of the social, where 'the constant struggle and tension between "equality" and "difference", as conceptualized by Arendt in both the social and the political domains, is characteristic of modernity'.[50] Benhabib continues her analysis on the grounds that 'distinction' and 'difference' in Arendt's social and cultural understanding cannot be only individual, for they 'always concern the identities and social positions of collectivities'.[51] Social, in this sense, 'signifies _civic and associational society_'.[52] On the other hand, 'politics' is always concerned with 'plurality, difference, perspectivality'.[53] However, Benhabib argues, it is not until Arendt is able to propose the concept of 'human plurality' at the centre of the experience of 'wordliness' that she finally overcomes Heidegger's 'Existenz philosophy' and gives place to her finished elaboration of action and identity in the category of 'world'.[54] Furthermore, in her attempt to depart from existential phenomenology, argues Benhabib, Arendt creates an empirical view of a 'sociology of associations' stimulated by her interpretation of Tocqueville.[55] Thus, the 'dialectics of equality and difference' are reconfigured as the narrative of the 'emergence of modern civil society'.[56] Therefore, it is through connecting Arendt to Tocqueville and in developing insight into the empirical evidences found in Arendt's work that Benhabib's effort can be found to draw a space for associationism in the public sphere. From this viewpoint, it can be inferred that it is not Habermas' idea of 'consensus' that plays a significant role in Benhabib's concern with the normative dimension but Tocqueville's idea of democratic institutions. Thus, for Benhabib, the last step should be to recover Arendt, not in the light of a new scientific effort but, rather, in her 'new narrative'. The normative dimension can be traced through Arendt's conception of storytelling: 'Historiography originates with the human desire to overcome oblivion and nothingness; it is the attempt to save, in the face of the fragility of human affairs and the inescapability of death, something "which is even more than remembrance" '.[57]

In this chapter, I have tried to demonstrate the relevance of feminist narratives to the problematic of multiculturalism. I have suggested that in the variety of their approaches they have described the public sphere as an arena of multiple foci protecting the diversity of points of view (Fraser) by highlighting the performative dimension of action (Honig) in a manner that seeks to bring to light a concept of 'mutuality and co-operation' (Benhabib) in matters of general interest. In each of these different approaches the public sphere plays a major role. It is important to stress that feminist discourses do not legislate; rather, they exert influence, transform public opinion, recompose views of life, and even allow legal ways out to be visualized. Once their illocutionary character is manifest, they can exert a positive influence on the broader 'public' involved in legislative process. Yet only if one emphasizes that illocutionary public understandings of 'different' groups are initially differentiated from the institutional sphere of law, can one realize the extent to which it is the cultural dynamics of civil society and its discourses[58] that first promote new and better interpretations of justice.

Conclusion

Having reached the final stage of this exploration of women's narratives, I would now like to offer a concluding assessment of the general approach to their struggles for identity. That women's struggles for recognition are not, in fact, only struggles for inclusion, but also efforts towards major cultural transformation, constitutes the main thesis of this book. To the degree that I have been successful in demonstrating this thesis, the model of women's illocutionary action in the public sphere can serve as an appropriate model for theorizing about other kinds of social movement, movements which have responded to other kinds of exclusion.

In drawing these implications, I will relate my model to Jean Cohen and Andrew Arato's discussion, in *Civil Society and Political Theory*, of the relation between social movements and civil society, one of the most important thematizations of this issue.[1] By problematizing social movements, Cohen and Arato show that the historical transformation of democratic institutions can provide an empirical demonstration that the existence of the normative public sphere does, indeed, allow for fundamental social change. Such movements, they argue, 'constitute the dynamic element in processes that might realize the positive potentials of modern civil societies'.[2] What is new about such processes, in their view, is the way in which they allow participants to engage in a continuous process of self-understanding, one which allows them simultaneously to search for novel ways of articulating contemporary claims with long-standing democratic promises and institutions: 'It implies continuity with the utopian perspective of an open horizon that is worth preserving (even if this is hotly contested) in the institutions, norms, and political cultures of contemporary civil societies, and transformation by means of critically assessing what is missing'.[3] They argue that the 'central question' for social movements 'is whether and in what way this theme [of continuity] has been connected to new identities, forms of organization, and scenarios of conflict'.[4]

The model of women's narrative interventions in the public sphere can offer answers to this central question about social movements. My argument has been that women's ability to conquer public opinion is based on the way they have narrated their identity as 'open', 'self-reflexive', and 'universal'. If, as I have tried to show, these features were performed as deconstructions of male notions of universality, these performances can be used to understand how other social movements have succeeded by narrating a similar dialectic between particularity and universality. Such a negotiation is precisely what Houston A. Baker, Jr, articulates in his study of the black public sphere published in 1995. Referring to white Americans' construction of black culture as antithetical to the public sphere – 'as an irrational, illiterate, owned, nonbourgeois community of chattel'[5] – Baker suggests that 'it is exactly because black Americans have so aptly read this flip side that they are attracted to a historically imagined "better time" of reason'.[6] Baker insists that this connection was achieved, moreover, via the very same kinds of public aesthetic interventions I have stressed here. 'Black cultural work', he writes, 'can be conceived as ceaselessly inventing its own modernity'.[7]

> In the concrete instance of southern Jim Crow legality, for example, it had to fashion a voice, songs, articulations, conversions of wish into politics. This creative agency enabled hundreds of thousands of black men, women, and children to gain access to basic public accommodations. The black civil rights struggle, and particularly during the decade from 1955–1965, exemplifies the active working of the imagination of a subaltern, black American counterpublic.[8]

For Baker, in other words, it is the aesthetic creativity of action that allowed continuity to be established – between newly emerging black identity and traditional American democratic culture and institutions – that allowed it, in my terms, to achieve illocutionary force. Black Americans were 'drawn to the possibilities of structurally and affectively transforming the founding notion of the bourgeois public sphere into an expressive and empowering self-fashioning'.[9]

In this contemporary intellectual narration of earlier movement narratives, there is not only empirical but theoretical confirmation of the interconnections between the moral and aesthetic spheres which I have insisted upon throughout this book. Just as women's projects of group identity contested the partialized universality of identity, so, Baker writes, did the 'performances' of Martin Luther King simultaneously appeal to black identity and to an enlarged, less partial universality. King's narratives were the 'agency of civil rights and the movement's efforts to recapture and recode all existing American arrangements of publicness'.[10] Much as I have described the great creative achievements of feminist narratives, Baker writes how King was able to 'convert the tortuous, complex, heterogeneous lines and images of United States race relations into a strategically and brilliantly articulated program of American social reform that led directly to a new and modern black publicity in America'.[11] This interweaving of the particular and the universal depended on King's ability to enter the moral sphere via the aesthetic. Baker writes that 'King reclaimed those imaginary racial traits of Uncle Tom': by 'dramatically and performatively refigur[ing] them', he 'metaphysically' transformed them into 'the terms of will, daring, spirit and institutional strengths of a new black public sphere'. In doing so, King 'brought this sphere to an intense consciousness of the immediate necessity to achieve full citizenship rights now, in this world'.[12]

While King made by far the most powerful illocutionary intervention into the American public sphere, other contemporary narrators of the black public sphere show that the same theoretical apparatus can be applied to African-American activists of very different persuasions. In her revealing study of the immensely influential autobiography of Malcolm X, for example, Manthia Diawara explores how the black leader and Alex Haley (co-author of the autobiography) succeeded in their effort to 'transform an intimate and personal story into a public and conversionist essay'.[13] On the one hand, she recounts how the autobiography related to, and helped reconstruct, the particularities of African-American identity – 'Black structures of feeling'.[14] On the other hand, she finds in the autobiography a strongly moral and universal emphasis which also originates in the aesthetic domain. Pointing to what she calls 'Malcolm's cosmopolitan artistic sensibility', she describes the young Malcolm Little (his original name) as 'a flâneur looking for modernism in the ballrooms, bars and streets frequented by the world's greatest and hippest musicians'.[15] Indeed, Diawara traces the universalizing, emancipatory implications of the autobiography – the tale of personal _Bildung_ that gave the book its public and political impact – to an aesthetic innovation. 'Malcolm X makes an important contribution to the art of autobiography', she writes, 'through his use of alienation, a trope which enables him to distance himself from Detroit Red [Malcolm's earlier persona] as another person in the text'.[16] The result of this aesthetic innovation was that the mature Malcolm, who embraced Islam and assumed the name Hajj Malik El-Shabazz, could produce 'an autobiographical account that sounds like a sermon'.[17]

To return to the level of social theory, it is clear that Cohen and

Arato's critical appraisal of earlier social movement literature gains strength from their insistence that inclusion into the public sphere (a moral event) is tied to the construction of new identities, a construction that, in my terms, suggests an aesthetic performance. Cohen and Arato describe Charles Tilly's historical work, for example, as having demonstrated 'that the transformation of the loci of power and the corresponding changes in forms of collective action presuppose the creation of new meanings, new organizations, new identities, and a social space (namely, civil society) in which these can appear'.[18] They read Tilly's empirical writings, in other words, as showing how social actors have acquired reflexivity in the construction of their identities in the space of a 'nonstrategic' action. At the same time, however, they observe that Tilly himself refuses to include 'identity politics' in his own theory. Because Tilly can refer only to strategies of social inclusion, his paradigm cannot clarify what Cohen and Arato call the 'politics of influence'. It is the more subjective medium of influence, tied to the cultural and symbolical contestation of meanings, which is at stake when social inclusion and personal identity transformation are viewed as two sides of the same historical process.

In their review of Alain Touraine's social movement theory, by contrast, Cohen and Arato argue that the latter paradigm focuses not only on the affirmation of group identities but also on the formal elements attached to them – 'the formal principle of an equal chance for all to participate in group processes through which identities are formed, and . . . have become self-reflective regarding the social processes of identity formation'.[19] Drawing an important conclusion from the Tourainean approach, they suggest that the 'creation of identity' also involves 'social conflict around the reinterpretation of norms, the creation of new meanings, and a challenge to the social construction of the very boundaries between public, private, and political domains of action'.[20] The idea that social actors are not only searching for material transformations in relation to money and power, but that they also employ influence to draw new ways to understand 'solidarity' and 'social relations' lends support to my thesis that social movements make 'altruistic' contributions even while engaging in struggles for recognition. My discussions of women's narratives have shown that Cohen and Arato are surely correct when they emphasize the normative contents of organized social action, insisting that 'associations are treated not as interest groups but as ends in themselves'.[21] My illocutionary model of women's emancipation provides both philosophical and empirical support for their thesis that 'autonomous, voluntary, and indigenous associations within civil society, using and expanding public discourse and public spaces for discourse, are the differentia specifica of contemporary social movements'.[22]

This analysis of Cohen and Arato's critical review of social movement theory leads back to Habermas, and to one final consideration of
what his contributions to the thematization of social movements might
be. Cohen and Arato view Habermas' understanding of action and self-
reflexiveness as two sides of his theory of communicative action, and
they suggest that the latter, at least in principle, can provide a broad
framework within which a variety of different kinds of social movement, and theoretical approaches to them, can be placed. Highlighting
the manner in which Habermas has appropriated Kenneth Burke's
conception of 'dramaturgical action', they suggest that 'this action involves the purposeful and expressive fabrication and disclosure of
one's subjectivity (feelings, desires, experiences, identity) to a set of
others who constitute a public'.[23] However, because the ontological
status of dramaturgy is fixed and given, Cohen and Arato worry that, as
in the early work of Erving Goffman, this approach can easily become
merely strategic or even cynical in its understanding of social action. In
order to sustain the dimension of normativity, they incorporate into
their new critical paradigm Neil Smelser's conception of normatively
oriented social movements.[24]

Yet, while Cohen and Arato believe that Habermas' communicative
action theory is by no means incompatible with an emphasis on creativity and signification, they are concerned about the dualistic tendencies
of his theoretical model. They distance themselves, for example, from
the manner in which Habermas divides social movements into 'traditionalist' ones that emphasize identity claims, and thus what he sees as
their inherent particularity, with those that are 'integrationist' and
universalizing and which, in his view, develop further the potential of
modernity and democracy as the true inheritors of the bourgeois public
sphere.[25] Cohen and Arato link this inability to see the emancipatory
and public role of identity claims with Habermas' sharp division between system and lifeworld, a separation that makes it impossible for
him to translate the subjectively oriented categories of lifeworld 'into a
full-fledged conceptualization of civil and political society'.[26] What Cohen
and Arato conclude – rightly, in my view – is that Habermas' analysis of
movements does not do justice to the potentials of his theory. To correct
this failure, they introduce the category of social movement 'associations' in order to refer to the dimensions of social movements that aim
at cultural reproduction, social integration and socialization. While this
proposal is welcome, it does not address the challenge of conceptualizing the cultural moment inside communicative action theory itself.
Precisely because the cultural contestation of meaning is a struggle in
which every social movement is intensively engaged, the philosophical
understanding of this cultural moment is absolutely necessary if a
communicative theory of public action is to succeed. What for Cohen

and Arato is Habermas' failure to establish a mediation between system and lifeworld has been redefined in this book as Habermas' failure to provide cultural grounding for his theory. Only by exploring how validity spheres communicate and interact with one another, I have argued, can one fully understand what a decentred notion of reason entails. Only from a cultural-communicative viewpoint can the public use of reason in both its agonistic and consensual aspects be understood. Focusing on the manner in which women's narratives expanded public subjectivity, I have shown how an analytical approach to the cultural moment of communicative action can cast light on just what 'institutional transformation' involves. In this way, I have aimed to show how and why the bourgeois public sphere has always carried such a great potential for reconfiguration, and how women's illocutionary interventions into this sphere could succeed in reconceptualizing its male particularity just as the illocutionary interventions of African-Americans were able to reconfigure its racial restrictions.[27]

If I have accomplished the tasks I have set myself in this book, I will have succeeded in presenting a model that provides a detailed account of how social movements enlarge, expand and transform democratic institutions by challenging previous collective meanings and self-representations. Cohen and Arato have developed an extensive criticism of the failure of previous approaches to understand that the emancipatory potential of social movements depends on mediations between system and lifeworld. They have not, however, thematized the cultural space in which this mediation takes place, an arena where societies can change their self-understandings precisely because moral, aesthetic and political issues are intertwined. Exposing different dimensions of what might be called this re-signifying aspect of social movements, I have tried to conceptualize the missing cultural dimension of illocutionary action. Habermas' failure to conceive the dynamic and complex ways in which issues of the good life and justice are interrelated can be overcome, I have argued, only if a much more cultural understanding of communicative action is introduced. The basic error in Habermas' dualistic conception of system and lifeworld stems from its inability to conceptualize the mediation between spheres that is provided by the cultural domain, where actions reveal their connection to communicative reason in a decentred way. By publicly thematizing their new identity projects, feminists have created mediations between particularistic and universal claims. By showing how societies had conceptualized the sphere of justice as deliberately separate from issues of the good life, they have revealed the restricted manner in which the political has been understood – as if it were communicatively unrelated to the moral and expressive domains. By contesting the spaces where 'private/public' meanings located differences, feminists have shown that these spaces and their boundaries cannot be taken as given facts but must be seen as arenas for re-signification. Social movements need to contest the spaces in which they can appear in order to be able to attract the attention of others, and in doing so they also contribute in concrete ways to designing the institutional changes they would like to effect. The restrictions and inequalities that have generated norms, interpreted traditions, and constructed identities all have cultural contents, the 'falsification' of which is a challenge that social movements always engage with. By showing how the women's movement has used the public sphere as a space for both integration and transformation, I have tried to clarify the mediating space within which processes of cultural contestation take place. In achieving success in their identity projects while transforming public space, women have demonstrated that the particularistic reconstruction of their identities has also promoted new conceptions of universality _vis-à-vis_ traditional notions of human beings. In doing so, they have enlarged their self-conceptions as social agents and displayed the emancipatory potentials of democratic institutions.

By conceiving their identities as flexible and self-reflexive tools for their performative actions, social movements achieve illocutionary force, connecting their particularities to the normative basis of more collective and universal self-understanding. In demanding solidarity, not only with one another but with others, social movements represent their claims for justice as an expanded horizon where needs can be reinterpreted, where new historical accounts can be drawn that reveal the bias and distortion of earlier narrations, and where the polluted representations of marginalized, excluded and oppressed groups can be challenged and set right. In creating a new vocabulary social groups provide for new descriptions that not only illuminate once repressed truths but create possibilities for relationships that were never envisioned before. In their struggles for recognition, women have achieved all of these tasks. Through their performances, they have themselves become the very subjects of collective action.

Notes

Introduction

1 On the other hand, once he had acknowledged his earlier failure, Habermas was able to assert in his 'Further Reflections on the Public Sphere', that he was not initially able to perceive the emancipatory content of groups to contest previous norms and injustices. See Habermas, Jürgen, 'Further Reflections on the Public Sphere' in *Habermas and the Public Sphere*, ed. Craig Calhoun. Cambridge, MA, MIT Press, 1996, pp. 421–57.

2 Habermas argues: 'We may use "excluded" in Foucault's sense when we are dealing with groups that play a constitutive role in the formation of a particular public sphere. "Exclusion" assumes a different and less radical meaning when the same structures of communication simultaneously give rise to the formation of several arenas where, beside the hegemonic bourgeois public sphere, additional subcultural or class-specific public spheres are constituted on the basis of their own initially not easily reconcilable premises'. Ibid., p. 425.

3 While I am aware of the critical responses of many feminists to Habermas' initial conception of the public sphere, I am arguing that it is precisely because of the 'illocutionary' strategies of feminism that it is possible to see what Habermas' initial view was covering up. In this book I aim to show that 'emancipatory' impulses from the feminist revolution have highlighted and enabled a new understanding of the public sphere and its capacity to contribute to a theory that sees the public sphere as an arena to develop communicative power to transform inequality and gain recognition. This is the reason why Habermas argues: 'I must confess, however, that only after reading Mikhail Bakhtin's book *Rabelais and His World* have my eyes become really opened to the inner dynamics of a plebeian culture. This culture of the common people apparently was by no means only a backdrop, that is, a passive echo of the dominant culture; it was also the periodically recurring violent revolt of a counterproject to the hierarchical world of domination, with its official celebrations and everyday disciplines. Only a stereoscopic view of this sort reveals how a mechanism of exclusion that locks out and

represses at the same time calls forth countereffects that cannot be neutralized. If we apply the same perspective to the bourgeois public sphere, the exclusion of women from this world dominated by men now looks different than it appeared to me at the time'. Ibid., p. 427. Different feminist narratives also drew his attention to this feature of the public sphere, and he has considered some of them as important to his own critical viewpoint. Ibid., p. 429.

4 In a similar manner Dana Villa argues that 'in order to grasp the atelic quality of action, we need a theory of presentation or appearance – a theory of performance in the aesthetic as opposed to the technical sense. . . . Arendt herself proposes the performing arts as the most apt analogy because their meaning, actuality, or "truth" is inseparable from the activity of presentation'. Villa, Dana, *Arendt and Heidegger: The Fate of the Political*. Princeton, NJ, Princeton University Press, 1996, p. 53.

5 Villa writes that 'in the same essay, Arendt notes the striking similarity between Benjamin's approach to the past, in which "the heir and preserver unexpectedly turns into a destroyer", and Heidegger's'. Ibid., p. 9.

6 Arendt, Hannah, *The Human Condition*. Chicago, University of Chicago Press, 1958, p. 175.

7 Ibid., pp. 244–5.

8 Lisa Jane Disch argues, for example, that 'Storytelling is thus one of the less exploited riches of Arendt's works. It demands serious attention because it is the closest she comes to explaining the relationship between her innovative approach to political theory and the experiences that move her to adopt it'. Disch, Lisa Jane, *Hannah Arendt and the Limits of Philosophy*. Ithaca and London, Cornell University Press, 1994, p. 2.

9 Villa argues that 'Arendt argues against Aristotle, and not merely against his philosophical prejudices. Her theory of action attempts a radical reconceptualization of action, one that proceeds, in part, through a critique and transformation of Aristotelian praxis': *Arendt and Heidegger*, p. 6. And again, 'Nevertheless, their [Habermas and Benhabib] mutual insistence against Arendt, that authentic processes of public dialogue yield a cognitively based agreement with the force of truth, marks them as inheritors of the rationalist attempt to reduce, if not eliminate, what Arendt calls the "incessant discourse" born of plurality', ibid., p. 71. See also Disch, 'Introduction: Storytelling and the Archimedean Ideal', in *Hannah Arendt*, pp. 1–19.

10 Villa, *Arendt and Heidegger*, p. 267.

11 As Clifford Geertz suggests, 'Culture is public because meaning is': *The Interpretation of Cultures*, New York, Basic Books, p. 12. Paul Ricoeur elaborates this kind of position in unusual terms: 'In this way, symbolism confers an initial readability of action. . . . If we may nevertheless speak of action as a quasi-text, it is insofar as the symbols, understood as interpretants, provide the rules of meaning as a function of which this or that behavior can be interpreted. . . . The term "symbol" further introduces the idea of a rule, not only in the sense that we have just spoken of about rules for description and interpretation of individual actions, but in the sense of a norm'. Ricoeur, Paul, *Time and Narrative*, vol. 1, trans. K. McLaughlin and D. Pellauer. Chicago and London, University of Chicago Press, 1984, p. 58.

12 Habermas, 'Further Reflections', p. 457.

13 Disch, *Hannah Arendt*, p. xi.

14 'With word and deed we insert ourselves into the human world, and this insertion is like a second birth, in which we confirm and take upon ourselves the naked fact of our original physical appearance. This insertion is not forced upon us by necessity, like labor, and it is not prompted by utility, like work. It may be stimulated by the presence of others whose company we may wish to join, but it is never conditioned by them; its impulse springs from the beginning which came into the world when we were born and to which we respond by beginning something new on our own initiative': Arendt, *Human Condition*, pp. 176–7.

15 Honig justifies her own position as follows: 'I turn to her not as a theorist of gender, nor as a woman, but as a theorist of an agonistic and performative politics that might stand a feminist politics in good stead. I turn to Arendt because of what she does include in her vision of politics, and also because (not in spite) of what she excludes from it'. Honig, Bonnie, 'Introduction: The Arendt Question in Feminism', in *Feminist Interpretations of Hannah Arendt*, ed. Honig. Pennsylvania, University of Pennsylvania Press, 1995, p. 136.

16 Arendt, *Human Condition*, p. 179.

17 With this, I hope to develop an explicit account of the cultural contents involved in the processes of telling stories, which Arendt never did.

18 Villa, *Arendt and Heidegger*, p. 71.

19 Ricoeur, *Time and Narrative*, 3 vols, trans. Kathleen McLaughlin [vol. 3: Kathleen Blamey] and D. Pellauer. Chicago and London, University of Chicago Press, 1984.

20 Ricoeur argues: 'This narrative interpretation implies that a life story proceeds from the untold and repressed stories in the direction of actual stories the subject can take up and hold as constitutive of his personal identity. It is the quest for this personal identity that assures the continuity between potential or inchoate story and the actual story we assume responsibility for'. Ibid., vol. 1, p. 74.

21 'Plot, says Aristotle, is the mimesis of an action. . . . I see in the plots we invent the privileged means by which we re-configure our confused, unformed, and at the limit mute temporal experience. "What then is time?" asks Augustine. . . . In the capacity of poetic composition to re-figure this temporal experience, which is prey to the aporias of philosophical speculation, resides the referential function of the plot'. Ibid., vol. 1, p. xi.

22 Ibid., vol. 1, p. 85.

23 Ibid., p. xi.

24 Benhabib, Seyla, *Situating the Self: Gender, Community and Postmodernism in Contemporary Ethics*. Cambridge, Polity Press, 1992.

25 Benhabib, Seyla, *The Reluctant Modernism of Hannah Arendt*. London, Sage, 1996.

26 Fraser, Nancy, *Justice Interruptus. Critical Reflections on the 'Postsocialist' Condition*. New York and London, Routledge, 1997.

27 Dean, Jodi, *Solidarity of Strangers: Feminism after Identity Politics*. Berkeley, Los Angeles and London, University of California Press, 1996.

28 Martha Nussbaum and Amartya Sen have worked together to bring to light the conception of 'human capabilities' into a broader discussion of economics, morality and the political policies that are best suited to make this approach a possibility in the future. See Nussbaum, Martha and Glover, Jonathan, eds, _Women, Culture and Development: A Study of Human Capabilities_, Oxford, Clarendon Press, 1995.

29 Rosi Braidotti has argued that it is necessary to be essentialist to avoid the problems of not addressing possibilities of transformation and change. See Braidotti, Rosi, 'The Politics of Ontological Difference', _Nomadic Subjects: Embodiment and Sexual Difference in Contemporary Feminist Theory_, ed. Carolyn C. Heilbrun and Nancy K. Miller, New York, Columbia University Press, 1994, pp. 173–90.

30 Alcoff, Linda, 'Cultural Feminism versus Poststructuralism' in _The Second Wave. A Reader in Feminist Theory_, ed. Linda Nicholson. New York, Routledge, 1997, p. 346.

31 Scott, Joan, 'The Evidence of Experience', _Critical Inquiry_, no. 17, 1991, p. 777.

32 Foucault states his field of research on what he calls the 'technologies of the self' as follows: 'Let's say very briefly that through studying madness and psychiatry, crime and punishment, I have tried to show how we have indirectly constituted ourselves through the exclusion of some others: criminals, mad people, and so on. How did we directly constitute our identity through some ethical techniques of the self which developed through antiquity down to now?' Foucault, Michel, 'The Political Technology of Individuals', in _Technologies of the Self: A Seminar with Michel Foucault_, ed. Luther H. Martin, Huck Gutman and Patrick Hutton. Amherst, MA, University of Massachusetts Press, 1988, p. 146.

33 De Lauretis, Teresa, _Technologies of Gender: Essays on Theory, Film, and Fiction_. Bloomington and Indianapolis: Indiana University Press, 1987, p. 2.

34 Julia Kristeva argues: 'A woman cannot be: it is something which does not even belong in the order of being. _It follows that a feminist practice can only be negative_, at odds with what already exists so that we may say "that's not it" and "that's still not"' (italics added). Kristeva, Julia, 'Woman can Never be Defined', in _New French Feminism_, ed. Elaine Marks and Isabelle Cortivron. New York, Schoken, 1981, p. 137.

35 Alcoff, 'Cultural Feminism', p. 339.

36 De Lauretis, Teresa, _Alice Doesn't: Feminism Semiotics, and Cinema_. Bloomington, Indiana University Press, 1984, p. 156.

37 Ricoeur argues: 'Another new source of complexity has appeared in the twentieth century, in particular with the stream-of-consciousness novel, so marvelously illustrated by a work of Virginia Woolf [_To the Lighthouse_], a masterpiece from the point of view of the perception of time . . . [in which what] holds the center of attention is the incompleteness of personality, the diversity of levels of the conscious, the subconscious, and the unconscious, the stirring of unformulated desires, the inchoactive and evanescent character of feelings. The notion of the plot here seems to be especially in trouble. . . . As the breadth of the plot increases, so does that of action. . . . Action, in this enlarged sense, also includes the moral tranformation of characters, their growth and education, and their initiation into the com-

plexity of moral and emotional purely internal changes affecting the temporal course of sensations, least conscious level introspection can reach' in:
Ricouer, Paul, *Time and Narrative*, vol. 3, pp. 9–10.
38 Ibid., p. 13.
39 Arendt argues: 'In other words, the stories, the results of action and speech,
reveal an agent, but this agent is not an author or producer. Somebody
began it and is its subject in the twofold sense of the word, namely, its actor
and sufferer, but nobody is its author', *Human Condition*, p. 184.
40 Alcoff, 'Cultural Feminism', p. 338.
41 'The problem of "difference" points to another layer of related issues: the
difference within each single woman, understood as the complex interplay
of differing levels of experience, which defer indefinitely any fixed notion of
identity. . . . The thinking/speaking "I" that signs this paper is neither the
owner nor the queen of the complex network of meanings that constitute the
text': Braidotti, in *Nomadic Subjects*, p. 184.
42 De Lauretis argued: 'The relevance to the theoretical feminism of the notion
of semiosis, such as I have outlined it, seems undeniable. In the first place,
semiosis specifies the mutual overdetermination of meaning, perception,
and experience, a complex nexus of reciprocally constitutive effects between
the subject and social reality, which, in the subject, entail a continual modification of consciousness; that consciousness in turn being the condition of
social change. In the second place, the notion of semiosis is *theoretically*
dependent on the intimate relationship of subjectivity and practices; and the
place of sexuality in that relationship, feminism has shown, is what defines
sexual difference *for women*, and gives femaleness its meaning as the experience of a female subject'. *Alice Doesn't*, p. 184.
43 De Lauretis, Teresa, 'Feminist Politics: What's Home Got to Do with It?', in
Feminist Studies/Critical Studies, De Lauretis. Bloomington, Indiana University Press, p. 194.
44 Ricoeur, *Time and Narrative*, vol. 1, p. 53.

Chapter 1   Autobiographies and Biographies

1 Alisdair MacIntyre is one of the main authors who saw this connection. See
MacIntyre, Alasdair, *After Virtue*. Notre Dame, IN, University of Notre
Dame Press, 1984. Charles Taylor, on the other hand, has always been
concerned with this specific connection. See Taylor, Charles, 'Self-interpret-
ing Animals', *Philosophical Papers: Human Agency and Language*, vol. 1. Cambridge, MA, Harvard University Press, pp. 45–76; *Sources of the Self: The
Making of Modern Identity*. Cambridge, MA, Harvard University Press, 1989;
and *The Ethics of Authenticity*. Cambridge, MA, Harvard University Press,
1991. In the important field of hermeneutics, particularly in the French
tradition, see Ricoeur, *Time and Narrative*, vol. 1. For views that relate the
continental tradition (German, French) with concerns and theories of
postmodernism, see Kerby, Anthony Paul, *Narrative and the Self*. Bloomington
and Indianapolis: Indiana University Press, 1991.
2 Kerby, *Narrative and the Self*, p. 1.
3 Habermas, Jürgen, *Moral Consciousness and Communicative Action*, trans.

Christian Lenhardt and Shierry Weber Nicholsen. Cambridge, Polity Press, 1990. See also Habermas, *Justification and Application: Remarks on Discourse Ethics*, trans. Ciaran P. Cronin. Cambridge, MA, MIT Press, 1993.

4 McCarthy,Thomas, 'Practical Discourse: On the Relation of Morality to Politics', *Ideals and Illusions: On Reconstruction and Deconstruction in Contemporary Critical Theory*. Cambridge, MA, MIT Press, 1991, p. 185.

5 Ibid., p. 187.

6 Wellmer, Albrecht, 'Ethics and Dialogue: Elements of Moral Judgement in Kant and Discourse Ethics', *The Persistence of Modernity: Essays on Aesthetics, Ethics, and Postmodernism*. Cambridge, MA, MIT Press, 1991, p. 197.

7 Ibid., p. 197.

8 Benhabib, Seyla, *Critique, Norm, and Utopia. A Study of the Foundations of Critical Theory*. New York, Columbia University Press, 1986, p. 300.

9 Michael Walzer, Charles Taylor, Michael Sandel, Bernard Williams and Alasdair MacIntyre are the representative figures that criticized 'procedural notions' of moral agents and their lack of contextualization, their emptiness, etc.

10 Habermas, *Moral Consciousness*.

11 Gilligan, Carol, *In a Different Voice: Psychological Theory and Women's Development*. Cambridge, MA, Harvard University Press, 1982.

12 Habermas, Jürgen, *The Structural Transformation of the Public Sphere: An Inquiry into the Category of Bourgeois Society*, trans. Thomas Burger with the assistance of Frederick Lawrence. Cambridge, Polity Press, 1989.

13 'To be sure, before the public sphere explicitly assumed political functions in the tension-charged field of state-society relations, the subjectivity originating in the intimate sphere of the conjugal family created, so to speak, its own public. Even before the control over the public sphere by public authority was contested and finally wrested away by the critical reasoning of private persons on political issues, there evolved under its cover a public sphere in apolitical form – the literary precursor of the public sphere operative in the political domain'. Ibid., p. 29.

14 'It provided the training ground for a critical public reflection still preoccupied with itself – a process of self-clarification of private people focusing on the genuine experiences of their novel privateness'. Ibid., p. 176.

15 'In January 1762 Rousseau writes M. de Malesherbes four letters in which he presents and projects himself as the *one who he is and who, with the will of authenticity, he wants to be.* With growing intensity and desperation, he continues this existential presentation of self in his *Confessions*, later in the *Dialogues*, and lastly in the *Reveries of a Solitary Walker*. But those initial letters already name the *communicative presuppositions for the public process of mercilessly reaching self-understanding and of assuring oneself of one's own identity.* Rousseau turns to Malesherbes with his revelations in order to justify himself before him. . . . Of course, the addressee is only representative of an omnipresent public. The form of the letter does indeed indicate the private character of the contents; but the *claim to radical sincerity with which Rousseau writes these letters requires unrestricted publicity.* The real addressee extends beyond the contemporary audience; *it is the universal public of a justly judging posterity*': Habermas, Jürgen, 'Individuation through Socialization: On Mead's

Theory of Subjectivity', *Postmetaphysical Thinking: Philosophical Essays*, trans. William Mark Hohengarten. Cambridge, MA, MIT Press, 1992, p. 166 (italics added).

16 Habermas, p. 42.

17 Ibid., p. 43.

18 Ibid., p. 27.

19 'Subjectivity, as the innermost core of the private, was already oriented to an audience [*Publikum*]. The opposite of the intimateness whose vehicle was the written word was indiscretion and not publicity as such. . . . Thus, the directly or indirectly audience-oriented subjectivity of the letter exchange or diary explained the origin of the typical genre and authentic literary achievement of that century: the domestic novel, the psychological description in autobiographical form'. Ibid., p. 49.

20 Ibid., p. 50.

21 'The reality as illusion that the new genre created received its proper name in English, "fiction": it shed the character of the *merely* fictitious'. Ibid., p. 50.

22 Ibid., p. 50 (italics added).

23 Ibid., p. 51.

24 'The circle of persons who made up the two forms of public were not even completely congruent. Women and dependents were factually and legally excluded from the political sphere, whereas female readers as well as apprentices and servants often took a more active part in the *literary public sphere* than the owners of private property and family heads themselves. Yet in the educated classes the one form of public sphere was considered to be identical with the other; in the self-understanding of public opinion the public sphere appeared as one and indivisible'. Ibid., p. 56 (italics added).

25 Habermas, *Postmetaphysical Thinking*, p. 151.

26 'Like the world-generating transcendental ego, Fichte's original ego comes on the scene in the singular, as one over and against everything; thus, "freely active" subjectivity, of which I want to reassure myself without illusion in the consciousness as something universal after all – as *Egohood* in general. . . . But Fichte himself already addresses this problem, namely the dynamic of reciprocal objectification that falls short of what is specific both to an intersubjectively shared understanding of language and to a communicative relationship between first person and second person. With his central argument Fichte does, it is true, lay claim to language as a medium through which one is able to demand independent activity of the other and to confront him with one's expectation'. Ibid., p. 161.

27 'These speaker and hearer perspectives no longer converge at the focal point of subjectivity centered in itself; they instead intersect at the focal point of language – and at this focal point Humboldt designates the "reciprocal conversation in which ideas and feelings are sincerely exchanged" '. Ibid., p. 163.

28 'And the idea that each individual must first make itself into that which it is would be honed by Kierkegaard into the act of taking responsibility for one's own life history'. Ibid., p. 162.

29 'From this secularized perspective, the *performatively employed* concept of individuality has been completely detached from its descriptive use. A totally different meaning is invested in the claim to individuality that is put

forth by a first person in dialogue with a second person. Justificatory confessions, through which the performatively raised claim to one's own identity can be authenticated, are not to be confused with the description, always selective, of an individual. The literary genre of the letter, the confession, the diary, the autobiography, the *Bildungsroman*, and the didactically recited self-reflection, which authors such as Rousseau and Kierkegaard favor, testifies to the transformated *illocutionary mode*: it is not a matter of *reports* and descriptions from the perspective of the observer, not even *self-observations*; rather, is it a matter of interested *presentations of the self*. Ibid., p. 167.

30 Ibid., p. 167.
31 Ibid., p. 167.
32 'Every attempt at the reassurance and justification of one's own identity must remain fragmentary. . . . It would be false to look on these exemplary attempts as substitutes for a *descriptive* explication of the ineffable individual that can never be completed'. Ibid., p. 169.
33 Ibid., p. 179.
34 Ibid., p. 180.
35 Ibid., p. 180 (italics added).
36 Ibid., p. 183.
37 Ibid., pp. 183–4.
38 Ibid., p. 185.
39 Habermas, Jürgen, *Between Facts and Norms: Contributions to a Discourse Theory of Law and Democracy*, trans. William Rehg. Cambridge, Polity Press, 1996.
40 'What was considered "ethics" since the time of Aristotle now assumed a new subjectivistic sense. This was true of both individual and life histories and of intersubjective shared traditions and forms of life. In connection with, and in reaction to, a growing autobiographical literature of confessions and self-examinations – running from Rousseau through Kierkegaard to Sartre – a kind of reflection developed that altered attitudes toward one's own life. To put it briefly, in place of exemplary instructions in the virtuous life and recommended models of the good life, one finds increasingly pronounced, abstract demand for a conscious, self-critical appropriation, the demand that one responsibly take possession of one's own individual, irreplaceable, and contingent life history. Radicalized interiority is burdened with the task of achieving a self-understanding in which self-knowledge and existential decision interpenetrate'. Ibid., p. 96.
41 Ibid., p. 96.
42 Ibid., p. 98.
43 Ibid., p. 103.
44 'Law is two things at once: a system of knowledge and a system of action. It is equally possible to understand law as a text, composed of legal propositions and their interpretations, and to view it as an institution, that is, as a complex of normatively regulated action'. Ibid., p. 79.
45 Ibid., p. 103.
46 Ibid., p. 301.
47 Ibid., p. 154.
48 Ibid., p. 306.

49 Schrag, Calvin O., *Communicative Praxis and the Space of Subjectivity*. Bloomington and Indianapolis, Indiana University Press, 1986, p. 23.

50 Ibid., p. 23.

51 Ibid., p. 24.

52 Arendt, *Human Condition*.

53 Canovan, Margaret, 'Politics as Culture: Hannah Arendt and the Public Realm', in *Hannah Arendt. Critical Essays*, ed. Lewis P. Hinchman and Sandra K. Hinchman. New York, State University of New York Press, 1994.

54 Canovan, Margaret, *Hannah Arendt: A Reinterpretation of her Political Thought*. Cambridge, MA, Harvard University Press, 1992.

55 Ibid., p. 181.

56 Ibid., p. 183.

57 Ibid., p. 191 (italics added).

58 Benhabib, Seyla, 'Hannah Arendt and the Redemptive Power of Narrative' in *Hannah Arendt: Critical Essays*, ed. Hinchman and Hinchman, pp. 111–37.

59 Richard J. Bernstein has focused on these issues. He writes: 'Arendt quite clearly and assertively affirmed herself as a Jewish pariah. She sought to accept the challenge and responsibility of being a member of the Jewish people. Not only in France, but also in the United States. For the next 20 years Arendt worked almost exclusively for Zionist and Jewish organizations in Paris and New York'. Bernstein, J. Richard, (1996), *Hannah Arendt and the Jewish Question*. Cambridge, Polity Press, 1996, p. 21.

60 Seyla Benhabib, Richard Bernstein and Dagmar Barnouw agree on this point. See Benhabib, 'The Pariah and her Shadow: Hannah Arendt's Biography' in *Feminist Interpretations*, ed. Honig, pp. 83–104. See also Bernstein, *Hannah Arendt*, where Bernstein forcefully argues (p. 19): 'Arendt does not really "narrate the story of Rahel's life as she herself might have told it", but rather as Arendt thinks she should have told it". Barnouw says: 'She relates her cultural-political criticism in the shape of stories that have as their source her own cultural experience as a Jew and a woman. "Bashed on the head by history" – as she said of Rahel Varnhagen, another German Jewess, and, by implication, of herself – she could not acknowledge the reality of historical experience, her own and others'. And such an acknowledgement sustained the personal quality of her narration'. Barnouw, Dagmar, *Visible Spaces: Hannah Arendt and the German-Jewish Experience*. Baltimore and London, Johns Hopkins University Press, 1990, pp. 13–14.

61 Benhabib, 'The Pariah and her Shadow: Hannah Arendt's Biography of Rahel Varnhagen', in *Feminist Interpretations*, ed. Honig, p. 90 (italics added).

62 Ibid., p. 91.

63 Ibid., p. 91.

64 Arendt, Hannah, *Rahel Varnhagen: The Life of a Jewish Woman*. New York: Harcourt Brace Jovanovich, 1974, p. xvi (italics added).

65 Ibid., p. xv.

66 'Actions, unlike things and natural objects, only live in the narratives of those who perform them and the narratives of those who understand, interpret, and recall them. This narrative structure of action also determines the identity of the self': Benhabib, 'Hannah Arendt', in *Critical Essays*, ed. Hinchman and Hinchman, p. 124.

67 Arendt, *Rahel Varnhagen*, p. 227.

68 Ibid., p. xvii.

69 Benhabib, 'Hannah Arendt', in *Critical Essays*, ed. Hinchman and Hinchman, p. 119.

70 Arendt, Hannah, *The Origins of Totalitarianism*. New York, Harcourt Brace Jovanovich, 1975, p. 9.

71 Arendt, Hannah, *Men in Dark Times*, New York, Harcourt Brace & World, 1968.

72 Obviously Arendt is connected with Aristotle mainly when she is interpreted as a premodern thinker, and with Kant when she is seen as a modern theorist.

73 Arendt, *Human Condition*, p. 175.

74 Ibid., p. 176.

75 Ibid., p. 178.

76 Ibid., p. 179.

77 Ibid., p. 180 (italics added).

78 Ibid., p. 183.

79 Ibid., p. 184.

80 Benjamin, Walter, 'The Storyteller: Reflections on the Work of Nikolai Leskov', in *Illuminations: Essays and Reflections*, ed. Hannah Arendt. New York, Shocken Books, 1968, pp. 83–110. Richard Wolin states: 'That meaning is immanent to life in the world of the story is apparent from the fact that the story always contains something *useful* – practical advice, a kernel of wisdom, or a conventional moral. That such a knowledge acquires an immediate self-evidence bespeaks of a situation in which there exists a *continuity and flow* to the continuum of experience, where time has the character of a meaningfully ordered, organic sequence of events, and where the phenomenon of death fits meaningfully within this sequence'. Wolin, Richard, *Walter Benjamin. An Aesthetic of Redemption*. Berkeley, CA, University of California Press, 1994, p. 219.

81 Benhabib, 'Hannah Arendt', in *Critical Essays*, ed. Hinchman and Hinchman, p. 115. It is well documented that Benjamin was unable to get an academic position because his research did not conform to rigid academic standards.

82 Ibid., p. 116.

83 Ibid., p. 116.

84 Ibid., pp. 116–17.

85 Ibid., p. 119.

86 Benjamin, Walter, 'Theses on the Philosophy of History', in *Illuminations*, ed. Arendt, pp. 254–6.

87 Ibid., thesis 2.

88 Wolin says: 'Faced with the seemingly inexplicable series of horrors and catastrophes of Jewish history (above all, the expulsion from Spain in 1492), the Kabbalists proceeded to attach an inverse, mystical significance to these events, which were assumed to represent signs of the impending Messianic age – its "birth pangs" '. *Benjamin: Aesthetic*, p. 62.

89 Wolin, Richard, *Benjamin, Aesthetic*, p. 36. Benjamin's *Gessamelte Schriften* has appeared in English as *Walter Benjamin, Selected Writings,* ed. Marcus Bullock and Michael W. Jennings. Cambridge, MA, and London, Belknap Press, 1996, vol. 1.

90 Arendt, *Rahel Varnhagen*, p. 16.

91 Arendt, *Human Condition*, p. 190.

92 According to Benhabib: 'The historical narrator no less than the moral actor had to engage in acts of judgement, for *Verstehen* as well was a form of judging – certainly not in the juridical or moralistic sense of the delivery of a value perspective but in the sense of the recreation of shared reality from the standpoint of all involved and concerned. Historical judgement revealed the perspectival nature of the shared social world by representing its plurality in narrative form'. Benhabib, 'Hannah Arendt', in *Critical Essays*, ed. Hinchman and Hinchman, p. 121.

93 Arendt, *Human Condition*, p. 192.

94 Arendt, *Eichmann in Jerusalem: A Report on the Banality of Evil*. New York, Penguin, 1992.

95 'Only the actors and speakers who re-enact the story's plot can convey the full meaning, not so much of the story itself, but of the "heroes" who reveal themselves': Arendt, *Human Condition*, p. 187.

96 Ibid., p. 189.

97 Ibid., p. 198.

98 Arendt, 'Rosa Luxemburg: 1817–1919', *Men in Dark Times*, pp. 33–56.

99 Dagmar Barnouw supports this interpretation when she argues that: 'Rahel herself proves Arendt to be right. Her letters to her friend Pauline Wiesel, the mistress of Prince Louis Ferdinand of Prussia, express precisely the almost physically oppressive "mood" of the "waiting distraught woman" which Arendt, to Bedford's dismay, forces on the reader'. Barnouw, *Visible Spaces*, p. 48.

100 Arendt, *Rahel Varnhagen*, p. 21.

101 Ibid., p. 20.

102 De Maio, Romeo, *Mujer y Renacimiento*. Madrid, Mondadori, 1987 (especially chapter VI: 'La mujer en la biografía', pp. 157–76).

103 Works on this subject include: Okin, Susan Moller, *Women in Western Political Thought*. New Jersey, Princeton University Press, 1979; Keohane, Nannerl O., 'But for her Sex . . . The Domestication of Sophie', in *Trent Rousseau Papers*, ed. MacAdam et al. Ottawa, University of Ottawa Press, 1980; Figes, Eva, *Patriarchal Attitudes*. London, Panther, 1972; Lange, Lynda, 'Rousseau and Modern Feminism', in *Feminist Interpretations and Political Theory*, ed. Mary Lyndon Shanley and Carole Pateman. Pennsylvania, Pennsylvania State University Press, 1991, pp. 95–111.

104 Farge, Arelette, and Zemon Davies, Natalie, directors, *Historia de las Mujeres: Del Renacimiento a la edad moderna. Discurso y disidencia*, ed. Georges Duby and Michelle Perrot. Madrid, Taurus, 1992.

105 Craft-Fairchild, Catherine, *Masquerade and Gender. Disguise and Female Identity in Eighteenth-century Fictions by Women*. University Park, PA: Pennsylvania State University, 1993; Gilmore, Leigh, *Autobiographics: A Feminist Theory of Women's Self-representation*. Ithaca and London, Cornell University Press, 1994; Webster Barbre, Joy *et al.*, *Interpreting Women's Lives: Feminist Theory and Personal Narratives*, ed. Personal Narratives Group. Bloomington and Indianapolis: Indiana University Press, 1989.

106 De Beauvoir, Simone, *The Prime of Life*, trans. Peter Green. Harmondsworth,

Penguin, 1965; *Force of Circumstance*, trans. Richard Howard. New York, Warner, 1968; *All Said and Done*, trans. Patrick O'Brien. New York, Warner, 1975.

107 De Beauvoir, Simone, *The Second Sex*, trans. H. M. Parshley. New York, Vintage, 1974. See Spelman, V. Elizabeth, 'Simone de Beauvoir and Women: Just Who Does She Think "We" Is?', in *Feminist Interpretations*, ed. Lyndon Shanley and Pateman, pp. 199–216.

108 That feminists are conscious of these strategies of self-presentation is proven by the many books already written on the subject. Gilmore defines it as follows: 'I offered autobiographics to describe those elements of self-representation which are not bound by a philosophical definition of the self derived from Augustine or the literary history or concept of the book which defines autobiography as a genre; instead, autobiographics marks a location in a text where self-invention, self-discovery, and self-representation emerge within the technologies of autobiography, namely, those legalistic, literary, cultural, and ecclesiastical discourses of truth and identity through which the subject of autobiography is produced'. Gilmore, *Autobiographics*, p. 185.

109 Calisher, Hortense, *Herself*. New York, Dell Publishing Co., 1972.

110 Ibid., p. 51.

111 Ibid., p. 356.

112 Ibid., p. 358.

113 Ibid., p. 392.

114 Lessing, Doris, *The Golden Notebook*. London, Michael Joseph, 1962.

115 Mary McCarthy is the example Leigh Gilmore gives that most resembles my own accounts of autobiographies. In referring to McCarthy's *Memories of a Catholic Girlhood* (1957) she claims: 'Between the numbered chapters, the purportedly truthful accounts drawn from life, is a sequence of italicized interchapters in which McCarthy distinguishes what she *really* remembers from what she invented to satisfy her own artistic sensibility: gaps in memory disappear into narrative continuity, conversations that never took place economically convey information, and characters behave as they must in a story even when they frustrate her with their "real" and unsassimilable actions. . . . That is, in telling the *truth*, autobiographers usually narrate, and thereby shift the emphasis to *telling* the truth'. Gilmore, *Autobiographics*, p. 121.

116 Nin, Anaïs, *The Diary of Anaïs Nin*. 6 vols, ed. Gunther Stuhlmann. New York, Harcourt Brace Jovanovich, 1966–76.

117 Herrera, Hayden, *Frida: A Biography of Frida Kahlo*. New York, Harper & Row, 1983.

118 Bradu, Fabienne, *Antonieta Rivas Mercado*. Mexico City, Vuelta.

119 Poniatowska, Elena, *La Vida de Tina Modotti*. Mexico City: Cal y Arena Press, 1993.

Chapter 2   Communicative Rationality

1 Habermas deals with this mainly in his *Theory of Communicative Action*, 2 vols, Cambridge, Polity Press, 1984–7.

2 'The term "faculty of judgement" carries the implication that the correct (i.e. justified) solutions which it is possible to find for the "mediation of moments of reason" are only ever valid "here and now"': Wellmer *Persistence of Modernity*. p. 229.

3 Adorno, Theodor, and Horkheimer, Max, *Dialectic of Enlightenment*, trans. J. Cumming. New York, London: Verso, 1979.

4 'The unity of reason can now be seen as a network of connecting lines and interchanges between theoretical, technical, moral and aesthetics issues of arguing': Wellmer, *Persistence of Modernity*, p. 229.

5 'Only as a medium of communicative mediation, as a medium that is both produced and received, can the work of art come to correspond formally to the changing forms of individuation and socialization': ibid., p. 20.

6 Adorno, Theodor, *Negative Dialectic*, trans. E. B. Ashton. New York, Routledge and Kegan Paul, 1973.

7 About this 'twist', Wellmer says: 'This is what happens in Adorno, his name for the realm of conceptual thought is *mimesis*. Reflection on the foundations of the instrumental spirit in terms of a philosophy of language, by contrast, requires us to acknowledge a "mimetic" moment within conceptual thought itself, for a mimetic moment is sublimated in everyday speech, just as it is in art and philosophy. This is something which must remain concealed from philosophy which understands the function of the concept in terms of the polarity between subject and object, it is capable of recognizing functions of language as a precondition of the possibility of those functions. *That is why it can only conceive mimesis as the Other of rationality, and the coming-together of mimesis and rationality as negation of historical reality'*. Wellmer, 'Truth, Semblance, Reconciliation: Adorno's Aesthetic Redemption of Modernity', in *The Persistence of Modernity*, p. 13.

8 Ibid., p. 8.

9 Ibid., p. 8.

10 Ibid., p. 8.

11 Ibid., p. 9.

12 It is very important to state that Adorno and Benjamin have similar concerns and that some of the most interesting features of their visions of art and philosophy are in this area. Wellmer thinks that Adorno was trying to fulfil the need postulated in one of the most famous philosophical theories of history written by Benjamin, namely the need to find a 'historical materialism' that would be at the service of theology, and which made his philosophical idea of reconciliation the most important theme in his work. Wellmer says: 'Walter Benjamin had argued in his "Thesis on the Philosophy of History" that the puppet of "historical materialism" needed to enlist the services of theology. Adorno's philosophy could be understood as the attempt to fulfil this postulated need. There is, however, a fissure between messianic-utopian and materialistic motifs in Adorno's thought, which cannot be overlooked'. Ibid., p. 11.

13 Ibid., p. 12.

14 Ibid., p. 11.

15 'The utopian projection is not the Other of discursive reason, but the idea which discursive reason has of itself. Since utopia is rooted in the conditions

of language, the utopia in question is of this world, and in this sense a "materialistic" one': ibid., p. 14.

16 'That is why it can only conceive mimesis as the Other of rationality, and the coming-together of mimesis and rationality only as a negation of historical reality. In order to recognize the _prior_ unity of the mimetic and the rational moment in the foundations of language, we need to change the philosophical paradigm': ibid., p. 13.

17 'This thesis is concerned with the differentiation of two types of rationalization in the modern world. It leaves open the question of the way in which the structures of communicative and instrumental functionalist rationality, which are certainly conceived as _conceptually_ complementary, will interpenetrate each other within the overarching structure of the living context of society at large': ibid., p. 15.

18 'It is the moments of _inauthenticity_ and _violence_ in traditional synthesis that Adorno has in mind when he characterizes modern art on the one hand as an "action against the work of art as a constellation of meaning", and on the other hand, claims for modern art a principle of individuation and of "an increasing elaboration" in detail': ibid., p. 19.

19 Ibid., p. 19.

20 Ibid., p. 20.

21 Ibid., p. 20.

22 Ibid., p. 20.

23 Schwab, Gabriele, _Subjects without Selves: Transitional Texts in Modern Fiction_. Cambridge, MA, Harvard University Press, 1994.

24 Ibid., p. 5.

25 Schwab's theory is closely linked to Kristeva's conception of language and the aesthetic experience. However, she prefers to recover theories of authors like Ehrensweig and Winnicott, because both develop a holistic model, 'presupposing a continual process of mediation between primary and secondary processes as indispensable for an "ecology of the subject" ' Ibid., p. 13.

26 Wellmer, _Persistence of Modernity_, p. 20.

27 Ibid., p. 20 (italics added).

28 Ibid., p. 20.

29 In writing about Samuel Beckett's _The Unnamable_, Schwab says: 'The literary subject of this text transgresses its own boundaries in a highly reflexive self-exploration. This creates the fictional paradox of a first person narrator who invents himself as the fiction of an Other, himself a fiction, can only come into existence by inventing other fictions or voices, one of whom is _The Unnamable_. Combining the features of literary characters, empirical subject, and transcendental subject of philosophy, the unnamable becomes a transitional character who challenges our most basic assumptions about subjectivity'. _Subjects without Selves_, p. 20.

30 Ibid., p. 22.

31 'For works of art which point towards an expansion of the boundaries of communication by virtue of their effect and not their being do not fulfil their enlightening cognitive function at the level of philosophical knowledge, but on that of the subjects' relationship to themselves and to the world where works of art intervene in a complex network of attitudes,

feelings, interpretations and evaluations. It is through this intervention that what we might call the cognitive character of art is fulfilled'. Ibid., p. 22.

32 Alan Singer criticizes Wellmer's interpretation, arguing that Wellmer puts too much weight on the concept of reconciliation and ignores the concept of 'tremor', which would enlighten the cognitive enterprise of Adorno's aesthetics. But in regard to the cognitive status of art, Singer agrees with Wellmer's interpretation and makes a similar statement about the cognitive status of literature. Singer, Alan, 'The Adequacy of the Aesthetic', *Philosophy and Social Criticism*, vol. 20, nos 1/2, 1994, pp. 39–72 (p. 66).

33 Wellmer, *Persistence of Modernity*, p. 22 (italics added).

34 Ibid., p. 25.

35 Ibid., p. 26 (italics added).

36 'The uncomprehended experience is illuminated by becoming condensed into an experience of a higher order: experience becomes experienceable': ibid., p. 26.

37 Schwab develops a very similar formulation to Wellmer's when she argues that: 'translated into a consciously shaped aesthetic production, primary processes do not merely represent the unconscious, but play a formational role by shifting the boundaries between unconscious modes of production and reception. Primary-processes operations in literary texts may thus shape unconscious material, but as textual figurations they pertain completely to neither the primary nor the secondary processes. . . . Seen from this perspective, cultural objects facilitate negotiations between inner and outer reality and between primary- and secondary-process experiences. Their specific achievement, then, does not lie primarily in what Freud emphasized – namely in their referring to a latent meaning and thus revealing the operations of the unconscious – but lies rather in their creating specific figurations of language able to provide an aesthetic formative for subjectivity'. *Subject without Selves*, p. 33.

38 'Aesthetic discourse is the mediating instance between the apophantic metaphors from which we started out, and questions of aesthetic rightness. That is why we can only understand the truth-*claim* of art if we start by looking at the complex relationship of interdependency between the various dimensions of truth in aesthetic discourse': ibid., p. 27.

39 Ibid., p. 28.

40 Ibid., p. 29.

41 Schwab argues that 'each new order at first appears as chaos, but the aesthetic experience of changing modes and sensibilities of perception is a fundamental process pertaining to the historical development of the transitional space of cultural objects. . . . In this respect, Ehrenzweig shares the assumptions of an aesthetics of reception that works with the notion of a horizon of expectation – as developed, for example, by Hans Robert Jauss. Ehrenzweig describes a dynamic in the aesthetics of reception according to which our conscious experience tries increasingly to integrate what is experienced as chaos and undifferentiation. This process becomes the basis for changes in our notions of order, our epistemologies, and the cultural forms of language and subjectivity'. *Subjects without Selves*, p. 44.

42 Ibid., p. 46.

43 Cornell, Drucilla, _Transformations: Recollective Imagination and Sexual Difference_. New York, Routledge, p. 1.
44 Cornell, Drucilla, 'Feminist Challenges: A Response', _Philosophy and Social Criticism_, vol. 22, no. 4, p. 113.
45 Wellmer, _Peristence of Modernity_, p. 30.
46 Wellmer, 'Ethics and Dialogue: Elements of Moral Judgement in Kant and Discourse Ethics', _Persistence of Modernity_, pp. 113–231.
47 See, for instance, the excellent critical review by Alessandro Ferrara, 'Critical Theory and its Discontents: On Wellmer's Critique of Habermas', _Praxis International_, vol. 9, no. 3, 1989, pp. 305–20.
48 'When I say that discourse ethics is _not Kantian enough_ I mean that it fails to come up to what Kant had already achieved in terms of differentiation. I am thinking in particular of differentiation between problems of morality and problems of law': Wellmer, _Persistence of Modernity_, p. 117.
49 'With my criticism that discourse ethics remains too close to Kant, then, I am proceeding on the assumption that ethics needs to advance beyond the false antithesis of absolutism and relativism, which is to say that morality and reason do not stand or fall with the absolutism of ultimate agreements or fundamental groundings': ibid., p. 116.
50 As Martin Seel has aptly argued: 'For it is both aspects together, namely difference and unity, which distinguish communicative reason from the one-dimensionality characteristic not only of instrumental rationality; _any_ form of one-sidedly restricting the plural meaning of validity would have to be understood as a sign of reification, even if in modernity theoretical rationality represents the foremost paradigm for such alienation' in: Seel, Martin, 'The Two Meanings of "Communicative" Rationality: Remarks on Habermas' Critique of a Plural Concept of Reason', in _Communicative Action_, ed. Axel Honneth and Hans Joas. Cambridge, MA, MIT Press, 1991, pp. 36–48 (p. 36).
51 'Cautionary use' is a concept explained by Richard Rorty in his essay 'Pragmatism, Davidson and Truth', _Philosophical Papers_, vol. 1. Cambridge, MA, Cambridge University Press, 1991, pp. 126–50. He discusses the concept of truth in terms of the 'endorsing use', 'disquotational truth' and 'cautionary truth', also arguing that the only concept of truth that could not be erased from our linguistic practices is the 'cautionary use'.
52 Wellmer, _Persistence of Modernity_, p. 169.
53 Ibid., p. 173.
54 Ibid., p. 173.
55 Ibid., p. 75.
56 'In both instances the idea of the absolute betokens the precondition for the possibility of truth': ibid., p. 178.
57 Ibid., p. 184.
58 Habermas clarified his position and argued in favour of this differentiation in _Between Facts and Norms_.
59 Ibid., p. 196.
60 Ibid., p. 197.
61 'The proponents of a universalistic morality (and it is with them that we are concerned here) never did believe that morality stops when it comes to

homosexuals, women or children. They believed rather that homosexuality was corrupting, that women were not capable of rational self-determination, or that children must learn obedience above all in order to become decent human beings. In proportion as such views become questionable, which is to say that it is no longer possible to advance good reasons in their defence, so, too, do the moral views change that are associated with them': ibid., p. 197.

62 Ibid., p. 198.
63 Ibid., p. 198.
64 Ibid., p. 202.
65 Ibid., p. 203 (italics added).
66 Ibid., p. 225.
67 As Martin Seel has rightly argued: 'This relation with the *Other* of each and every justifiable orientation is now visibly related to our dealings with the *Others*. It derives from the interactive relationships in which we acquire the ability to justify, and grows – as it then does – out of communicative dealings with subjects *vis-à-vis* whom we represent the validity of our assumptions and the soundness of our reasons. The constitutive perspectival character of reason cannot be thought without at the same time conceiving of a plurality of subjects who depend on coordinating their actions in language'. Seel, 'Two Meanings' in *Communicative Action*, ed. Honneth and Joas, p. 47.
68 Wellmer, *Persistence of Modernity*, p. 29.
69 Seel, 'Two Meanings'.
70 Ibid., p. 39.
71 Mary Hesse has dealt extensively with this dimension of language used in scientific explanations. Hesse, Mary, 'Socializing Epistemology', in *Construction and Constraint: The Shaping of Scientific Rationality*, ed. Ernau McMullin. Notre Dame, Indiana, University of Notre Dame Press, 1988, pp. 97–122.
72 Kant, Immanuel, *Elements of Pure Practical Reason*, ed. William Benton. Chicago, Encyclopedia Britannica, 1952. See Part II: 'Of the Right that Pure Reason in its Practical Use has to an Extension which is not Possible to it in its Speculative Use'.
73 Seel, 'Two Meanings', p. 41.
74 Schwab argues: 'My own readings focus on the new ties woven between language and the subject in order to elucidate the new notions of literary subjectivity implied in the experimental language games in modernism and postmodernism . . . in order to investigate the dynamic relationship they entertain with the cultural system from which they emerge and to which they react in a transformative way'. *Subjects without Selves*, p. 10.

Chapter 3   Feminism as an Illocutionary Model

1 Schrag, Calvin O., *The Self after Postmodernity*. New Haven and London, Yale University Press, 1997, p. 24.
2 Arendt, *Human Condition*, p. 179.
3 Lisa J. Disch has drawn attention to Arendt's own way of performing her

identity as a 'political fact' when receiving the Lessing Prize: 'The Lessing Address is a performance that dramatizes how to acknowledge an identity as a "political fact" and, at the same time, to refute it . . . [thus] identity is not the standpoint or ultimate ground it is so often posited to be; when it comes "under attack" it becomes a political fact, undeniable in a specific situation but also refutable in terms of that situation. As such, it may be a positive site of both resistance and collective agency'. Disch, Lisa J., 'On Friendship in "Dark Times" ', in _Feminist Interpretations_, ed. Honig, pp. 286, 287.

4 Ricoeur argues: 'Unlike the abstract identity of the Same, this narrative identity, constitutive of self-constancy, can include change, mutability, within the cohesion of one lifetime. The subject then appears both as a reader and the writer of its own life, as Proust would have it. As the literary analysis of autobiography confirms, the story of a life continues to be refigured by all truthful or fictive stories a subject tells about himself or herself. The refiguration makes this life itself a cloth woven of stories told'. Ricoeur, _Time and Narrative_. vol. 3, p. 246.

5 Arendt, _Human Condition_, p. 184.

6 Schrag describes this process as follows: 'A storyteller finds herself by emplotting herself in stories in the making. To be a self is to be able to render account of oneself, to be able to tell the story of one's life. Sometimes we are at the mercy of stories that we tell, and at other times the stories suffer the inscription of our own agenda'. _Self after Postmodernity_, p. 26.

7 'Narrative in the stronger sense of the term is a form and dynamics of the self as life-experiencing subject . . . on the other hand is narrative as expressive of an ontological claim': ibid., p. 42.

8 Ricoeur formulates the question 'Is it not the narrative praxis at work in all emplotment that recruits, so to speak, by way of the semantics of action, the predicates capable of defining narrative roles due to the capacity of bringing the structures of human action within the realm of narratives?': _Time and Narrative_, vol. 2, p. 44.

9 Schrag, for example, explains that 'the self as concretely embodied motility, exhibiting lines of active and reactive forces and displaying the power to initiate action exercises a peculiar claim on praxis-oriented reason. In such a gestural comportment as caressing the arm of a beloved and in such skilled performance as swimming the length of the stadium we observe a bodily comprehension of the world, a dynamics of discernment, an economy of practical wisdom that exhibits its own insight without needing to wait on the determinations of pure cognition and pure theory': _Self after Postmodernity_, p. 57.

10 Ibid., p. 61.

11 'The future of narrative time is the self as possibility, as the power to be able to provide new readings of the script that has already been inscribed and to mark out new inscriptions of a script in the making': ibid., p. 37.

12 'With this, the phenomenon of reading became the necessary mediator of refiguration': Ricoeur, _Time and Narrative_, vol. 3, p. 159.

13 Habermas, _Structural Transformation_.

14 Joan Landes, whose work has been of major importance to gender studies within the realm of the public sphere, says about this Habermasian

conceptualization: 'Anticipating what Stephen Greenblatt has termed "self-fashioning", Habermas describes the interplay between the codes of intimacy characteristic of fiction (the novel), the forms of subjectivity that were fitted to print, and the appeal of literature to a widening public of readers. Likewise, by appropriating aspects of the Frankfurt School's account of "authority and the family", Habermas concludes that the experiential complex of audience oriented privacy affected the political realm's public sphere', Landes, Joan, 'The Public and the Private Sphere: A Feminist Reconsideration', in: *Feminist Reading Habermas: Gendering the Subject of Discourse*, ed. Johanna Meehan. New York and London, Routledge, p. 95.

15 Geoff Eley argues: 'But on the other hand, the beauty of Landes's analysis is to have shown how this pattern of subordination was reformulated and recharged in the midst of the major political cataclysm, the French Revolution, through which the ideal of human emancipation was otherwise radically enlarged'. Eley, Geoff, 'Nations, Publics, and Political Cultures: Placing Habermas in the Nineteenth Century', in *Habermas and the Public Sphere*, ed. Craig Calhoun. Cambridge, MA, MIT Press, 1996, p. 310.

16 Landes, B. Joan, *Women in the Public Sphere in the Age of the French Revolution*. Ithaca and London, Cornell University Press, 1988.

17 Landes says: 'I insist that the eighteenth century marked a turning point for women in the construction of modern identity: public-private oppositions were being reinforced in ways that foreclosed women's earlier independence in the street, the marketplace, and, for elite women, in the public spaces of the court and the aristocratic household. But we also need to account for the emergence of a very impressive social institution in which women exercised a considerable degree of power – unmatched in subsequent or prior eras. Women appeared to organize according to certain fixed rules of comportment and speech, a terrain upon which manners and talk were decisively altered. In the salons, men of the aristocracy mingled with writers, artists, scholars, merchants, lawyers, and officeholders. A novel pattern of interchange existed between educated men and literate, informed women who functioned not just as consumers but as purveyors of culture'. Ibid., p. 22.

18 Ibid., p. 24.

19 Landes claims: 'Thus Diderot accuses women of suppressing the reign of reasoned argument, while Rousseau worries over speech's lost ability to a world of deep human significance'. Ibid., p. 45.

20 Ibid., p. 25.

21 Ricoeur describes this process: 'On the one hand, it is through the individual process of reading that the text reveals its "structure of appeal"; on the other hand, it is inasmuch as readers participate in the sedimented expectations of the general reading public that they are constituted as competent readers. The act of reading thus becomes one link in the chain of history of the reception of a work by the public. Literary history, renovated by the aesthetic of reception, may thus claim to include the phenomenology of the act of reading'. *Time and Narrative*, vol. 3, p. 167.

22 Ricoeur argues: 'But we added that reading also includes a moment of impetus. This is when reading becomes a provocation to be and to act

differently. However this impetus is transformed into action only through a decision whereby a person says Here I stand! So narrative identity is not equivalent to true self-constancy except through this decisive moment, which makes ethical responsibility the highest factor in self-constancy'. _Time and Narrative_, vol. 3, p. 249.

23 See, for example, the eloquence of Mary Ryan's claim that we need to 'insert women and gender into the historical space of the "public"': Ryan, Mary P., _Women in Public: Between Banners and Ballots, 1825–1880_. Baltimore and London, Johns Hopkins University Press, 1990, p. x.

24 Landes asserts: 'I have already observed the extent to which women excelled in the categories of speech and letter writing; as a result of this excellence, they helped to shape an aesthetic of preciosity or wordliness'. _Women in the Public Sphere_, p. 53.

25 Landes claims: 'The habit of letter writing was another important manifestation of this new symbolic culture. In letters, men and women explored their unique subjectivity and shared it intimately with a sympathetic Other'. Ibid., p. 62.

26 'The salon offered one way of getting around the problem of censorship, by holding public discussion in private': ibid., p. 57.

27 Arendt, Hannah, 'Berlin Salon', in _Essays in Understanding, 1930–1954_, ed. Jerome Kohn. New York and London, Harcourt Brace & Co., 1993, p. 58.

28 The major development of Lucinde's character in Friedrich Schlegel's novel of 1799 lies in the intensity and importance granted to the dimensions of intimacy and privacy. Arendt also alludes to the fact that a narrative like Schlegel's would be regarded as a typical product of a feminine mind, if this shift in literature and subjectivity had not taken place: ibid., p. 61.

29 See, for example, Landes' chapter 'Rousseau's Reply to Public Women', in her _Women in the Public Sphere_, pp. 66–89.

30 Ibid., p. 63.

31 Ibid., p. 61.

32 Ibid., p. 61.

33 'Indeed', says Landes, 'Sévigné's letters made an enormous impact on militant writers such as Voltaire, Diderot, and Rousseau, all of whom practiced epistolary activity as a privileged form of literary expression': ibid., p. 63.

34 Ricoeur argues: 'What the strategy of persuasion, wrought by the implied author, seeks to impose on the reader is, precisely, the force of conviction – _the illocutionary force_, we might say in the vocabulary of speech-act theory – that upholds the narrator's vision of the world'. _Time and Narrative_, vol. 1, p. 177.

35 Landes expresses this point of view: 'Virtually everything is perverted, but worst of all are the political consequences of this overly feminized atmosphere: a king and a kingdom ruled by women'. _Women in the Public Sphere_, p. 33.

36 Denby, David J., _Sentimental Narrative and the Social Order in France. 1760–1820_. Cambridge, MA, Cambridge University Press, 1994, p. 198.

37 Ibid., pp. 198–9.

38 Ibid., pp. 204–5 (italics added).

39 In doing so, Denby says, she also manages to 'transform this tradition (the

sentimental), not least by virtue of her very great talent. The transformation is both an intellectual and an aesthetic one': ibid., p. 207.

40 Gutwirth, Madelyn, *Madame de Staël, Novelist: The Emergence of the Artist as Woman*. Chicago and London, Urbana, 1978, p. 150.

41 Ibid., p. 150.

42 Lori J. Marso has also pointed out Madame de Staël's importance as a political thinker. See Marso, Lori J., 'The Loving Citizen: Germaine de Staël's *Delphine*', *Journal of Political Philosophy*, vol. 5, no. 2, 1997, pp. 109–31.

43 Joyce, Patrick, *Democratic Subjects: The Self and the Social in Nineteenth-Century England*. Cambridge, MA, Cambridge University Press, 1994.

44 Hunt, Lynn, *The Family Romance of the French Revolution*. Berkeley and Los Angeles, University of California Press, 1992.

45 Joyce, *Democratic Subjects*, p. 157.

46 Walkowitz, Judith R., *City of Dreadful Delight: Narratives of Sexual Danger in Late Victorian London*. Chicago: Chicago University Press, 1992.

47 Ibid., pp. 157–8.

48 See also Outram, Dorinda, *The Body and the French Revolution*. New Haven, Yale University Press, 1989; and Hesse, Carla, 'Kant, Foucault, and Three Women', in *Foucault and the Writing of History*, ed. Jan Goldstein. Oxford and Cambridge, Blackwell, 1994, pp. 81–97.

Chapter 4   Autonomy and Authenticity

1 One of the key thinkers to develop the concept of autonomy in the Kantian tradition is Jürgen Habermas, with his intersubjective constitution of the self and the evolution of self-identity through communicative interaction with others. As discussed in chapter 2 above, Habermas conceives a simultaneous process of socialization and individuation, adopting Mead's and Durkheim's notions. However, like Rawls, Habermas defends an ontological outlook and, with it, the priority of the right over the good.

2 Michael Sandel has written a critique of Rawls' conception of moral agents. Sandel, Michael J., *Liberalism and the Limits of Justice*. Cambridge, MA, Cambridge University Press, 1982.

3 Taylor, *Sources of the Self*; and Taylor, *Ethics of Authenticity*.

4 The origins of this tradition, although not homogenous, could be traced back to authors such as Rousseau, Kierkegaard, Nietzsche, Heidegger and Sartre.

5 Even sociologists and political theorists have tried to thematize such a category and the importance that it has in a normative sense. See, for example, David Held's statement that 'the idea of democracy derives its power and significance from the idea of self determination': Held, David, *Democracy and the Global Order: From the Modern State to Cosmopolitan Governance*. Cambridge, Polity Press, 1995, p. 145.

6 Taylor says: 'The notion of authenticity develops out of a displacement of the moral accent in this idea. On the original view, the inner voice is important because it tells us what is the right thing to do. Being in touch with our moral feelings would matter here, as a means to the end of acting rightly. What I'm calling the displacement of the moral accent comes about

when being in touch takes on independent and crucial moral significance. It comes to be something we have to attain to be true and full human beings. . . . This is part of the massive subjective turn of modern culture, a new form of inwardness, in which we come to think of ourselves as beings with inner depths'. _Ethics of Authenticity_, p. 26.

7 Ferrara, Alessandro, _Modernity and Authenticity: A Study of the Social and Ethical Thought of Jean-Jacques Rousseau_. New York, State University of New York Press, 1993, p. 149.

8 Habermas, _Between Facts and Norms_, p. 93.

9 Held, _Democracy and the Global Order_, p. 155.

10 Raz, Joseph, _The Morality of Freedom_. Oxford, Clarendon Press, 1986, p. 387.

11 Held, _Democracy and the Global Order_, p. 156.

12 Habermas, _Between Facts and Norms_, p. 96.

13 Ibid., p. 96.

14 Habermas states that there is a correlation between private and public autonomy which is manifest in the system of law: _Between Facts and Norms_, chapter 3, pp. 82–131. Held conceptualizes this interrelation in a very similar fashion, and he argues that this particular connection between the system of law and the collective understanding of the principle of autonomy could be regarded as 'democratic autonomy': _Democracy and the Global Order_, p. 156.

15 Habermas, _Between Facts and Norms_, p. 98.

16 Habermas argues: 'To the extent that moral and ethical questions have been differentiated from one another, the discursively filtered substance of norms finds expression in the two dimensions of self-determination and self-realization'. Ibid., p. 99.

17 As Anthony Giddens argues: 'It is generally accepted among historians that the writing of autobiographies (as well as biographies) only developed during the modern period. . . . Yet autobiography – particularly in the broad sense of an interpretative self-history produced by the individual concerned, whether written down or not – is actually at the core of self-identity in modern social life. Like any other formalised narrative, it is something that has to be worked at, and calls for creative input as a matter of course'. Giddens, Anthony, _Modernity and Self-Identity: Self and Society in the Late Modern Age_. Cambridge, Polity Press, 1991, p. 76.

18 Taylor, Ferrara and Habermas agree on proposing Rousseau as the first author to exemplify the authenticity project.

19 Habermas, _Postmetaphysical Thinking_, p. 167.

20 Taylor, _Ethics of Authenticity_, p. 27.

21 Habermas adds: 'The authentic individual has himself to thank for his individuation; as this determinate product of determinate historical surroundings, he has made himself responsible for himself: "in choosing himself as product he can just as well be said to produce himself". For Kierkegaard, spontaneous activity is tied up with the "avowal" of individuality because it must prove itself in the recalcitrant material of one's own life'. _Postmetaphysical Thinking_, p. 165.

22 Kierkegaard, Søren, _Either/Or_, ed. and trans. Howard V. Hong and Edna H. Hong. Princeton, NJ, Princeton University Press, 1987, Part II. 52, p. 167.

23 Ibid., II. 160, p. 176 (italics added).

24 Seel, 'Two Meanings', in *Communicative Action,* ed. Honneth and Joas, p. 38.

25 See Kagan, L. Richard, *Los sueños de Lucrecia. Política y profecía en la España del siglo XVI.* Madrid, Nerea, 1991.

26 Von der Recke, Elisa, *Aufzeichnungen und Briefe aus ihren Jugendtagen,* ed. Paul Rachel. Leipzig, Dieterich, 1902.

27 'Oh! Sternheim was much better, more lovable and more unhappy than I. I will try to imitate her virtues, but I can never become as happy as Sternheim was at the end! For – Ah! Recke has no similarities with Seymour'. Cited from the English translation by Katherine R. Goodman, 'Poetry and Truth: Elisa von der Recke's Sentimental Autobiography' in *Interpreting Women's Lives: Feminist Theory and Personal Narratives,* ed. Personal Narratives Group. Bloomington and Indianapolis, Indiana University Press, 1989, p. 122.

28 Ibid., p. 118.

29 Ibid., p. 127.

30 See the example of Rebecca Cox Jackson, *Gifts of Power: The Writings of Rebecca Jackson, Black Visionary,* ed. Jean MacMahon Humey. Amherst, University of Massachusetts Press, 1981. See also Andrews, William L., *To Feel a True Story: The First Century of Afro-American Autobiography, 1760–1865.* Urbana, University of Illinois Press, 1986; Andrews, William, ed., *Three Black Women's Autobiographies of the Nineteenth Century.* Bloomington, Indiana University Press, 1986; Bromberg, Pamela S., 'The Development of Narrative Technique in Margaret Drabble's Novels', *Journal of Narrative Technique,* vol. 16, no. 3, 1986, pp. 179–91; Decker, Jeffrey Louis, 'Reconstructing Enterprise: Madam Walker, Black Womanhood and the Transportation of the American Culture of Success', in *The Seductions of Biography,* ed. Mary Rhiel and David Suchoff. New York and London, Routledge, 1996, pp. 99–111; Epstein, Barbara Leslie, *The Politics of Domesticity: Women, Evangelism, and Temperance in Nineteenth-century America.* Middletown, Wesleyan University Press, 1981; Gilkes, Cheryl, 'Together in Harness: Women's Tradition in the Sanctified Church', *Signs: Journal of Women in Culture and Society,* vol. 10, no. 4, 1985, pp. 678–99; McKay, Nellie J., 'Nineteenth-century Black Women's Spiritual Autobiographies: Religious Faith and Self-empowerment', in *Interpreting Women's Lives: Feminist Theories and Personal Narratives,* ed. Personal Narratives Group. Bloomington, Indiana University Press, pp. 139–54; Stone, Albert, *Autobiographical Occasions and Original Acts: Versions of American Identity from Henry Adams to Nate Shaw.* Philadelphia, University of Pennsylvania Press, 1982.

31 Elizabeth Hampstead, for example, argues that: 'In black autobiography, to a greater degree than in white, author and white reader, with separate racial identities within the same culture, are forced toward a common reading of experience': Hampstead, Elizabeth, 'Considering more than a Single Reader', in *Interpreting Women's Lives,* p. 140.

32 As Hampstead argues, 'the nineteenth century black writer, in telling her story, had to be sufficiently imaginative to avoid the pitfall of boring "facts", even while she remained true to her personal history': ibid., p. 140.

33 Ibid., p. 141.

Chapter 5 Narrative Cultural Interweavings

1 See, for example, the imaginative research of Gabriele Schwab about 'otherness in literary language': Schwab, _The Mirror and the Killer Queen_. Bloomington, Indiana University Press, 1996, esp. 'Witches, Mothers, and Male Fantasies: The Otherness of Women', pp. 103–24.

2 Arendt, _Human Condition_, p. 187.

3 Ibid., p. 192.

4 Ricoeur, _Time and Narrative_, vol. 1.

5 As Ricoeur has argued: 'action is the object in the expression _mimesis praxeos_. . . . The action is the "construct" of that construction that the mimetic activity consists of'. Ibid., vol. 1, pp. 34–5.

6 Ricoeur says: 'I named mimesis 1, mimesis 2, and mimesis 3. I take it as established that mimesis 2 constitutes the pivot of this analysis. By serving as a turning point it opens up the world of a plot and institutes . . . the literariness of the work of literature. But my thesis is that the very meaning of the configurating operation constitutive of emplotment is a result of its intermediary position between the two operations I am calling mimesis 1 and mimesis 3, which constitute the two sides of mimesis 2. By saying this, I propose to show that mimesis 2 draws its intelligibility from its faculty of mediation, which is to conduct us from the one side of the text to the other, transfiguring the one side into the other through its power of configuration'. Ibid., vol. 1, p. 53.

7 Kerby, _Narrative and the Self_, p. 44.

8 Margaret Kirkham argues: 'In these circumstances it is not surprising that the first major woman novelist to make her mark on English literature in a powerful way was a moralist, acutely interested in moral discourse as it affected the status of women in society and bore their representations in literature'. . . . '[her work] was concerned with establishing the moral equality of men and women and the proper status of individual women as accountable beings'. Kirkham, Margaret, _Jane Austen, Feminism and Fiction_. London, Athlone Press, 1977, p. 3.

9 Ricoeur defines 'mimesis 1' thus: 'To imitate or represent action is first to preunderstand what human acting is, in its semantics, its symbolic system, its temporality. Upon this preunderstanding, common to both poets and readers, emplotment is constructed and, with it, textual and literary mimetics'. _Time and Narrative_, vol. 1, p. 64.

10 Kirkham argues: 'Through her own practice as a novelist she criticises Johnson as well as Richardson and Fielding, giving her heroines sound heads as well as warm, susceptible hearts, and generally discerning taste in literature'. _Jane Austen_, p. 18.

11 Sulloway, Allison G., _Jane Austen and the Province of Womanhood_. Philadelphia, University of Pennsylvania Press, 1989, p. 4.

12 Ricoeur defines 'mimesis 2' thus: 'By placing mimesis 2 between an earlier and a later stage of mimesis in general, I am seeking not just to locate and frame it. I want to understand better the mediating function between what precedes fiction and what follows it. Mimesis 2 has an intermediary position

because it has a mediating function. . . . The dynamism lies in the fact that a plot already exercises, within its own textual field, an integrating and, in this sense, a mediating function, which allows it to bring about, beyond this field, a mediation of a larger amplitude between the preunderstanding and, if I may dare to put it this way, the postunderstanding of the order of action and its temporal features'. *Time and Narrative*, vol. 1, p. 65.

13 'Her novels are the culmination of a line of development in thought and fiction which goes back to the start of the eighteenth century, and which deserves to be called *feminist* since it was concerned with establishing the equality of men and women and the proper status of individual women as accountable beings': Kirkham, *Jane Austen*, p. 3.

14 Ely, John, 'Jane Austen: A Female Aristotelian', *Thesis Eleven*, no. 40, 1995, p. 94.

15 Ryle, Gilbert, 'Jane Austen and the Moralists', *Collected Papers*. London, Hutchinson, 1971, vol. 1, pp. 287.

16 MacIntyre, Alasdair, *After Virtue*, Notre Dame, IN, University of Notre Dame Press, 1984.

17 'Mimesis 3 marks the intersection of the world of the text and the world of the hearer or reader; the intersection, therefore, of the world configured by the poem and the world wherein real action occurs and unfolds its specific temporality': Ricoeur, *Time and Narrative*, vol. 1, p. 71.

18 Ely, John, 'Jane Austen', p. 95.

19 'Austen mocks those who fear that women could not be trusted as readers, and she makes sure that critics, as well as novelists, are included in her attack': Kirkham, *Jane Austen*, p. 17.

20 Kirkham agrees with this connection when she further explains that 'The disagreement [between herself and Dr Marilyn Butler] turns on how one sees Jane Austen's insistence upon Reason as the supreme guide to conduct, from which follow her criticism of Romanticism and her belief that sexual passion ought to be subjected to rational restraint': *Jane Austen*, p. xxii. It is known that Jane Austen read Hume. See Tucker, George Holbert, *Jane Austen, the Woman: Some Biographical Insights*. New York, St Martin's Griffin, 1994, p. 133.

21 Kirkham adds: 'but through participation in the new fiction women were to acquire a public voice, and the authority of moral teachers. The "female philosopher", who was never anything but a joke while she attempted the kinds of discourse from which her education disqualified her, was to become a powerful and respected influence through the novel'. Ibid., p. 14.

22 Ely, 'Jane Austen', p. 94.

23 For a feminist outlook on Hume's work, see Baier, C. Annette, *Moral Prejudices*. Cambridge, MA, Harvard University Press, 1994.

24 Smith, Adam, *The Theory of Moral Sentiments*, ed. D. D. Raphael and A. L. Macfie. Indianapolis, Liberty Fund, 1984.

25 Ely argues : 'The Aristotelian ethical principle of *habit* becomes, in Austen, the cultivation of feeling; and the heart is for Austen a morally educated organ. The heart is the source of "active kindness"'. 'Jane Austen', p. 95.

26 Ibid., p. 94.

27 Austen, Jane, *Sense and Sensibility*, with introduction by Tony Tanner. Lon-

don, Penguin, p. 38 (italics added).

28 Ely, 'Jane Austen', p. 94.

29 Ibid., p. 95.

30 Kirkham also focuses her defence of Austen's work on this particular scene: 'In Sanditon the avarice and pretentiousness of a minor seaside resort, aping the Prince Regent's Brighton, is satirised. In both strictures are made, or implied, on the most fashionable Romantic authors, Lord Byron and Scott. In both, the burlesque stereotype of a young woman deluded by romantic reading and corrected by a hero of sense *is reversed*. Anne Elliot advises the self-dramatising Captain Benwick to read less poetry; Charlotte Heywood begins to think Sir Edward Denham deranged when she hears the way he talks about Wordsworth, James Montgomery, Burns and Scott'. *Jane Austen*, p. 145.

31 Austen, Jane, *Persuasion*, ed. and with introduction by D. W. Harding. Harmondsworth, Penguin, 1965, p. 122.

32 Austen, *Sense and Sensibility*, p. 47.

33 Ibid., p. 52.

34 Austen, Jane, *Emma*, ed. and with introduction by Ronald Blythe. Harmondsworth, Penguin, 1971, p. 42.

35 Kirkham, *Jane Austen*, p. 133.

36 See, for example, the passage in which Elinor listens to the confession of Willoughby, the character who deceived her sister, Marianne, and who confesses to her why he did so: 'Willoughby, he, whom only half an hour ago she had abhorred as the most worthless of men, Willoughby, in spite of all his faults, excited a degree of commiseration for the sufferings produced by them, which made her think of him now as separated for ever from her family with a tenderness, a regret, rather in proportion, as she soon acknowledged within herself, to his wishes than to his merits. She felt that his influence over her mind was heightened by circumstances which ought not in reason to have weight; by that person of uncommon attraction, that open, affectionate, and lively manner which it was no merit to possess; and by that still ardent love for Marianne, which it was not even innocent to indulge. But she felt that it was so, long, long before she could feel his influence less'. Austen, *Sense and Sensibility*, p. 341.

37 Sulloway argues: 'The signature of all these women is also an Austenian signature: they all insisted that the mind thinks through the heart as often as the heart thinks through the mind'. *Jane Austen*, p. 120.

38 Booth, Wayne, *The Company We Keep: An Ethics of Fiction*. Berkeley, University of California Press, 1988, p. 432 (italics added).

39 Kirkham argues: 'Such a view arises from failure to recognise the author's feminist point of view and the play of ironic allusion upon the whole construction, plot and characterisation'. *Jane Austen*, p. 101.

40 Booth, *Ethics of Fiction*, p. 433.

41 Sulloway, *Jane Austen*, p. 63.

42 Kirkham, *Jane Austen*, p. 162.

43 Booth, *Ethics of Fiction*, p. 435 (italics added).

44 Nussbaum, Martha, *The Therapy of Desire: Theory and Practice in Hellenistic Ethics*. Princeton, NJ, Princeton University Press, 1994.

45 Ibid., p. 80.

46 Nussbaum argues: 'Thus, rather than having a simple dichotomy between the emotional and the (normatively) rational, we have a situation in which all emotions are to some degree "rational", in a descriptive sense – all are to some degree cognitive and based upon belief – and they are to be assessed, as beliefs are assessed, for their normative status'. Ibid., p. 81.

47 Nussbaum goes on to clarify that *philia* 'strictly speaking, is not an emotion at all, but a relationship with emotional components'. Ibid., p. 90.

48 Nussbaum had already dealt with these elements in her earlier works, for example, *The Fragility of Goodness: Luck and Ethics in Greek Tragedy and Philosophy*. Cambridge, MA, Cambridge University Press, 1986, and *Love's Knowledge: Essays on Philosophy and Literature*. Cambridge, MA, Oxford University Press, 1990. In the latter, she points out (p. 41): 'Because the emotions have the cognitive dimension in their very structure, it is very natural to view them as intelligent parts of our ethical agency, responsive to the workings of deliberation and essential to its completion'.

49 'One obvious answer was suggested already by Aristotle: we have never lived enough. Our experience is, without fiction, too confined and too parochial. Literature extends it, making us reflect and feel about what might otherwise be too distant for feeling. The importance of this for both morals and politics cannot be overestimated': Nussbaum, *Love's Knowledge*, p. 47. Compare how Austen felt about her world, and how her heroines felt the need to compensate their lack of experience with literature as a source of moral learning.

50 A similar idea is expressed by Iris Murdoch in her essay 'The Idea of Perfection': 'But the most essential and fundamental aspect of culture is the study of literature, since this is an education in how to picture and understand human situations. We are men and we are moral agents before we are scientists, and the place of science in human life must be discussed in words. This is why it is and always will be more important to know about Shakespeare than to know about any scientist: and if there is a "Shakespeare of science" his name is Aristotle'. *The Sovereignty of Good*. New York, Routledge, 1970 p. 35.

51 This connection has also been brilliantly appraised by Booth in *Ethics of Fiction*. Nussbaum recognizes that her formulation is similar to Booth's: 'although, as "Discernment", most novels focus in some manner on our common humanity, through their structures of friendship and identification, and thus make some contribution to the pursuit of those projects'. *Love's Knowledge*, p. 45.

52 Gilligan, *In a Different Voice*.

53 See, for example, Tronto, C. Joan, *Moral Boundaries: A Political Argument for an Ethic of Care*. New York, Routledge, 1993.

54 Lawrence Blum has drawn attention to this issue in *Moral Perception and Particularity*. Cambridge, MA, Cambridge University Press, 1994, esp. Part III, 'The Morality of Care', pp. 173–237.

55 As Blum rightly argues: 'this binary conception of morality is a very misleading way to think about morality and the moral life. . . . It overemphasizes the differences that do exist between men and women, and potentially contributes both to further divisions between them and to unequal treat-

ment of women'. _Moral Perception_, p. 241. Similar objections based on strong arguments that justice and care are complementary have been offered by Benhabib in her essay 'The Debate over Women and Moral Theory Revisited', in _Feminists Read Habermas: Gendering the Subject of Discourse_, ed. Johanna Meehan. New York, Routledge, 1995, pp. 181–203.

56 Benhabib defends Gilligan on grounds similar to the outlook I am developing here. She has also argued against criticism from feminists who think that Gilligan's findings are not relevant because she did not address 'gender difference' in her psychological explanation of moral development. Benhabib also answered the opposite charge from feminists who believe terms such as care will mean that women again submit themselves to the features which men have considered the signs of woman's inferiority. See Benhabib, 'Debate over Women'.

57 Nussbaum, Martha, 'Human Capabilities, Female Human Beings' in _Women, Culture and Development_, ed. Nussbaum and Glover, pp. 61–104.

58 Nussbaum, 'Human Capabilities', p. 74.

59 Nussbaum also argues: 'The result of this inquiry is, then, not a list of value-neutral facts, but a normative conception. . . . The account is meant to be both tentative and open-ended. It claims only that in these areas there is considerable continuity and overlap, sufficient to ground a working political consensus'. Ibid., p. 74.

60 Murdoch, _Sovereignty_, p. 97.

Chapter 6   Justice and Solidarity

1 See, Habermas, Jürgen, 'Three Normative Models of Democracy', _Constellations_, vol. 1, no. 1, 1994, pp. 1–10.

2 See Rawls, John, _Political Liberalism_. New York, Columbia University Press, 1993; and Habermas, _Between Facts and Norms_.

3 Benhabib, Seyla, 'Deliberative Rationality and Models of Democratic Legitimacy', _Constellations_, vol. 1, no. 1, 1994, pp. 26–52.

4 Niklas Luhmann is one of the social theorists who has expressed scepticism about representative democracy under modern conditions of extreme complexity.

5 Among feminist theorists, Iris Young is concerned about the enlightened version of the 'civil' public, arguing that such a public is partial in its claim of universalism and proposing instead a heterogeneous public sphere. See Young, Iris Marion, _Justice and the Politics of Difference_. Princeton, NJ, Princeton University Press, 1990.

6 Habermas, _Between Facts and Norms_, p. 371.

7 Fraser, Nancy, 'Rethinking the Public Sphere', in _Justice Interruptus_, 1997, pp. 69–98.

8 See, for example, Alexander, Jeffrey C., 'Civil Society I, II, III: Constructing an Empirical Concept from Normative Controversies and Historical Transformations', in _Real Civil Societies_, ed. Alexander, London, Sage Publications, London, 1998. Cohen, Jean, and Arato Andrew, _Civil Society and Political Theory_. Cambridge, MA, MIT Press, 1992.

9 Claus Offe, for example, argues: 'From that perspective, associative rela-

tions fulfil the function of a filter *vis-à-vis* the moral dimension of action. The selectivity of this filter determines whether and to what extent the application and development of legally guaranteed freedoms of action plus cognitive and moral capacities of individual actors, as constituted in socialization processes and by cultural transmission, are encouraged and fostered'. Offe, Claus, *Modernity and the State: East, West*. Cambridge, Polity Press, 1996, p. 45.

10 Bohman, James, *Public Deliberation: Pluralism, Complexity, and Democracy*. Cambridge, MA, MIT Press, 1996.

11 Alexander, Jeffrey C., 'The Paradoxes of Civil Society', in *International Sociology*, vol. 12, no. 2, 1995, pp. 115–33.

12 Offe says: 'As examples of this need, consider seemingly trivial contexts of action in the areas of education, health, consumption, and transportation, and, more generally, the regulation of relations between genders, between generations, between indigenous and immigrant populations, between professionals and their clients. There are countless other cases where so-called problems of the collective good and of systemic control cannot be resolved by price regulation or by coercion. . . . If such problems can be resolved at all, it can only be by the informed and circumspect, yet abstract development of solidarity and of a civilized public spirit. In all these spheres of action, the common moral problem revolves around the constitutive 'vulnerability' of individuals, and the need to compensate for it by protecting their physical integrity and by respecting their dignity'. *Modernity and the State*, p. 44.

13 See, for example, Landes, *Women in the Public Sphere*; Benhabib, Seyla, 'Models of Public Space: Hannah Arendt, the Liberal Tradition and Jürgen Habermas', *Situating the Self*, pp. 89–120; Yeatman, Anna, 'Beyond Natural Right: The Conditions for Universal Citizenship', *Postmodern Revisionings of the Political*. New York, Routledge, 1994, pp. 57–79; Young, Iris Marion, 'The Ideal of Impartiality and the Civic Public', in *Justice and the Politics of Difference*, pp. 96–121; Fleming, Marie, 'Women and the "Public Use of Reason"', *Feminists Read Habermas*, ed. Meehan, pp. 117–38. Chambers, Simone, 'Feminist Discourse/Practical Discourse', in *Feminists Read Habermas*, ed. Meehan, pp. 163–80.

14 Jane Mansbridge argues: 'We need communities of discourse, oppositional communities, to keep alive, nourish, analyze, and rework our understandings of the injustices that went into making up the very people we are now, at the same time that the people we are now go about acting in the world as it is. We go forward, but instead of putting our compromises with justice behind us, we keep them with us, in nagging tension, not disabling us but reminding us that all is not as it should be.' Mansbridge, Jane, 'Using Power and Fighting Power', *Constellations*, vol. 1, no. 1, 1994, p. 55.

15 Axel Honneth claims: 'Generalizing these results beyond their particular research context, we arrive at the conclusion that the normative presupposition of all communicative action is to be seen in the acquisition of social recognition: Subjects encounter each other within the parameters of their reciprocal expectation that they receive recognition as moral persons and for their life achievements'. Honneth, Axel, 'The Social Dynamics of Disrespect:

On the Location of Critical Theory', _Constellations_, vol. 1, no. 2, 1994, p. 262.

16 Bohman, _Public Deliberation_, p. 200.

17 Dean, _Solidarity of Strangers_, p. 45.

18 Bohman, _Public Deliberation_, p. 213 (italics added).

19 Ibid., p. 213.

20 Ibid., p. 214.

21 Ibid., p. 214.

22 See, for example, Rorty's use of this concept: Rorty, Richard, _Contingency, Irony, and Solidarity_. Cambridge, MA, Cambridge University Press, 1989.

23 Wellmer has argued: 'Art does not merely disclose reality, it also opens our eyes. This opening of eyes (and ears), this tranformation of perception, is the healing of a partial blindness (and deafness), of an incapacity to perceive and experience reality in the way that we learn to perceive and experience it through the medium of aesthetic experience'. Wellmer, Albrecht, 'Truth, Semblance, Reconciliation: Adorno's Aesthetic Redemption of Modernity', _Persistence of Modernity_, p. 26.

24 Bohman, _Public Deliberation_, p. 215.

25 It has long been known among literary critics that novels and fiction are usually more alive and imaginative in countries where there are enormous problems in terms of social justice, democracy and institutions. Latin American fiction, for example, has been among the most powerful of the twentieth century, with an abundance of utopias and social criticism. During various military governments in Latin America, a great many novels critical towards them appeared, notably those of Gabriel García Márquez (from Colombia), Alejo Carpentier (from Cuba), Augusto Roa Bastos (from Paraguay) and Arguedas (from Guatemala). This could be interpreted as paralleling Central Europe of the 1930s, when such writers as Hermann Broch, Robert Musil, Franz Kafka, Joseph Roth and Elias Canetti dealt with the disappearance of a world and the collapse of morality in the total horror of the holocaust.

26 According to Wellmer: 'Schwab's idea is that reflexive opening-up of literary forms of representation triggers a playful to and fro between identification and differentiation on the part of the reader, which effectively works towards a genuine expansion of subjective boundaries. In this sense one might also say that new forms of aesthetic synthesis in modern art point towards new forms of psychic and social "synthesis" '. 'Truth, Semblance, Reconciliation', p. 20.

27 Wellmer also says: 'The connection between the expansion of the work of art on the one hand and of the subject on the other shows that what Adorno called "aesthetic synthesis" can after all be ultimately linked up with a real utopia of non-violent communication. But this is true only if we acknowledge that art has a _function in connection with_ forms of non-aesthetic communication or of a real change in ways of understanding ourselves and the world'. Ibid., p. 21.

28 Wellmer argues: 'But if we allow the course of history such a degree of ambiguity that we can still see it as possessing a potential for emancipation, then it is also possible to discover traces of a transformation of the relationship between art and the life-world in reality. On the basis of these traces we

can defend the idea of an altered relationship between art and the life-world in which a democratic praxis would be able to draw productively on the innovative and communicative potential of art. My reflections on the truth of art were intended to show, amongst other things, that the perspective of *this sort* of "sublation" of art in the praxis of life really is present in the concept of artistic beauty'. Ibid., pp. 31–2.

29 Bohman, *Public Deliberation*, p. 218.
30 Ibid., p. 223.
31 Bohman, *Public Deliberation*, p. 225.
32 Ibid., p. 229.
33 Ibid., p. 230 (italics added).
34 MacKinnon, Catharine, *Feminism Unmodified: Discourses of Life and Law*. Cambridge, MA, Harvard University Press, 1987, p. 77.
35 Gilligan, *In a Different Voice*.
36 Benhabib, 'Debate over Women', in *Feminists Read Habermas*, ed. Meehan, p. 181.
37 As Benhabib puts it: 'Even in highly rationalized modern societies where most of us are wage earners and political citizens, the moral issues which preoccupy us most and which touch us most deeply derive not from problems of justice in the economy and the polity, but precisely from the quality of our relations with others in the "spheres of kinship, love, friendship, and sex"'. 'The Debate over Women', p. 187.
38 Ibid., p. 187.
39 Ibid., p. 189.
40 Nussbaum, *Love's Knowledge*, p. 50.
41 Ibid., pp. 66–7.
42 Ibid., p. 67.
43 Ibid., p. 75.
44 Nussbaum argues: 'Emotion can play a cognitive role, and cognition, if it is to be properly informed, must draw on the work of the emotive elements'. Ibid., p. 78.
45 Cornell, Drucilla, *The Imaginary Domain. Abortion, Pornography and Sexual Harassment*. New York, Routledge, 1995, p. 4.
46 Ibid., p. 4.
47 Cornell states: 'I use the word "degradation" to specify what I mean by the primary good of self-respect for each one of us as a sexual being. It should go without saying that hierarchical gradations of any of us as unworthy of personhood violates the postulation of each one of us as an equal called for by a democratic and modern legal system'. Ibid., p. 10.
48 Ibid., p. 10.
49 Dean 'Discourse in Different Voices', in *Feminists Read Habermas*, ed. Meehan, p. 205.
50 Dean, *Solidarity of Strangers*, p. 49.
51 Dean believes that 'these motivational questions become issues of socialization and personality formation on the one hand, and the appropriate social and democratic institutions on the other': ibid., p. 206.
52 Dean, 'Reflective Solidarity', *Constellations*, vol. 2, no. 1, 1995, p. 123.
53 Ibid., p. 123.

54 Ibid., p. 126.
55 Ibid., p. 126.
56 Dean, _Solidarity of Strangers_, p. 174.
57 Ibid., p. 129.
58 Ibid., p. 174.

Chapter 7   The Moral Foundation of Recognition

1 Nancy Fraser argues: 'The struggle for recognition is fast becoming the paradigmatic form of political conflict in the late twentieth century. Demands for recognition of difference fuel struggles for groups mobilized under the banners of nationality, ethnicity, "race", gender and sexuality'. 'From Redistribution to Recognition?', in _Justice Interruptus_, p. 11.
2 Taylor, Charles, 'The Politics of Recognition', in _Multiculturalism and 'The Politics of Recognition'_, ed. Amy Gutmann. Princeton, NJ, Princeton University Press, 1992.
3 Taylor says: 'I should note here that Herder applied his conception of originality at two levels, not only to the individual person among other persons, but also to the culture-bearing people among other cultures'. He adds 'The projection of an inferior or demeaning image on another can actually distort and oppress to the extent that the image is internalized. Not only contemporary feminism but also race relations and discussions of multiculturalism are undergirded by the premise that the withholding of recognition can be a form of oppression'. Ibid., p. 31.
4 Taylor, _Sources of the Self_, p. 373.
5 Taylor says: 'In realizing my nature, I have to define it in the sense of giving it some formulation. . . . I am realizing this formulation and thus giving my life a definite shape. A human life is seen as manifesting a potential which is also being shaped by this manifestation'. Ibid., p. 375.
6 Taylor says: 'Just because it is a theory of freedom, the Kantian moral philosophy finds it hard to ignore the criticism that the rational agent is not the whole person. This didn't lead Kant to want to alter his definition of autonomy, but he did see that the condition of polar opposition between reason and nature was somehow non-optimal, that the demands of morality and freedom point towards a fulfilment in which nature and reason would once more be in alignment'. Ibid., p. 385.
7 Taylor, Charles, _The Ethics of Authenticity_. Cambridge, MA, Harvard University Press, 1991.
8 Taylor says: 'I'd like to maintain that there is something valid in this presumption, but that it is by no means unproblematic and involves something like an act of faith. As a presumption, the claim is that all human cultures that have animated whole societies over some considerable stretch of time have something important to say to all human beings'. 'The Politics of Recognition', _Philosophical Arguments_. Cambridge, MA, Harvard University Press, p. 253.
9 What Taylor ignores, in other words, is the possibility of this problematic relation between our feelings and our rationality, the fact that no one can assure us that our feelings are in a way truer than our rationality. This is one

of the major rationales of pyschoanalytic therapy, for example.

10 See Giddens, *Modernity and Self-Identity*.

11 Habermas, Jürgen, 'Struggles for Recognition in Constitutional States', *European Journal of Philosophy*, vol. 1, no. 2, 1993, p. 133.

12 Ibid., p. 144.

13 Honneth, Axel, *The Struggle for Recognition: The Moral Grammar of Social Conflict*. Cambridge, Polity Press, 1995. In our review of this book, in *New Left Review*, no. 220, 1996, pp. 126–36, Jeffrey C. Alexander and I elaborated the criticism to Honneth's anthropological model. I thank the *New Left Review* for permission to use this material. I am also grateful to Jeffrey C. Alexander for allowing me to use our work as part of my argument in this chapter.

14 Honneth says: '[Hegel] sees a society's ethical relations as representing forms of practical intersubjectivity in which movements of recognition guar-antee the complementary agreement and the necessary mutuality of opposed subjects. To the degree that a subject knows itself to be recognized by another subject with regard to certain of its (the subject's) abilities and qualities and is thereby reconciled with the other, a subject always comes to know its own distinctive identity and thereby comes to be opposed once again to the other as something particular', pp. 16–17.

15 Hegel's 'idea leads to the further conclusion that an individual that does not recognize its partner to interaction to be a certain type of person is also unable to experience itself completely or without restriction as that type of person. The implication of this for the relationship of recognition can only be that an obligation to reciprocity is, to a certain extent, built into such relations'. Honneth, ibid., p. 37.

16 See, for example, the essay on Mead in Habermas, 'Individuation through Socialization: On George Herbert Mead's Theory of Subjectivity', in *Postmetaphysical Thinking*, 1992, pp. 149–204 (p. 180).

17 Honneth, *Struggle for Recognition*, p. 131.

18 The following discussion is drawn from Alexander, Jeffrey C., and Lara, Maria Pia, 'Honneth's New Critical Theory', *New Left Review*, no. 220, 1996, pp. 126–36.

19 Ibid., p. 131.

20 Honneth, *Struggle for Recognition*, p. 172.

21 Ibid., pp. 172–3.

22 Freud, Anna, *The Ego of the Mechanisms of Defense*, vol. 2 of *The Writings of Anna Freud*, New York, International Universities Press, 1936.

23 Chodorow, Nancy, *The Reproduction of Mothering: Psychoanalysis and the Sociology of Gender*. Berkeley and Los Angeles, University of California Press, 1978.

24 Honneth, *Struggle for Recognition*, p. 128.

25 Ibid., p. 129.

26 Ricoeur, Paul, *Oneself as Another*. Chicago, University of Chicago Press, 1992. Ricoeur points out (p. 3): 'Oneself as another suggests from the outset that the selfhood of oneself implies otherness to such an intimate degree that one cannot be thought of without the other, that instead one passes into the other, as we might say in Hegelian terms.'

27 Ricoeur, *Time and Narrative*, vol. 1.
28 Ricoeur writes: 'in this way, self-esteem and self-respect together will represent the most advanced stages of the growth of selfhood, which is at the same time its unfolding'. Ibid., p. 171.
29 Ricoeur says: 'In this sense, equality is presupposed by friendship. This is why friendship alone can aim at the familiarity of a shared life'. Ibid., p. 184.
30 Ricoeur claims: 'What it adds is the idea of reciprocity in the exchange between human beings who each esteem themselves. As for the corollary of reciprocity, namely equality, it places friendship on the path of justice, where the life together shared by few people gives way to the distribution of shares in a plurality on the scale of a historical, political community'. Ibid., p. 188.
31 Ricoeur says: 'Equality, however it is modulated, is to life in institutions what solicitude is to interpersonal relations. Solicitude provides the self another who is a face, in the strong sense that Emmanuel Levinas has taught us to recognize. Equality provides to the self another who is an each. In this, the distributive character of "each" passes from the grammatical plane. Because of this, the sense of justice takes nothing away from solicitude; the sense of justice presupposes it, to the extent that it holds persons to be irreplaceable. Justice, in turn, adds to solicitude, to the extent that the field of application of equality is all of humanity'. Ibid., p. 202.
32 Ibid., p. 215.
33 Ricoeur claims: 'Now humanity, taken not in the extensive or enumerative sense of the sum of human beings but in the comprehensive or fundamental sense of that by reason of which one is made worthy of respect, is nothing other than universality considered from the viewpoint of the multiplicity' of persons: what Kant termed 'object' or 'matter'. Ibid., p. 223.
34 Ibid., p. 226.
35 Ibid., p. 179.
36 Ibid., p. 179.
37 Kosselleck, Reinhart, *Futures Past: On the Semantics of Historical Time*. Cambridge, MA, MIT Press, 1985, pp. 272–3.
38 Ricoeur, *Time and Narrative*, vol. 1, p. 163.
39 Ibid., p. 164.
40 Ibid., p. 164.
41 Ricoeur, *Oneself as Another*, p. 181.
42 Ibid., p. 182.
43 Ricoeur finishes this paragraph with the words: 'which, in the hour of agony, find refuge in the shared whisper of voices or the feeble embrace of clasped hands'. Ibid., p. 191.
44 Ricoeur says: 'According to Arendt, power stems directly from the category of action as irreducible to those of labour and work: this category has a political significance, in the broad sense of the word, irreducible to the state, if one stresses, on the one hand, the condition of plurality and, on the other, *action in concert*'. Ibid., p. 195.
45 Ibid., p. 196.
46 Ricoeur says: 'However illusive power may be in its fundamental structure, however weak it may be without the help of authority that articulates it on

ever more ancient foundations, it is power, wanting to live and act together, that brings to the ethical aim the point of application of its indispensable third dimension: justice'. Ibid., p. 197.

Chapter 8 Feminist Models of Recognition

1 Parekh, Bhikhu, 'Dilemmas of a Multicultural Theory of Citizenship', *Constellations*, vol. 4, no. 1, 1997, p. 54.
2 In several ways Young's ideas resemble those of Charles Taylor in his 'Politics of Difference'. They both value cultures equally, they regard Modernity and liberal theory with suspicion, they will not provide for transcultural criteria for moral worthness.
3 These 'practical vicious circles' are described by Wellmer as tensions between liberal rights and the democratic praxis derived from them. See Wellmer, Albrecht, 'Bedingungen einer demokratischen Kultur: Zur Debatte zwischen "Liberalen" und "Kommunitaristen" ', *Endspiele: Die unversöhnliche Moderne. Essays und Vorträge*. Frankfurt am Main, Suhrkamp, 1993, p. 64.
4 In this respect, see Pateman, Carole, *The Problem of Political Obligation. A Critique of Liberal Theory*. Berkeley, University of California Press, 1985; *The Disorder of Women*. Cambridge, Polity Press, 1988; and *The Sexual Contract*. Cambridge, Polity Press, 1988. See also Okin, Susan Moller, *Women in Western Political Thought*, esp. Part III: 'Rousseau' pp. 99–197; and Benhabib, 'Deliberative Rationality'.
5 Butler, A. Melissa, 'Early Liberal Roots of Feminism: John Locke and the Attack on Patriarchy', in *Feminist Interpretations*, ed. Lyndon Shanley and Pateman, pp. 74–94. See also Pateman, *Sexual Contract*; Parry, Geraint, 'Individuality, Politics and the Critique of Paternalism in John Locke', *Political Studies*, no. 12, June 1964, pp. 163–77.
6 For critical examination of all these issues, see Phillips, Anne, *Democracy and Difference*. University Park, PA, Pennsylvania State University Press, 1993.
7 The work of Catharine MacKinnon has been very important in this sense, first, through her struggle for recognition of sexual harassment as a legal crime and, later, with her projected law for the prohibition of pornography as a right of women to safeguard their dignity and to avoid the degrading image that these practices exercise on the self-conception of women. See MacKinnon, Catharine, *Sexual Harassment and the Working Woman: A Case of Working Women*. New Haven, Yale University Press, 1979. See also Schroeder, Jane, 'Feminism Historicized: Medieval Misogynist Stereotypes in Contemporary Feminist Jurisprudence', *Iowa Law Review*, vol. 75, 1990, p. 1135; Cornell, 'Sex Discrimination Law and Equivalent Rights', in *Transformations*, pp. 147–55.
8 See Landes, *Women and the Public Sphere*; Benhabib, 'Models of Public Space', in *Situating the Self*; Fraser, 'Rethinking the Public Sphere'; Yeatman, Anna, 'Beyond Natural Right: The Conditions for Universal Citizenship', *Postmodern Revisionings of the Political*. New York, Routledge, 1994, pp. 57–79; and Young, *Justice and the Politics of Difference*.
9 Fraser, Nancy, 'Multiculturalism and Gender Equity: The U.S. "Difference" Debates Revisited', *Constellations*, vol. 3, no. 1, 1996, pp. 61–72.

10 Ibid., p. 64.

11 Ibid., p. 66.

12 Ibid., p. 67.

13 Fraser, _Justice Interruptus_, esp. 'Multiculturalism, Antiessentialism, and Radical Democracy', pp. 173–88.

14 The line that needs to be drawn between forms of difference which foster democracy and those which reflect anti-democratic aspirations has to be made on the normative dimension, which links the aspiration for the recognition of difference with the solidarity of addressing others in the claim for the recognition of what makes human life worth living.

15 Fraser, for example, argues: 'Deconstructive antiessentialists appraise identity claims on ontological grounds alone. They do not ask, in contrast, how a given identity or difference is related to social structures of domination and to social relations of inequality. . . . They risk succumbing, as a result, to a night in which all cows are gray: all identities threaten to become equally fictional, equally repressive, and equally exclusionary'. _Justice Interruptus_, p. 183.

16 Butler, Judith, 'Imitation and Gender Insubordination', in _The Second Wave: A Reader in Feminist Theory_, ed. Linda Nicholson. New York and London, Routledge, 1997, p. 301; see also Butler, _Gender Trouble: Feminism and the Subversion of Identity_. New York and London, Routledge, 1990, p. 101.

17 Thus Bonnie Honig: 'This notion of an agonistic politics of performativity situated in the self evidences of the private realm is explored by Judith Butler, who focuses in particular on the construction and constitution of sex and gender. Butler unmasks the private realm's constatations . . . and redescribes them as performativities that daily (re)produced sex/gender identities. Honig, Bonnie, 'Towards an Agonistic Feminism: Hannah Arendt and the Politics of Identity' in _Feminist Interpretations of Hannah Arendt_, ed. Honig, pp. 147–8.

18 Fraser, Nancy, 'False Antitheses: A Response to Seyla Benhabib and Judith Butler', _Justice Interruptus_, p. 214.

19 Ibid., p. 214.

20 Fraser, 'From Redistribution to Recognition', _Justice Interruptus_, pp. 11–40.

21 Ibid., p. 15.

22 This distinction is derived from Seyla Benhabib's analysis of these two conceptions; see Benhabib, Seyla, 'Democracy and Difference: Reflections on the Metapolitics of Lyotard and Derrida', _Journal of Political Philosophy_, vol. 2, no. 1, 1994, pp. 1–23.

23 See, for example, the criticisms developed by Benhabib, ibid.

24 A similar point is made by Judith Butler when she argues that cultural deconstructions are healthy for the envisioning and enlarging of our conceptions of universality: 'In this sense, being able to utter the performative contradiction is hardly a self-defeating enterprise; on the contrary, it is crucial to the continuing revision and elaboration of historical standards of universality proper to the futural movement of democracy itself. To claim that the universal has not yet been articulated is to insist that the 'not yet' is proper to an understanding of the universal itself: that which remains 'unrealized' by the universal constitutes it essentially'. Butler, Judith, 'Uni-

versality in Culture' in Nussbaum, C. Martha, and respondents, *For Love of Country: Debating the Limits of Patriotism*, ed. Martha C. Joshua Cohen. Boston, Beacon Press, 1996, p. 48.

25 Benhabib argues: 'Only through the perpetual asking and answering of the relevant questions through publicly accessible channels can new identities come to the fore, delegitimization processes be aired and the meaning of sovereignty be re-established'. 'Democracy and Difference', p. 21.

26 Young argues: 'An emancipatory politics that affirms group difference involves a reconception of the meaning of equality. The assimilationist ideal assumes that equal social status for all persons requires treating everyone according to the same principles, rules, and standards. A politics of difference argues, on the other hand, that equality as the participation and inclusion of all groups sometimes requires different treatment for oppressed or disadvantaged groups. To promote social justice, I argue, social policy should sometimes accord special treatment to groups. I explore pregnancy and birthing rights for workers, bilingual-bicultural rights, and American Indian rights as three cases of such a special treatment. Finally, I expand the idea of a heterogeneous public here by arguing for a principle of representation for oppressed groups in democratic decisionmaking bodies'. *Justice and the Politics of Difference*, p. 158.

27 Freud's theory deals extensively with the notion of bisexuality and the repression of the other. In the case of Jung, for example, and his notions of archetypes, feminine figures play important roles in the formation of the self. And Lacan has had a great impact among feminists precisely because of his understanding of the roles of the masculine seeking the feminine and placing women as myth. Drucilla Cornell synthesizes Lacan's conception as follows: 'Indeed, Woman as lack, as the impossible, the unreachable projection of an inexpressible desire, is constitutive of genderized subjectivity. Even so, Woman does not exist as a 'reality', present to the subject, but as a loss. . . . Lacan explains some of the great myths of the quest in which masculine identity seeks to ground itself as a quest for Her. The feminine becomes the Holy Grail. Within the Lacanian framework, the myths of Woman are about this quest to ground masculine subjectivity'. Cornell, *Transformations*, p. 75.

28 Young argues the contrary: 'The requirements of justice, then, concern less the making of cultural rules than providing institutional means for fostering politicized discussion, and making forums and media available for alternative experiment and play'. *Justice and the Politics of Difference*, p. 152.

29 Fraser suggests: 'There are different kinds of differences. Some differences are of type 1 and should be eliminated (as artefacts of oppression); others are of type 2 and should be universalized (differences as new evaluations of worth); still others are of type 3 and should be enjoyed (differences as cultural variation). This position implies that we can make judgements about which differences fall into which categories. It also implies that we can make normative judgements about the relative value of alternative norms, practices, and interpretations, judgements that could lead to conclusions of inferiority, superiority, and equivalent value. It militates against any politics of difference that is wholesale and undifferentiated. It entails a

more differentiated politics of difference'. _Justice Interruptus,_ p. 204.

30 I refer to the example of the United States mainly because Iris Young takes it as her basic empirical ground for asserting her thesis about the 'difference' strategies claims for recognition. But I am sure that there are other good examples of how a group, in a society, has built up its strength by claiming its difference as something worthy and with the aim of it being accepted as a universal feature. However, my interpretation of how this has been achieved differs from Young's, because I think that when those differences become part of the revalued judgement of other cultures, they have succeeded through a universalizing process. That is certainly the case of the basic characteristics that Jewishness has presented to the public in several films: the iconic figure of Woody Allen, for example, representing Jewish existential insecurity, dark and light humour, all the various stereotypes of the Jewish family, has an international appeal. This is part of a much wider process, including the general availability of Jewish religious food for everyday consumption in the United States and elsewhere. See Katz, Eliha, _The Voyage of the Bagel._ Tel Aviv, University of Tel Aviv, 1995.

31 Fanon, Franz, _The Wretched of the Earth._ New York: Grove Press, 1965.

32 Those achievements have been made through a deconstruction of the category 'race', and also, by thematizing other interpretations of different categories such as 'caste'. See, for example, Dollard, John, _Caste and Class in a Southern Town._ New York, Doubleday, 1957.

33 Ricoeur, _Oneself as Another,_ p. 161.

34 Habermas, Jürgen. 'Struggles for Recognition in the Democratic Constitutional State', in, _Multiculturalism,_ ed. Gutmann, pp. 107–48.

35 Benhabib, _Situating the Self._

36 Villa, _Arendt and Heidegger,_ p. 69.

37 Ibid., p. 70.

38 Honig, _Feminist Interpretations,_ p. 156.

39 Arendt, _Human Condition,_ p. 186.

40 Ibid., p. 136.

41 Ibid., p. 140.

42 Ibid., p. 146.

43 Ibid., p. 147.

44 Ibid., p. 155.

45 Ibid., p. 159.

46 Honig argues: 'The emphasis of agonistic feminism on the development of individuality as an effect of participation in concerted political action restores Arendt's original partnering of agonism and associationism'. _Feminist Interpretations,_ p. 160.

47 Lisa Jane Disch has also noticed this problem: 'Honig offers no account of "virtuosic" citizenship to explain how an individual who braves the risks of the public space out of an "agonal passion for distinction and outstanding achievement", would act in concert with others. Whether out of fear or delight, proponents of the "agonistic" interpretation play up the disruptive implications that natality and plurality have on the model of the political actor as responsible, self-contained subject at the expense of attending to the ways in which Arendt's concept of publicity counters the subjectivism and

narcissism of the agonistic model'. Disch, *Hannah Arendt*, p. 84.
48 Honig, *Feminist Interpretations*, p. 158.
49 Landes, *Women and the Public Sphere*, p. 27.
50 Benhabib, *Reluctant Modernism*, p. 27.
51 Ibid., p. 28.
52 Ibid., p. 28.
53 Ibid., p. 42.
54 Benhabib argues: 'In Arendt's later terminology, the world is always a world shared with others because "plurality" is the fundamental human condition, that is, because humans inhabit a space with others to whom they are both equal and from whom they are distinct'. Ibid., p. 53.
55 Ibid., p. 71.
56 Ibid., p. 82.
57 Ibid., p. 87.
58 I am grateful to Jeffrey C. Alexander for discussions about, and readings of, his forthcoming book, *Possibilities of Justice: A Sociological Theory of Civil Society*.

Conclusion

1 Cohen and Arato, *Civil Society and Political Theory*, esp. chapter 10, 'Social Movements and Civil Society,' pp. 492–563.
2 Ibid., p. 492.
3 Ibid., p. 494.
4 Ibid., p. 494.
5 Baker, Houston A., Jr, 'Critical Memory and the Black Public Sphere', in *The Black Public Sphere: A Public Culture Book*, ed. Black Public Sphere Collective, Chicago and London, University of Chicago Press, p. 13.
6 Ibid., p. 13.
7 Ibid., p. 16.
8 Ibid., p. 16.
9 Ibid., p. 13.
10 Ibid., p. 16.
11 Ibid., pp. 22–3.
12 Ibid., p. 29.
13 Diawara, Manthia, 'Malcolm X and the Black Public Sphere: Conversionists versus Culturalists', in *Black Public Sphere*, p. 29.
14 Ibid., p. 49.
15 Ibid., p. 49.
16 Ibid., p. 43.
17 Ibid., p. 43.
18 Cohen and Arato, *Civil Society*, p. 503; Tilly, Charles, et al., *The Rebellious Century: 1830–1930*. Cambridge, MA, Harvard University Press, 1975; Tilly, Charles, *From Mobilization to Revolution*. Reading, MA, Addison Wesley, 1978.
19 Cohen and Arato, *Civil Society*, p. 511; Touraine, Alain, *The Voice and the Eye*. Cambridge, Cambridge University Press, 1981.
20 Cohen and Arato, *Civil Society*, p. 511.

21 Ibid., p. 505.
22 Ibid., p. 507.
23 Ibid., p. 523; Burke, Kenneth, _Language as Action: Essays on Life, Literature and Method_. Berkeley, University of California Press, 1966.
24 'For it is perfectly conceivable that a concrete social movement can involve all the forms of action. This is obvious in the case of contemporary collective actions. Key sectors of the new movements, from feminism to ecology, have a self-reflective relation to the objective, subjective, and social worlds insofar as they thematize issues of personal and social identity, defend existing norms, contextualize social interpretations of norms, communicatively create new norms, and propose alternative ways of relating to the environment. [Because] all collective action . . . involves strategic, instrumental, and norm oriented activity [,] there is no reason why the analysis of the various logics of collective action should be construed as the sole form of rationality of collective action to the exclusion of others. Moreover, on the basis of this analysis, one can see that movements can struggle simultaneously for the defense and democratization of civil society and for inclusion within and expansion of political society'. Cohen and Arato, _Civil Society_, p. 523. Smelser, Neil, _The Theory of a Collective Behavior_. New York, Free Press, 1962.
25 'The only exception he sees is the feminist movement. It alone has a dual logic and clear emancipatory potential: an offensive, universalist side concerned with political inclusion and equal rights, along with a defensive, particularist side focusing on identity, alternative values, and the overturning of concrete forms of life marked by male monopolies and a one-sidedly rationalized everyday practice. The first dimension links feminism to the tradition of bourgeois-socialist liberation movements and to universalist moral principles. The second links it to the new social movements. [As Habermas sees it,] however, the new resistance movements, including the second dimension of feminism, involve exclusively defensive relations to colonization. Hence [his] label "particularist" for the concern with identities, norms, and alternative values, and hence [his] charge of a "retreat" into ascriptive or biologistic categories of gender. According to Habermas, the emancipatory dimension of feminism [thus] suffers from the same drawbacks as the other new movements'. Cohen and Arato, _Civil Society_, p. 529.
26 Ibid., p. 530.
27 These examples of how cultural narration allows the opening up of restrictions in the bourgeois public sphere can be multiplied by considering not only other kinds of social movements in developed countries but movements in less developed countries as well. In relation to Mexico, see Lara, Maria Pia, 'The Frail Emergence of Mexico's Democracy: Conquering the Public Sphere', London: Sage. In relation to social movements in other Latin American countries, one could point to the impact of Rigoberta Menchú's story; see Burgos, Elizabeth, ed., _Me llamo Rigoberta Menchú y así me nació la conciencia_. Mexico City, Siglo Veintiuno Editores, 1985. Winner of the Nobel Peace Prize in 1992, this Guatemalan Indian dictated her autobiography to Elizabeth Burgos, as a narration of her life, but also, as a claim for justice and recognition for the Indians in her country. The power of her performative claim compelled international public opinion to investigate conditions of

oppression, inequality and injustice in Central America on newly univer-salistic grounds. The illocutionary force that Menchú gained from this aesthetic intervention had tremendous public-political impact (the book has been reprinted fourteen times), giving her a stature that allowed her to promote a peace treaty between the repressive military government and the guerrillas in Guatemala. She has now become a powerful symbol mediating every struggle by Indians in Latin America.

Bibliography

Adorno, Theodor, *Negative Dialectic*, trans. E. B. Ashton. London: Routledge and Kegan Paul, 1973.

Adorno, Theodor, *Aesthetic Theory*, trans. Robert Hullor-Kentor et al. Minneapolis, University of Minnesota Press, 1997.

Adorno, Theodor, and Horkheimer, Max, *Dialectic of Enlightenment*, trans. J. Cumming. London: Verso, 1979.

Alcoff, Linda, 'Cultural Feminism versus Post-structuralism: The Identity Crisis in Feminist Theory' in *The Second Wave: A Reader in Feminist Theory*, ed. Linda Nicholson. New York and London, Routledge, 1997, pp. 330–55.

Alexander, Jeffrey C., 'Bringing Democracy Back In: Universalistic Solidarity and the Civil Sphere', *Intellectuals and Politics: Social Theory in a Changing World*, ed. C. Lemert. London, Sage, pp. 157–76.

Alexander, Jeffrey C., 'Citizen and Enemy as Symbolic Classification: On the Polarizing Discourse of Civil Society', in *Where Culture Talks: Exclusion and the Making of Society*, ed. M. Fournier and M. Lamot. Chicago, Chicago University Press, 1993, pp. 289–308.

Alexander, Jeffrey C., 'The Paradoxes of Civil Society', in *International Sociology*, vol. 12, no. 2, 1995, pp. 319–39.

Alexander, Jeffrey C., 'Collective Action, Culture and Civil Society: Secularizing, Updating, Inverting, Revising and Displacing the Classical Model of Social Movements', in *Alain Touraine*, ed. M. Diani and J. Clarke. Palmer Press, 1996, pp. 205–34.

Alexander, Jeffrey C., 'After Neofunctionalism: Action, Culture and Civil Society', in *Neofunctionalism and After*. London, Sage, 1997.

Alexander, Jeffrey C., 'Civil Society I, II, III: Constructing an Empirical Concept from Normative Controversies and Historical Transformations', in *Real Civil Societies*. London, Sage Publications (forthcoming).

Alexander, Jeffrey C., *Possibilities of Justice: A Sociological Theory of Civil Society* (forthcoming).

Alexander, Jeffrey C., and Lara, Maria Pia, 'Honneth's New Critical Theory', *New Left Review*, no. 220, 1996, pp. 126–36.

Alexander, Jeffrey C., and Smelser, N. J., 'The Discourse of Discontent: A

Sociological Rejoinder', in *Social Diversity and Cultural Conflict: Is Solidarity Possible?*, ed. Alexander and Smelser. Princeton, NJ, Princeton University Press (forthcoming).

Andrews, William L., *To Feel a True Story: The First Century of Afro-American Autobiography, 1760–1865*. Urbana, University of Illinois Press, 1986.

Andrews, William, ed., *Three Black Women's Autobiographies of the Nineteenth Century*. Bloomington, Indiana University Press, 1986.

Arendt, Hannah. 'Understanding and Politics'; 'The Great Tradition and the Nature of Totalitarianism.' MSS Box 68, lecture 1, 1953.

Arendt, Hannah, *The Human Condition*. Chicago, The University of Chicago Press, 1958.

Arendt, Hannah, *Between Past and Future: Eight Exercises in Political Thought*. Harmondsworth, Penguin, 1968.

Arendt, Hannah, *Men in Dark Times*. New York, Harcourt Brace & World, 1968.

Arendt, Hannah, *Rahel Varnhagen: The Life of a Jewish Woman*. New York, Harcourt Brace Jovanovich, 1974.

Arendt, Hannah, *The Origins of Totalitarianism*. New York, Harcourt Brace Jovanovich, 1975.

Arendt, Hannah, *The Jew as Pariah: Jewish Identity and Politics in the Modern Age*, ed. Ron Feldman. New York, Grove Press, 1978.

Arendt, Hannah, *Eichmann in Jerusalem: A Report on the Banality of Evil*. New York, Penguin, 1992.

Arendt, Hannah, 'Berlin Salon', in *Essays in Understanding, 1930–1954*, ed. Jerome Kohn. New York and London, Harcourt Brace & Co., 1993.

Arendt, Hannah, and McCarthy, Mary, *Between Friends: The Correspondence of Hannah Arendt and Mary McCarthy, 1949–1975*, ed. Carel Brightman. New York, Harcourt Brace & Co., 1995.

Austen, Jane, *Persuasion*, ed. and with introduction by D. W. Harding. Harmondsworth, Penguin, 1965.

Austen, Jane, *Emma*, ed. and with introduction by Ronald Blythe. Harmondsworth, Penguin, 1971.

Austen, Jane, *Sense and Sensibility*, with introduction by Tony Tanner. London, Penguin, 1986.

Baier, C. Annette, *Moral Prejudices*. Cambridge, MA, Harvard University Press, 1994.

Baker, Houston A., Jr, 'Critical Memory and the Black Public Sphere', in *The Black Public Sphere: A Public Culture Book*, ed. Black Public Collective. Chicago and London, University of Chicago Press, 1995, pp. 5–38.

Barnouw, Dagmar, *Visible Spaces. Hannah Arendt and the German-Jewish Experience*. Baltimore and London, Johns Hopkins University Press, 1990.

Beiner, Ronald, ed., *Hannah Arendt's Lectures on Kant's Political Philosophy*, with introduction by the editor. Chicago: University of Chicago Press, 1982.

Benhabib, Seyla, *Critique, Norm, and Utopia: A Study of the Foundations of Critical Theory*. New York, Columbia University Press, 1986.

Benhabib, Seyla, *Situating the Self: Gender, Community and Postmodernism in Contemporary Ethics*. Cambridge, Polity Press, 1992.

Benhabib, Seyla, 'Deliberative Rationality and Models of Democratic Legitimacy', *Constellations*, vol. 1, no. 1, 1994, pp. 26–52.

Benhabib, Seyla, 'Democracy and Difference: Reflections on the Metapolitics of Lyotard and Derrida', _Journal of Political Philosophy_, vol. 2, no. 1, 1994, pp. 1–23.

Benhabib, Seyla, 'Hannah Arendt and the Redemptive Power of Narrative', in _Hannah Arendt: Critical Essays_, ed. Lewis P. Hinchman and Sandra K. Hinchman. New York, State University of New York Press, 1994, pp. 111–37.

Benhabib Seyla, 'The Debate over Women and Moral Theory Revisited', in _Feminists Read Habermas: Gendering the Subject of Discourse_, ed. Johanna Meehan, New York, Routledge, 1995, pp. 181–203.

Benhabib, Seyla, 'The Pariah and her Shadow: Hannah Arendt's Biography of Rahel Varnhagen', in _Feminist Interpretations of Hannah Arendt_, ed. Honig; also in _Political Theory_, vol. 23, no. 1, 1995, pp. 3–24.

Benhabib, Seyla, _The Reluctant Modernism of Hannah Arendt_. London, Sage, 1996.

Benjamin, Walter, _Illuminations: Essays and Reflections_, ed. Hannah Arendt, trans. by Harry Zohn. New York, Shocken Books, 1968.

Benjamin, Walter. _Selected Writings_, ed. Marcus Bullock and Michael W. Jennings. Cambridge, MA, and London, Belknap Press, 1996.

Berlin, Isaiah, _Four Essays on Liberty_. Oxford, Oxford University Press, 1988.

Bernstein, Richard J., _Hannah Arendt and the Jewish Question_. Cambridge, Polity Press, 1996.

Blum, A. Lawrence, _Moral Perception and Particularity_. Cambridge, MA, Cambridge University Press, 1994.

Bobbio, Norberto, 'Equaglianza' and 'Libertà', in _Enciclopedia del novecento_. Rome, Istituto dell'Enciclopedia Italiana, 1977.

Bohman, James, _Public Deliberation: Pluralism, Complexity, and Democracy_. Cambridge, MA, MIT Press, 1996.

Booth, Wayne, _The Company We Keep: An Ethics of Fiction_. Berkeley, University of California Press, 1988.

Braidotti, Rosi, 'The Politics of Ontological Difference', in _Nomadic Subjects: Embodiment and Sexual Difference in Contemporary Feminist Theory_, ed. Carolyn C. Heilbrun and Nancy K. Miller. New York, Columbia University Press, 1994, pp. 173–90.

Bromberg, Pamela S., 'The Development of Narrative Technique in Margaret Drabble's Novels', _Journal of Narrative Technique_, vol. 16, no. 3, 1986, pp. 179–91.

Burgos, Elizabeth, ed. _Me llamo Rigoberta Menchú y así me nació la conciencia_. Mexico City, Siglo Veintiuno Editores, 1985.

Burke, Kenneth, _Language as Action: Essays on Life, Literature and Method_. Berkeley, University of California Press, 1996.

Butler, A. Melissa, 'Early Liberal Roots of Feminism: John Locke and the Attack on Patriarchy', in _Feminist Interpretations and Political Theory_, ed. Mary Lyndon Shanley and Carole Pateman. Pennsylvania State University Press, 1995, pp. 74–94.

Butler, Judith, _Gender Trouble: Feminism and the Subversion of Identity_. New York and London, Routledge, 1990.

Butler, Judith, _Bodies that Matter. On the Discursive Limits of 'Sex'_. New York and London, Routledge, 1993.

Butler, Judith, 'Imitation and Subordination', in _The Second Wave: A Reader in_

Feminist Theory, ed. Linda Nicholson. New York and London, Routledge, 1997, pp. 300–16.

Butler, Judith, *Excitable Speech: A Politics of the Performative*. New York and London, Routledge, 1997.

Calhoun, Craig, ed. *Habermas and the Public Sphere*. Cambridge, MA, MIT Press, 1996.

Calisher, Hortense, *Herself*. New York, Dell Publishing Co., 1972.

Canovan, Margaret, *Hannah Arendt: A Reinterpretation of her Political Thought*. Cambridge, MA, Harvard University Press, 1992.

Canovan, Margaret, 'Politics as Culture: Hannah Arendt and the Public Realm', in *Hannah Arendt: Critical Essays*, ed. Lewis P. Hinchman and Sandra K. Hinchman. New York, State University of New York Press, 1994.

Chodorow, Nancy, *The Reproduction of Mothering: Psychoanalysis and the Sociology of Gender*. Berkeley and Los Angeles, University of California Press, 1978.

Cohen, Jean, and Arato, Andrew, *Civil Society and Political Theory*. Cambridge, MA, MIT Press, 1992.

Cornell, Drucilla, *Beyond Accommodation: Ethical Feminism, Deconstruction and the Law*. New York, Routledge, 1991.

Cornell, Drucilla, *Transformations. Recollective Imagination and Sexual Difference*. New York, Routledge, 1993.

Cornell, Drucilla, *The Imaginary Domain: Abortion, Pornography and Sexual Harassment*. New York, Routledge, 1995.

Cornell, Drucilla, 'Feminist Challenges: A Response', *Philosophy and Social Criticism*, vol. 22, no. 4, 1996, p. 113.

Craft-Fairchild, Catherine, *Masquerade and Gender: Disguise and Female Identity in Eighteenth-century Fictions by Women*. University Park, PA, Pennsylvania State University Press, 1993.

De Beauvoir, Simone, *The Prime of Life*, trans. Peter Green. Harmondsworth, Penguin, 1965.

De Beauvoir, Simone, *Force of Circumstance*, trans. Richard Howard. New York, Warner, 1968.

De Beauvoir, Simone, *The Second Sex*, trans. H. M. Parshley. New York, Vintage, 1974.

De Beauvoir, Simone, *All Said and Done*, trans. Patrick O'Brien. New York, Warner, 1975.

De Lauretis, Teresa, *Alice Doesn't: Feminism, Semiotics, and Cinema*. Bloomington, Indiana University Press, 1984.

De Lauretis, Teresa, ed., *Feminist Studies/Critical Studies*. Bloomington, Indiana University Press, 1986.

De Lauretis, Teresa, *Technologies of Gender: Essays on Theory, Film, and Fiction*. Bloomington and Indianapolis: Indiana University Press, 1987.

De Maio, Romeo, *Mujer y Renacimiento*. Madrid, Mondadori, 1987 (esp. chapter VI: 'La mujer en la biografía', pp. 157–76).

Dean, Jodi, 'Reflective Solidarity', *Constellations*, vol. 2, no. 1, 1995, pp. 114–40.

Dean, Jodi, *Solidarity of Strangers: Feminism after Identity Politics*. Berkeley, Los Angeles and London: University of California Press, 1996.

Decker, Jeffrey Louis, 'Reconstructing Enterprise: Madam Walker, Black Womanhood and the Transportation of the American Culture of Success', in *The Seductions of Biography*, ed. Mary Rhiel and David Suchoff. New York and London, Routledge, 1996, pp. 99–111.

Denby, David, J., *Sentimental Narrative and the Social Order in France, 1760–1820*. Cambridge, MA, Cambridge University Press, 1994.

Diawara, Manthia, 'Malcolm X and the Black Public Sphere: Conversionists versus Culturalists', in *The Black Public Sphere: A Public Culture Book*, ed. Black Public Sphere Collective. Chicago and London, University of Chicago Press, 1995, pp. 39–52.

Disch, Lisa Jane, *Hannah Arendt and the Limits of Philosophy*. Ithaca and London, Cornell University Press, 1994.

Dollard, John, *Caste and Class in a Southern Town*. New York, Doubleday, 1957.

Dworkin, Andrea, *Pornography: Men Possessing Women*. New York, Perigee, 1981.

Dworkin, Andrea and MacKinnon, Catharine, *Pornography and Civil Rights: A New Day for Women's Equality*. Minneapolis, Anti-Pornography Civil Rights Ordinance, 1988.

Dworkin, Ronald, *A Matter of Principle*. Cambridge, MA, Harvard University Press, 1985.

Dworkin, Ronald, *Foundations of Liberal Equality*. Salt Lake City, University of Utah Press, 1990.

Dworkin, Ronald, 'Pornography, Feminism and Freedom', in *Isaiah Berlin: A Celebration*, ed. Edna and Avishai Margalit. Chicago, University of Chicago Press, 1992.

Dworkin, Ronald, *Law's Dominion: An Argument about Abortion, Euthanasia, and Individual Freedom*. New York, Alfred A. Knopf, 1993.

Dworkin, Ronald. 'Feminism and Abortion', *New York Review of Books*, 10 June 1993, pp. 27–9.

Dworkin, Ronald, and MacKinnon, Catharine, correspondence in *New York Review of Books*, 3 March 1994, p. 48.

Ely, John, 'Jane Austen: A Female Aristotelian', *Thesis Eleven*, no. 40, 1995, pp. 93–111.

Epstein, Barbara Leslie, *The Politics of Domesticity: Women, Evangelism, and Temperance in Nineteenth-century America*. Middletown, Wesleyan University Press, 1981.

Fanon, Frantz, *The Wretched of the Earth*, trans. C. Farrington. New York: Grove Press, 1965.

Farge, Arelette, and Zemon Davies, Natalie, directors, *Historia de las Mujeres: Del Renacimiento a la edad moderna. Discurso y disidencia*, ed. Georges Duby and Michelle Perrot. Madrid, Taurus, 1992.

Ferrara, Alessandro, 'Critical Theory and its Discontents: On Wellmer's Critique of Habermas', *Praxis International*, vol. 9, no. 3, 1989, pp. 305–20.

Ferrara, Alessandro, *Modernity and Authenticity: A Study of the Social and Ethical Thought of Jean-Jacques Rousseau*. New York, State University of New York Press, 1993.

Figes, Eva, *Patriarchal Attitudes*. London, Panther, 1972.

Foucault, Michel, 'The Political Technology of Individuals', in *Technologies of the Self: A Seminar with Michel Foucault*, ed. Luther H. Martin, Huck Gutman and Patrick Hutton. Amherst, MA, University of Massachusetts Press, 1988, pp. 16–49.

Fraser, Nancy, 'Foucault's Body Language: A Posthumanist Political Rhetoric?' in *Unruly Practices: Power, Discourse and Gender in Contemporary Social Theory*. Minnesota, University of Minnesota Press, 1989.

Fraser, Nancy, 'Rethinking the Public Sphere: A Contribution to the Critique of Actually Existing Democracy'. *Social Text*, nos. 25–6, 1990, pp. 56–80.

Fraser, Nancy, 'Multiculturalism and Gender Equity: The U.S. "Difference" Debates Revisited', *Constellations*, vol. 3, no. 1, 1996, pp. 61–72.

Fraser, Nancy, *Justice Interruptus: Critical Reflections on the 'Postsocialist' Condition*. New York and London, Routledge, 1997.

Freud, Anna, *The Ego of the Mechanisms of Defense*, vol. 2 of *The Writing of Anna Freud*. New York, International Universities Press, 1936.

Geertz, Clifford, *The Interpretation of Cultures*. New York, Basic Books, 1973.

Giddens, Anthony, *Modernity and Self-Identity: Self and Society in the Late Modern Age*. Cambridge, Polity Press, 1991.

Gilkes, Cheryl, 'Together in Harness: Women's Tradition in the Sanctified Church', *Signs: Journal of Women in Culture and Society*, vol. 10, no. 4, 1985, pp. 678–99.

Gilligan, Carol, *In a Different Voice: Pyschological Theory and Women's Development*. Cambridge, MA, Cambridge University Press, 1982.

Gilmore, Leigh, *Autobiographics: A Feminist Theory of Women's Self-representation*. Ithaca and London, Cornell University Press, 1994.

Goodman, Katherine R., 'Poetry and Truth: Elisa von der Recke's Sentimental Autobiography', in *Interpreting Women's Lives: Feminist Theory and Personal Narratives*, ed. Personal Narratives Group. Bloomington and Indianapolis, Indiana University Press, 1989.

Grosvenor Myer, Valerie, *Jane Austen, Obstinate Heart: A Biography*. New York, Arcade Publishing, 1997.

Gutmann, Amy, ed., *Multiculturalism and 'The Politics of Recognition'*. Princeton, NJ, Princeton University Press, 1992.

Gutwirth, Madelyn, *Germaine de Staël, Novelist: The Emergence of the Artist as Woman*. Urbana, University of Illinois Press, 1978.

Habermas, Jürgen, *The Theory of Communicative Action*, vol. 1: *Reason and the Rationalization of Society*; vol. 2: *System and Lifeworld: A Critique of Functionalist Reason*. Cambridge, Polity Press, 1984–7 (German original, 1981).

Habermas, Jürgen, *The Structural Transformation of the Public Sphere: An Inquiry into the Category of Bourgeois Society*, trans. Thomas Burger with the assistance of Frederick Lawrence. Cambridge, Polity Press, 1989.

Habermas, Jürgen, *Moral Consciousness and Communicative Action*, trans. Christian Lenhardt and Shierry Weber Nicholsen. Cambridge, Polity Press, 1990.

Habermas, Jürgen, *Postmetaphysical Thinking: Philosophical Essays*, trans. William Mark Hohengarten. Cambridge, MA, MIT Press, 1992.

Habermas, Jürgen, 'Struggles for Recognition in Constitutional States', *European Journal of Philosophy*, vol. 1, no. 2, 1993, pp. 128–55.

Habermas, Jürgen, *Justification and Application: Remarks on Discourse Ethics*, trans. by Ciaran P. Cronin. Cambridge, MA, MIT Press, 1993.

Habermas, Jürgen, 'Three Normative Models of Democracy', _Constellations_, vol. 1, no. 1, 1994, pp. 1–10.

Habermas, Jürgen. 'Struggles for Recognition in the Democratic Constitutional State', in _Multiculturalism and 'The Politics of Recognition'_, ed. Amy Gutmann. Princeton, NJ, Princeton University Press, 1994, pp. 107–48.

Habermas, Jürgen, 'Further Reflections on the Public Sphere', in _Habermas and the Public Sphere_, ed. Craig Calhoun. Cambridge, MA, MIT Press, 1996, pp. 421–57.

Habermas, Jürgen, _Between Facts and Norms: Contributions to a Discourse Theory of Law and Democracy_, trans. William Rehg. Cambridge, Polity Press, 1996.

Hampstead, Elizabeth, 'Considering more than a Single Reader', in _Interpreting Women's Lives: Feminist Theory and Personal Narratives_, ed. Personal Narratives Group. Bloomington and Indianapolis, Indiana University Press, 1989.

Held, David, _Democracy and the Global Order: From the Modern State to Cosmopolitan Governance_. Cambridge, Polity Press, 1995.

Hesse, Carla, 'Kant, Foucault, and Three Women', in _Foucault and the Writing of History_, ed. Jan Goldstein. Oxford and Cambridge, Blackwell, 1994.

Hesse, Mary, 'Socializing Epistemology', in _Construction and Constraint: The Shaping of Scientific Rationality_, ed. Ernan McMullin. Notre Dame, Indiana, University of Notre Dame Press, 1988.

Hinchman, Lewis P., and Hinchman, Sandra K., _Hannah Arendt: Critical Essays_. New York, State University of New York Press, 1994.

Honig, Bonnie, ed., _Feminist Interpretations of Hannah Arendt_, University Park, University of Pennsylvania Press, 1995.

Honneth, Axel, 'The Social Dynamics of Disrespect: On the Location of Critical Theory', _Constellations_, vol. 1, no. 2, 1994, pp. 255–69.

Honneth, Axel, _The Struggle for Recognition: The Moral Grammar of Social Conflict_. Cambridge, Polity Press, 1995.

Hunt, Lynn, _The Family Romance of the French Revolution_. Berkeley and Los Angeles, University of California Press, 1992.

Jackson, Rebecca Cox, _Gifts of Power: The Writings of Rebecca Jackson, Black Visionary_, ed. Jean MacMahon Humey. Amherst, University of Massachusetts Press, 1981.

Joyce, Patrick, _Democratic Subjects: The Self and the Social in Nineteenth-century England_. Cambridge, MA, Cambridge University Press, 1994.

Kagan, L. Richard, _Los sueños de Lucrecia: Política y profecía en la España del siglo XVI_. Madrid, Nerea, 1991. _Lucrecia's Dreams: Politics and Prophecy in Sixteenth-Century Spain_. Berkeley: University of California Press, 1990.

Kant, Immanuel, _Elements of Pure Practical Reason_, ed. William Benton. Chicago, Encyclopedia Britannica, 1952.

Katz, Eliha, _The Voyage of the Bagel_. Tel Aviv, University of Tel Aviv, 1995.

Keohane, Nannerl O., 'But for Her Sex . . . The Domestication of Sophie', in _Trent Rousseau Papers_, ed. MacAdam et al. Ottawa, University of Ottawa Press, 1980.

Kerby, Anthony Paul, _Narrative and the Self_. Bloomington and Indianapolis, Indiana University Press, 1980.

Kierkegaard, Søren, _Either/Or_, Part II, ed. and trans. Howard V. Hong and Edna H. Hong. Princeton, NJ, Princeton University Press, 1987.

Kirkham, Margaret, *Jane Austen: Feminism and Fiction*. London, Athlone Press, 1997.

Kosselleck, Reinhart, *Futures Past: On the Semantics of Historical Time*. Cambridge, MA, MIT Press, 1985.

Kristeva, Julia, 'Women can never be Defined', in *New French Feminism*, ed. Elaine Marks and Isabelle Cortivon. New York, Shocken, 1981.

Landes, B. Joan, *Women in the Public Sphere in the Age of the French Revolution*. Ithaca and London, Cornell University Press, 1988.

Landes, Joan, 'The Public and the Private Sphere: A Feminist Reconsideration', in *Feminist Reading Habermas: Gendering the Subject of Discourse*, ed. Johanna Meehan. New York and London, Routledge, 1995.

Lange, Lynda, 'Rousseau and Modern Feminism', in *Feminist Interpretations and Political Theory*, ed. Mary Lyndon Shanley and Carole Pateman. Pennsylvania, Pennsylvania State University Press, 1991, pp. 95–111.

Lapone, Ernesto, ed., *Truth and Interpretation: Perspectives of the Philosophy of Donald Davidson*. Oxford, Blackwell, 1986.

Lessing, Doris, *The Golden Notebook*. London, Michael Joseph, 1962.

Lyndon, Shanley, Mary, and Pateman, Carole, eds, *Feminist Interpretations and Political Theory*, University Park, PA, Pennsylvania State University Press, 1977.

McCarthy, Thomas, *Ideals and Illusions: On Reconstruction and Deconstruction in Contemporary Critical Theory*. Cambridge, MA, MIT Press, 1991.

MacIntyre, Alasdair, *After Virtue*. Notre Dame, IN, University of Notre Dame Press, 1984.

McKay, Nellie J., 'Nineteenth-century Black Women's Spiritual Autobiographies: Religious Faith and Self-empowerment', in *Interpreting Women's Lives: Feminist Theories and Personal Narratives*, ed. Personal Narratives Group. Bloomington, Indiana University Press, 1989, pp. 139–54.

MacKinnon, Catharine, *Sexual Harassment and the Working Woman: A Case of Working Women*. New Haven, Yale University Press, 1979.

MacKinnon, Catharine, *Feminism Unmodified: Discourses of Life and Law*. Cambridge, MA, Harvard University Press, 1987.

Mansbridge, Jane, 'Using Power and Fighting Power', *Constellations*, vol. 1, no. 1, 1994, pp. 53–73.

Marso, Lori J., 'The Loving Citizen: Germaine de Staël's *Delphine*', *Journal of Political Philosophy*, vol. 5, no. 2, 1997, pp. 109–31.

Meehan, Johanna, ed., *Feminists Read Habermas: Gendering the Subject of Discourse*. New York, Routledge, 1995.

Michaelman, Frank, 'Conceptions of Democracy in American Constitutional Argument: The Case of Pornography Regulation', *Tennessee Law Review*, vol. 56, no. 291, 1989, pp. 303–4.

Murdoch, Iris, *The Sovereignty of Good*. New York, Routledge, 1970.

Nin, Anaïs, *The Diary of Anaïs Nin*. 6 vols, ed. Gunther Stuhlmann. New York, Harcourt Brace Jovanovich, 1966–76.

Nussbaum, Martha, *The Fragility of Goodness: Luck and Ethics in Greek Tragedy and Philosophy*. Cambridge, MA, Cambridge University Press, 1986.

Nussbaum, Martha, *Love's Knowledge: Essays on Philosophy and Literature*. Cambridge, MA, Oxford University Press, 1990.

Nussbaum, Martha, _The Therapy of Desire: Theory and Practice in Hellenistic Ethics_. Princeton, NJ, Princeton University Press, 1994.

Nussbaum, C. Martha, and respondents, _For Love of Country: Debating the Limits of Patriotism_, ed. Martha C. Joshua Cohen. Boston, Beacon Press, 1996.

Nussbaum, Martha, and Sen, Amartya, _The Quality of Life_. Oxford, Clarendon Press, 1993.

Nussbaum, Martha, and Glover, Jonathan, eds, _Women, Culture and Development: A Study of Human Capabilities_. Oxford, Clarendon Press, 1995.

Offe, Claus, _Modernity and the State: East, West_. Cambridge, Polity Press, 1996.

Okin, Susan Moller, _Women in Western Political Thought_. Princeton, NJ, Princeton University Press, 1979.

Outram, Dorinda, _The Body and the French Revolution_. New Haven, Yale University Press, 1989.

Parekh, Bhikhu, 'Dilemmas of a Multicultural Theory of Citizenship', _Constellations_. vol. 4, no. 1, 1997, pp. 54–62.

Parry, Geraint, 'Individuality, Politics and the Critique of Paternalism in John Locke', _Political Studies_, no. 12, June 1964, pp. 163–77.

Pateman, Carole, _The Problem of Political Obligation: A Critique of Liberal Theory_. Chichester, NY, Wiley, 1979.

Pateman, Carole, _The Disorder of Women_. Cambridge, Polity Press, 1988.

Pateman, Carole, _The Sexual Contract_. Cambridge, Polity Press, 1988.

Phillips, Anne, _Democracy and Difference_. University Park, PA, Pennsylvania State University Press, 1993.

Poniatowska, Elena, _La vida de Tina Modotti_. Mexico City, Cal y Arena Press, 1993.

Poniatowska, Elena (1993), _Tinísima_, Mexico City, Cal y Arena Press, 1993.

Rawls, John, _Political Liberalism_. New York, Columbia University Press, 1993.

Raz, Joseph, _The Morality of Freedom_. Oxford, Clarendon Press, 1986.

Rhiel, Mary, and Suchoff, David, ed., _The Seductions of Biography_. New York and London, Routledge, 1996.

Ricoeur, Paul, _Time and Narrative_, 3 vols, trans. Kathleen McLaughlin [vol. 3: Kathleen Blamey] and D. Pellauer. Chicago and London, University of Chicago Press, 1984–8.

Ricoeur, Paul, _Oneself as Another_. Chicago, University of Chicago Press, 1992.

Rorty, Richard, and Skinner, Quentin, eds, _Philosophy in History_, Cambridge, MA, University Press, 1986.

Rorty, Richard, _Contingency, Irony, and Solidarity_. Cambridge, MA, Cambridge University Press, 1989.

Rorty, Richard, _Philosophical Papers_, vol. 1. Cambridge, MA, Cambridge University Press, 1991.

Rousseau, Jean-Jacques, _The Confessions_, trans. with introduction by J. M. Cohen. London and New York, Penguin, 1953.

Ryan, Mary P., _Women in Public: Between Banners and Ballots, 1825–1880_. Baltimore and London, Johns Hopkins University Press, 1990.

Ryle, Gilbert, 'Jane Austen and the Moralists', _Collected Papers_. London, Hutchinson, vol. 1, p. 287.

Sandel, Michael J., _Liberalism and the Limits of Justice_. Cambridge, MA, Cambridge University Press, 1982.

Schrag, Calvin O., *Communicative Praxis and the Space of Subjectivity*. Bloomington and Indianapolis: Indiana University Press, 1986.

Schrag, Calvin O., *The Self after Postmodernity*. New Haven and London, Yale University Press, 1997.

Schroeder, Jane, 'Feminism Historicized: Medieval Misogynist Stereotypes in Contemporary Feminist Jurisprudence', *Iowa Law Review*, vol. 75, 1990, p. 1135.

Schwab, Gabriele, *Subjects without Selves: Transitional Texts in Modern Fiction*. Cambridge, MA, Harvard University Press, 1994.

Schwab, Gabriele, *The Mirror and the Killer Queen*. Bloomington, Indiana University Press, 1996.

Scott, Joan, 'The Evidence of Experience', *Critical Inquiry*, no. 17, 1991, p. 777.

Seel, Martin, 'The Two Meanings of "Communicative" Reality: Remarks on Habermas' Critique of a Plural Concept of Reason', in *Communicative Action*, ed. Axel Honneth and Hans Joas. Cambridge, MA, MIT Press, 1991, pp. 36–48.

Seel, Martin, *Ethisch-ästhetische Studien*. Frankfurt, Seelekamp, 1996.

Singer, Alan, 'The Adequacy of the Aesthetic', *Philosophy and Social Criticism*, vol. 26, nos 1–2, 1994, pp. 39–72.

Smelser, Neil, *The Theory of a Collective Behavior*. New York, Free Press, 1962.

Smith, Adam, *The Theory of Moral Sentiments*, ed. D. D. Raphael and A. L. Macfie. Indianapolis, Liberty Fund, 1984.

Spelman, V. Elizabeth, 'Simone de Beauvoir and Women: Just Who Does She Think "We" Is?', in *Feminist Interpretations and Political Theory*, ed. Mary Lyndon Shanley and Carole Pateman. University Park, PA, Pennsylvania State University Press, 1977, pp. 199–216.

Stone, Albert, *Autobiographical Occasions and Original Acts: Versions of American Identity from Henry Adams to Nate Shaw*. Philadelphia, University of Pennsylvania Press, 1982.

Sulloway, G. Allison, *Jane Austen and the Province of Womanhood*. Philadelphia, University of Pennsylvania Press, 1989.

Taylor, Charles, *Philosophical Papers: Human Agency and Language*, vol. 1. Cambridge, MA, Harvard University Press, 1985.

Taylor, Charles, *Philosophical Papers*, vol. 2. Cambridge, MA, Cambridge University Press, 1988.

Taylor, Charles, *Sources of the Self: The Making of Modern Identity*. Cambridge, MA, Harvard University Press, 1989.

Taylor, Charles, *The Ethics of Authenticity*. Cambridge, MA, Harvard University Press, 1991.

Taylor, Charles, *The Politics of Recognition*. Princeton, New Jersey, Princeton University Press: 1992.

Taylor, Charles, *Philosophical Arguments*. Cambridge, MA, Harvard University Press, 1995.

Tilly, Charles, et al., *The Rebellious Century: 1830–1930*. Cambridge, MA, Harvard University Press, 1975.

Tilly, Charles, *From Mobilization to Revolution*. Reading, MA, Addison Wesley, 1978.

Touraine, Alain, _The Voice and the Eye_. Cambridge, Cambridge University Press, 1981.

Tronto, C. Joan, _Moral Boundaries. A Political Argument for an Ethic of Care_. New York, Routledge, 1993.

Tucker, George Holbert, _Jane Austen, the Woman: Some Biographical Insights_. New York, St Martin's Griffin, 1994.

Villa, Dana, _Arendt and Heidegger: The Fate of the Political_. Princeton, NJ, Princeton University Press, 1996.

Von der Recke, Elisa, _Aufzeichnungen und Briefe aus ihren Jugendtagen_, ed. Paul Rachel. Leipzig, Dieterich, 1902.

Walkowitz, Judith R., _City of Dreadful Delight: Narratives of Sexual Danger in Late Victorian London_. Chicago: Chicago University Press, 1992. (Cf. Chap. 3, n. 46).

Webster Barbre, Joy et al., _Interpreting Women's Lives: Feminist Theory and Personal Narratives_, ed. Personal Narratives Group. Bloomington and Indianapolis, Indiana University Press, 1989.

Wellmer, Albrecht, _The Persistence of Modernity: Essays on Aesthetics, Ethics, and Postmodernism_. Cambridge, MA, MIT Press, 1991.

Wellmer, Albrecht, _Endspiele: Die unversöhnliche Moderne. Essays und Vorträge_. Frankfurt am Main, Suhrkamp, 1993.

Wolin, Richard, _Walter Benjamin: An Aesthetic of Redemption_. Berkeley, University of California Press, 1994.

Yeatman, Anna, _Postmodern Revisionings of the Political_. New York, Routledge, 1994.

Young, Iris Marion, _Justice and the Politics of Difference_. Princeton, NJ, Princeton University Press, 1990.

Index of Names

Index of Subjects

social movements 7, 120, 134, 165,
    166, 168, 169, 170, 171, 211
solidarity 108, 109, 110, 117, 135,
    157, 171
  and justice 110, 114, 118, 126
speech-act, Austin's theory of 2
  Habermas's approach 2, 4
*Structural Transformation of the Public
    Sphere, The* (Habermas) 26,
    27
  see also Habermas, Jürgen, on the
    public sphere

Theory of Communicative Action
    (Habermas) 53, 54

Wellmer, Albrecht
  on Adorno's aesthetic theory 51–9
  reformulation of Habermas'
    conception of communicative
    rationality 51–4
  role of narratives 64, 65
  validity spheres 60–6
women's movement 1, 7, 15, 133,
    171, 211